Advance praise for

FICTIONAL BLUES

"The perspective Mack offers on blues mythology is fresh and compelling. *Fictional Blues* is well-researched, engaging, clear, confident, and important."
—EMILY J. LORDI, author of *Black Resonance: Iconic Women Singers and African American Literature*

"Mack provides a complex mapping of American blues music to investigate the work it does as a multifaceted cultural trope, from its inception in the Jim Crow South to its global dissemination in the twenty-first century. *Fictional Blues* is certain to make an impact in African American studies, along with American literary and cultural studies writ large."
—CAROLINE A. STREETER, author of *Tragic No More: Mixed-Race Women and the Nexus of Sex and Celebrity*

FICTIONAL BLUES

A VOLUME IN THE SERIES
African American Intellectual History
EDITED BY
Christopher Cameron

Fictional Blues

Narrative Self-Invention from Bessie Smith to Jack White

KIMBERLY R. MACK

University of Massachusetts Press
AMHERST AND BOSTON

Printed in the United States of America
ISBN 978-1-62534-550-9 (paper); 549-3 (hardcover)
Designed by Kristina Kachele Design, llc
Set in Alegreya ht Pro with Benton Sans Extra Compressed, Breakers and Breakers Slab display
Printed and bound by Books International, Inc.
Cover design by Kristina Kachele Design, llc
Cover art by Faith Ringgold, *Jazz Series: Mama Can Sing #7*, 2001–2004.
© 2020 Faith Ringgold / Artists Rights Society (ARS), New York,
Courtesy ACA Galleries, New York.

Library of Congress Cataloging-in-Publication Data
Names: Mack, Kimberly, author.
Title: Fictional blues : narrative self-invention from Bessie Smith to Jack White / Kimberly Mack.
Identifiers: LCCN 2020019281 | ISBN 9781625345493 (hardcover) | ISBN 9781625345509 (paperback) | ISBN 9781613767955 (ebook) | ISBN 9781613767962 (ebook)
Subjects: LCSH: Blues (Music)—History and criticism. | Blues musicians—United States. | African Americans—Folklore. | Music and folklore.
Classification: LCC ML3521 .M23 2020 | DDC 781.64309—dc23
LC record available at https://lccn.loc.gov/2020019281

British Library Cataloguing-in-Publication Data
A catalog record for this book is available from the British Library.

Portions of chapter 4 were published in a previous form in "'There's No Home for You Here': Jack White and the Unsolvable Problem of Blues Authenticity" in *Popular Music & Society* 38, no. 2 (March 15, 2015): 176, 179–91. Used by permission of Taylor & Francis. Portions of chapter 5 were published in a previous form in "'She's a Country Girl All Right: Rhiannon Giddens's Powerful Reclamation of Country Culture," *Journal of Popular Music Studies* 32, no. 2 (June 2020): 144–61. Used by permission of University of California Press.

The verses from Stagolee Version B in chapter 1 were drawn from recorded or transcribed performances by Ivy Joe White (likely Ivory Joe Hunter), Alexander "Little Alex" Wells, Sullivan Rock, and Windy Billy, documented by John A. Lomax and Alan Lomax in 1933 for the Library of Congress and published in *American Ballads and Folk Songs* (1934). The precise source for each verse is unattributed in the printed text.

For Mom

Contents

Preface and Acknowledgments ix

Introduction 1

CHAPTER 1
The Narrative Blues Tradition 25
Tall Tales, Myths, and Black American Folklore

CHAPTER 2
Shug, Big Mama, and Amy 67
Autobiographical Fictions and Addictions

CHAPTER 3
"I Was Astounded at What I Heard" 109
Robert Johnson's Autobiographical and Biographical Afterlives

CHAPTER 4
From John Anthony Gillis to Jack White 143
A Study in Blues Self-Invention

CHAPTER 5
The Blues Apprenticeship 183
Racialized Conventions of the Acolyte

Afterword 213

Notes 221
Index 247

Preface and Acknowledgments

Fictional Blues evolved out of my profound interest in stories and storytelling, particularly of the autobiographical variety. Tales told through words in books and magazines, as well as in music—lyrics, sounds, and the crafted personas of musicians as seen in interviews and live performances—have always proved especially fascinating to me. As a rock music–loving child growing up in Brooklyn, New York, I spent as much time reading the lyrics and liner notes for my favorite records as I did listening to their fierce sounds. I reveled in the wild tales of rock and roll excess as rendered by the (mostly) white male rockers and critics I admired in magazines such as *Rolling Stone* and *Creem.* As an adult I eventually, and perhaps not surprisingly, became a rock music critic myself. Later I decided to tell my own stories using the memoir form. And it is stories and storytelling, by others and myself, that continues to hold my interest today. In *Fictional Blues,* I have endeavored to learn *why*. What is it about a well-told story that motivates listeners to share it with others? And how do these stories circulate in musical forms and styles—in this case, with a specific focus on the blues?

In 2006, I attended the venerable EMP Pop Conference (now renamed the MoPOP Pop Conference) in Seattle for the first time. I had been writing about music—including for some of the magazines I grew up reading, such as *Relix* and *Hot Press*—since 2002. I had completed an M.F.A. in creative writing in 2003, and I was considering my next steps. My Pop Conference abstract was not chosen—it hewed a little too close to memoir to fit—but I showed up at EMP anyway. I had a feeling that I might find my people there. And I did. It was there that I met Daphne Brooks, who warmly welcomed me into the popular music studies fold, and has been a wonderful mentor and supporter ever since. Not long after returning home to Los Angeles, I realized that I wanted to pursue a Ph.D. in English, and I hoped to approach literary studies in an interdisciplinary way—perhaps even putting it into conversation with music.

This book has distant origins—with few traces left—as research I completed at UCLA in 2015. While about one-third of my original text remains, the theoretical framework was sturdy, and has supported my new research and writing since 2016. *Fictional Blues* began as a series of conversations with my chair, Richard Yarborough, who affirmed what I did not yet have the courage to suggest myself: that it might be possible to combine my various interests—twentieth- and twenty-first-century African American literature, American popular music, and life writing—into one project. I will be forever grateful for his generous support and capacious vision for what this (at the time embryonic) enterprise could be. Beyond that, Richard's intellectual rigor and extremely high standards for his graduate students' research and writing, coupled with his kind and compassionate nature, served as a helpful model for how to be a force for good in the academy. His mentorship has had a profound impact on my growth and development as a scholar and teacher, and it has informed my approach to mentoring my own undergraduate and graduate students.

I would like to also thank my other committee members, Bob Fink, James Goodwin, and Caroline Streeter. Caroline was particularly supportive while I was on the academic job market, notably helping me to refine my job talk, while James offered forward-thinking critiques for my research in anticipation of its movement toward a book. Bob has remained a committed mentor whose opinions about popular music, and advice about life inside and outside of the academy, have proven invaluable to me. While I was at UCLA, he, like Richard, showed me the possibilities of what my work could be, bringing his considerable knowledge of popular music, his insatiable intellectual curiosity, and his amiability and wonderful sense of humor to bear. Since beginning my faculty position at the University of Toledo, and becoming his colleague in popular music studies, Bob has been a guide for the field, and a committed champion of my work.

My research received critical financial support from various institutions on the UCLA campus, including the Center for the Study of Women, the Department of English, Graduate Division, the Institute of American Cultures, and the Ralph J. Bunche Center for African American Studies. Furthermore, I am grateful for having traversed many wonderful intellectual communities at UCLA. In particular, I treasure happy memories of my six summers working as a graduate student mentor for the Ralph J. Bunche Center Summer Humanities Institute in the company of Veronica Benson-Cole, Jan Freeman, Darnell Hunt, Dalena Hunter, Dawn Jefferson, Yolanda Jones, and Ana-Christina Ramon.

I would also like to thank all of the supportive professors I have had the great pleasure of knowing and learning from during my years as a graduate student at UCLA's Department of English. I am delighted to extend my gratitude to Ali Behdad, Helen Deutsch, Lowell Gallagher, Yogita Goyal, Ursula Heise, Louise Hornby, Arthur Little, Christopher Looby, Uri McMillan, Chris Mott, Harryette Mullen, and Mona Simpson. I also wish to thank Janet Bishop, Nora Elias, Rick Fagin, Jeanette Gilkison, Mike Lambert, and Bronson Tran for all of their advice, help, and encouragement along the way.

I owe a tremendous debt to my graduate school friends who assisted and inspired me during my time at UCLA. I am very grateful to Nasia Anam, Jonathan Collins, Guadalupe Escobar, Brandon Harrison, Laura Haupt, Renee Hudson, Courtney Marshall, Hannah Nahm, Therí Pickens, Erica Powe-Onugha, Maureen Shay, Melanie Masterton Sherazi, Erin Suzuki, Dennis Tyler, Brandy Underwood, Marilú Utomi, and Joyce Pualani Warren. The members of my Revolutionary Women writing group—Juliann Anesi, Carolina Beltrán, Isabel Gómez, Yvette Martínez-Vu, Erica Powe-Onugha, Sandra Ruiz, Ester Trujillo, Brandy Underwood, Marilú Utomi, and Joyce Pualani Warren—provided insightful feedback on my work and welcome emotional support during the last two years of my Ph.D. program.

I wrote *Fictional Blues* in Toledo, Ohio. After completing my Ph.D. in the summer of 2015, I happily accepted a tenure-track position as assistant professor of African American literature at the University of Toledo that began in the fall. My mother passed away after a brief battle with cancer three weeks after my start date. Facing a challenge of that magnitude, while trying to navigate a new job in a new city, would have felt impossible without the kindness and generosity of my new colleagues in the department of English. And they—along with recent additions—have been a pleasure to work with. A warm thank you to Teresa Boyer, Jane Bradley, Tyler Branson, Dan Compora, Anthony Edgington, Christina Fitzgerald, Joey Gamble, Tim Geiger, Melissa Gregory, Sara Lundquist, Andrew Mattison, Melinda Reichelt, Russ Reising, Parama Sarkar, and Ben Stroud. Other associates at UT, both past and present, who have enriched my time here include Dean Adams, Gbenga Ajilore, Tom Barden, Liat Ben-Moshe, Shara Crookston, Ally Day, Rachel Dudley, Jim Ferris, Charlene Gilbert, Catherine Harrington, Renée Heberle, Tammy Kinsey, Jean Kusina, Joel Lipman, Sam Nelson, Mysoon Rizk, Barbara Schneider, and Yerra Sugarman. And every day I appreciate Natalie Bullock's and Cathy Chengges's efforts toward making the English department run smoothly.

Thank you to my incredible graduate students at the University of Toledo, specifically students in my fall 2016 grad seminar "The Autobiographical Impulse in 20th-Century American Blues Literature, Drama, and Music," who helped me to think through my theorizing about unconventional autobiographical articulation, and where I had the chance to revisit some key literary and musical texts for *Fictional Blues*. Thank you also to the students in my spring 2020 "Contemporary Literary Theory and Criticism" graduate seminar who reminded me to clarify a key idea in the introduction to this book.

I am especially grateful to colleagues inside and outside of my disciplinary fields of American and African American literature and popular music studies who read portions of my book-in-progress and offered constructive critiques, including Liat Ben-Moshe, Bob Fink, Adam Gussow, Craig Howes, Meta DuEwa Jones, Andrew Mattison, Angela Nelson, Erica Powe-Onugha, Barry Shank, Melanie Masterton Sherazi, Erin Suzuki, Brandy Underwood, Elijah Wald, Joyce Pualani Warren, and Lisa Ze Winters.

A special thank you is in order to Brian Halley, my editor at the University of Massachusetts Press, who has enthusiastically shared his knowledge with me, and been patient and helpful, never failing to answer my numerous questions from the day he offered me an advance contract to the delivery of my final manuscript. *Fictional Blues* is part of Christopher Cameron's African American Intellectual History series. He has been a wonderful series editor, providing me with helpful feedback along the way. Thank you also to the two anonymous readers who vetted my draft manuscript, offering thoughtful suggestions for improvement. Finally, a big thank you to Rachael DeShano, the best production editor a first-time book author could hope for. I am so grateful for the extraordinary amount of time and care she took with my manuscript.

Presenting my work in progress to new audiences was vital to its success. While writing *Fictional Blues* I was invited to share my research at the Arnold Shaw Popular Music Center Lecture Series at the University of Nevada, Las Vegas; the Bowling Green State University Ethnomusicology Department Colloquium in Bowling Green, Ohio; the Everyday Humanities Series at Way Public Library in Perrysburg, Ohio; the Ralph Ellison Seminar at the Library of Congress's Ralph Ellison Reading Room in Washington, D.C.; and the Ralph Ellison and the Territory Symposium at Lewis and Clark College in Portland, Oregon. Thank you to all of my peers who invited me and/or provided constructive criticism that revealed new insights. I deeply appreciate the kind support of Herman Beavers, Adam Bradley, John F. Callahan, Marc Conner, Natalie Dielman, Christina Fitzgerald, Tracy Floreani, Michael Germana, Lena Hill, Sidra Lawrence, Jonathan Rhodes Lee, Kathy Meizel, Lucas Morel, Timothy Parrish, and Eric Sundquist.

I also presented my research at symposia and conferences, benefitting from intellectual exchanges between my fellow panelists, the audiences, and myself, organized by the American Literature Association, the American Studies Association, the Futures of American Studies Institute at Dartmouth College, the International Association for the Study of Popular Music (U.S. and Canada branches), the International Ralph Ellison Symposium at Oxford University, the Modern Language Association, the Modernist Studies Association, the MoPOP Pop Conference, the Popular Culture Association/American Culture Association, the Society for the Study of the Multi-Ethnic Literature of the United States Conference, and the U2 Conference. I also participated in the Popular Music

Study Group of the American Musicological Society 2016 Junior Faculty Symposium, workshopping part of what became chapter 5 of *Fictional Blues* with senior faculty and the other participants.

Through participation in these organizations, and scholarly engagement with my fields of African American literature and American popular music, I have gained much from the intellectual exchange, advice, and generosity of a number of critics and scholars. Thank you to Badia Ahad, Laila Amine, Alexandra Apolloni, Jackie Ardam, Gina Arnold, Stephanie Batiste, Herman Beavers, Ben Blackwell, Adam Bradley, Daphne Brooks, Daphne Carr, Theo Cateforis, Norma Coates, Soyica Colbert, Ali Colleen, Alex Corey, Laina Dawes, Josh Duchan, Erica Edwards, Mike D'Errico, Duncan Faherty, Daniel Goldmark, Adam Gussow, James Hall, Jason Hanley, Anthony Kwame Harrison, Craig Howes, Nadine Hubbs, Eric Hung, Tsitsi Ella Jaji, Robin James, Tyehimba Jess, A Yemisi Jimoh, Sherry Johnson, Julie Kae, Tammy Kernodle, Josh Kun, M. L. Liebler, Elizabeth Lindau, Emily Lordi, Eric Lott, Jarvis McInnis, Uri McMillan, Laurie McNeill, Kathy Meizel, Leah Milne, Koritha Mitchell, Chris Molanphy, Kevin Moore, Esther Morgan-Ellis, Tiffany Naiman, Mark Anthony Neal, Lauren Onkey, Therí Pickens, Ann Powers, Sonnet Retman, Francesca Royster, Barry Shank, Melanie Masterton Sherazi, David Shumway, RJ Smith, Sidonie Smith, Ben Swank, Victor Szabo, Greg Tate, Kyla Tompkins, Steve Waksman, Elijah Wald, Eric Weisbard, Lisa Ze Winters, and Brian Wright.

My first serious foray into blues history happened in 2013 during my seventeen-day research trip to Chicago, Illinois; Clarksdale, Mississippi; Memphis, Tennessee; Nashville, Tennessee; and Oxford, Mississippi. It was during that trip that I visited the Harold Washington Library Center–Visual and Performing Arts Chicago Blues Archives at the Chicago Public Library and the Center for Black Music Research at Columbia College Chicago, both of which I returned to in 2016 and 2019; and the Blues Archive at the University of Mississippi. I owe much to Greg Johnson at the Blues Archive at Ole Miss, and Melanie Zeck at the Columbia College Black Music Research Center, for their aid in finding archival materials for this book. I also participated in the PCA-BGSU Summer Research Institute at Bowling Green State University in 2017 to conduct research for *Fictional Blues* at the Music Library and Bill Schurk Sound Archives. Thank you to Dave Lewis, sound archivist at the Music Library and Bill Schurk Sound Archives, research archivist Anne Rhodes and director Libby Van Cleve at the Oral History of American Music at Yale University, and Todd Harvey, Lomax curator at the American Folklife Center at the Library of Congress, for their research assistance. Thank you as well to Valerie Brown at the University of Toledo Carlson Library for her assistance with the microfilm equipment for reading John Russell David's 1976 work for the discussion about Stagolee in chapter 1. And I am grateful to Janet Douglas and the staff at the UT Carlson Library for helping me to find and manage the large rotation of library books for this project.

I would not have been able to visit these archives, conduct vital research, or present my findings for *Fictional Blues* without support from the following University of Toledo grants and fellowships: Center for International Studies and Programs' Kohler International Travel Grants; College of Arts and Letters Faculty Development Grants; Department of English Language and Literature travel funds; Office of the Provost's Faculty Professional Development Grants; and Office of Research and Sponsored Programs' URFO Small Awards and URFO Summer Research Fellowships. I also received helpful stipends as a 2016–18 Duke University Summer Institute on Tenure and Professional Activity (SITPA) Scholar.

I would be remiss not to express my humble thanks to my friends outside of the academy—Terry and Jeff Beamsley, Jamie Birdwell-Branson, David Brandenburg, Susan Chen, Nzingha Clarke, Eric Craig, Matt DeMerritt, Gary Edelstone, Cindy Elden, Adam Kalesperis, Andrew Kasson, Deborah Lott, Paul Malcolm, Jessica and Alan Matkovic, Amanda Mosher, Tim Panek, Eric Pfeffinger, Joe Quintero, Keiya Rayne, Jill Rothenberg, Erica Ruiz, Matt Sarrel, Vijay Shanmugam, and Sunita Suryanarayan—for providing unflagging affection, comfort, and good cheer.

I am extremely grateful to my in-laws—Ann and Norm, and Alex, Hillary, Lola, Liv, and Peaches—whose warmth, love, and generosity know no bounds. I could not have asked to marry into a better family, one that feels exactly like home.

I do not know how to properly thank my husband, Adam Ginsburg, who has stood by me in every way imaginable—helping me through a long and arduous journey as a graduate student; joining me in Toledo, Ohio, as I began a new chapter in my career; consoling me in the aftermath of my mother's sudden and devastating passing; and sharing an immeasurable amount of love and emotional support during the drawn-out process of creating this book. Adam is an incredible friend, an indefatigable cheerleader, and a trusted reader of my work. It is important to note that he took on all sorts of tasks, small and large, as I wrote *Fictional Blues*—including, but not limited to, making sure I ate healthy meals and providing unpaid copyediting services.

And, finally, I would like to thank my dear mother, Jennifer whose love, support, encouragement, and many, many sacrifices along the way have helped me to become the person that I am. She would have been so happy to see this book in print. *Fictional Blues* is humbly dedicated to her.

FICTIONAL BLUES

Introduction

In 2007, blues-rock singer, songwriter, and guitarist Jack White told the *New York Times*, "Everything from your haircut to your clothes to the type of instrument you play to the melody of a song to the rhythm—they're all tricks to get people to pay attention to the story. If you just stood up in a crowd and said your story—'I came home, and this girl I was dating wasn't there, and I was wondering where she was'—it's not interesting. But give it a melody, give it a beat, build it all the way up to a haircut. Now people pay attention."[1]

As a member of the White Stripes, White told a story about "this girl" he was not only dating but who he married and divorced, his bandmate Meg White. Onstage, and in interviews, this autobiographical misdirection by White involved encouraging ambiguity about the very nature of his relationship. By referring to his ex-wife as his "big sister," he engaged rural stereotypes focused on sexual intrigue, family kinship, and transgressive desire that are part of blues mythology and legend. It is this kind of trickery in the realms of autobiographical and biographical narrative that this book explores. *Fictional Blues* asks readers to pay attention to the kinds of deliberate fabrications that are inherent in traditional autobiographical blues self-invention. These autobiographical falsehoods exist not only in White's words, sounds, and visuals but also in the lives and works of multiple real-life blues musicians, such as Mance Lipscomb, Bessie Smith, and Peetie Wheatstraw—who famously renamed himself the Devil's Son-in-Law—as well as in the narratives of fictional blues makers such as Shug Avery and Squeak in Alice Walker's *The Color Purple.*

I introduce this book incongruously with a *white* blues-rock artist, John Anthony Gillis, who became Jack White after taking his ex-wife Meg White's last name—his racially-inflected moniker serving as a model of reinvention and a subversion of the heteronormative tradition of the wife taking her husband's surname. I offer this example to explore autobiographical blues self-fashioning in American literary and musical texts because *Fictional Blues* engages the aural, spoken, embodied, and written languages and idioms of race, gender, class, and place in the blues, and their fabrications, in varied dimensions. Further, using White as a starting point underscores the ways in which I am contesting racially essentialist notions of blues authenticity, and recasts the blues as a narrative tradition cutting across traditional boundaries of race.

Fictional Blues is the story of how a range of blues artists, both real and imagined, invented their own personas independent of the so-called authentic blues, which is often predicated on the notion that Black men and women from poor or working-class backgrounds are more naturally suited to understand, and thus perform, the blues honestly. The familiar stories of Delta Blues musician Robert Johnson selling his soul to the devil at a Mississippi crossroads in exchange for his guitar virtuosity, and the violent, Black bad man of the early twentieth-century American imagination—represented by the mythical figure Stagolee, who murdered a man over a Stetson hat—undergird persistent racial myths surrounding "authentic" blues expression that are beloved by many blues fans and critics. As this opening example featuring Jack White briefly suggests, far from having ready-made racial and cultural identities, these blues makers have instead fashioned worlds through their own fictionalized autobiographical and biographical storytelling and self-made personas.

EMBEDDED NARRATIVES

In *Fictional Blues,* when the real-life contemporary blues performers, or the fictive blues narrators and characters, tell stories—songs, musical performances, and interviews are all examples too—about their familial lineages, childhood memories, past experiences, and even the origins of their names, they use literary devices, such as description or dialogue, to define their lives and personalities. Of course, for blues artists such as Gary Clark Jr. and Jack White, there is an expectation that they will engage in these types of storytelling—they share autobiographical narratives about themselves through song lyrics, onstage banter between songs, social media, and in print, online, and video interviews. Blues musicians within their fictive worlds do the same, and the stories told by narrators and characters in these realms that are created by real-life authors can be read as second-level stories, or embedded narratives. *Fictional Blues'* definition of narrative is grounded in Mieke Bal's understanding of it as "a text in which an agent or subject conveys to an addressee ('tells' the reader, viewer, or listener) a story in a medium, such as language, imagery, sound, buildings, or a combination thereof."[2] This capacious definition allows for a multidisciplinary approach to narrative in which words, sounds, and embodied performances can all tell a story, offering an expansive way of engaging autobiographical blues self-fashioning across different platforms.

My approach to engaging embedded narratives owes a debt to the work of Gérard Genette, with updates by Bal, William Nelles, and John Barth.[3] In what Barth refers to as "frametale literature" we encounter "the phenomenon of framed tales—that is, of stories within stories, which always to some degree imply stories *about* stories and even stories about story*telling*."[4] These narratives offer multiple levels of storytelling in which it is possible for the characters within a fictive world to tell a new story, introducing a new set of characters who in turn might tell further stories.[5] The concept of the embedded narrative is rooted in structuralist narratological theory; therefore, the author of a literary work does not serve a role in the criticism of a text. My primary interest is in the structure and function of the narratives through which fictional and nonfictional blues figures invent and reinvent themselves, but I am also interested in examples—such as the womanist philosophy that connects Alice Walker to characters in *The Color Purple*—in which the circumstances of an author shed light on those of a character or vice versa. But these authorial circumstances will not be primary here. Rather than focusing, for example, on Walker's intentions for her characters, or using her biography to interpret Shug Avery's rendering as a blueswoman, *Fictional Blues* instead considers Celie's autobiographical self-fashioning, and her biographical invention of others through her diary entries. This approach allows for a productive reading on another narrative level when, for instance, Celie describes a moment when Shug tells her own account of the early days of Shug's relationship with Albert. These embedded narratives, or "stories within stories," constitute complete autobiographical or biographical works, even if they are not long-form or generically marked as conventional life writing forms.[6] And rather than viewing embedded narratives as Bal does, when she suggests that "when the embedded text is kept to a minimum, its importance for the primary story diminishes," *Fictional Blues* argues that these stories, by literary and real-life narrators and characters, no matter how long or short, are not only important modes of autobiographical and biographical expression for the tellers but are also inextricable from the "primary story" of the narrative blues tradition in which informal autobiographical utterances fuel the blues musicians' reclamation of their power and agency.[7] *Fictional Blues* is indeed a book about "story*telling*."[8]

Fictional Blues questions racial, sociocultural, temporal, and gendered blues tropes by shifting blues expression from an innate, racially naturalized skill to a storytelling art form, which is one way through which its makers invent themselves. This book also allows for a new, interdisciplinary approach to autobiographical and biographical expression. I reframe traditional ideas of what autobiography, biography, and even narrative itself are in order to shift ideas about how blues music and blues people are made. *Fictional Blues* expands the variety of texts that constitute the blues, allowing for a wider group of people to participate in the tradition. By focusing on blues performers' paramusical narratives—literary depictions, lyrics, interviews, and more—in addition to music and musical performances, I demonstrate that it is storytelling in varied dimensions that undergirds the blues. This book tells an important new story: that the contemporary, multiracial, literary and musical characters who participate in so-called authentic blues expression actually create a fiction on top of a fiction. That is, they create their own literary, musical, or artistic visions, through autobiographical fictionality and persona building, within the works in which they appear, and they are autonomous in this creation, just like the early twentieth-century blues makers. While their expressive autonomy does not free them from oppressive forces based on their race, gender, or class, it does allow them to fully participate in the fictionalized, narrative blues tradition. And, of course, this claim to power and agency is most urgent for the Black blues figures in my book, with the blueswomen carrying the heaviest load as they fight to make their voices heard. Using examples culled from literature and contemporary music—close readings of literary passages, historical and contemporary interviews, live concert performances, music videos, and songs—my book shows how fictional and real-life blues artists create these self-made identities in the works of American writers as disparate as Sherman Alexie, Alice Walker, and Walter Mosley, and in the music of modern acts such as Amy Winehouse, Jack White, and Gary Clark Jr.

It is through their storytelling, both as fictional narrators and in real-life artists' song lyrics and constructed public personas—Shug Avery and Big Mama Thornton self-fashion in similar ways—that these artists resist racial, social, economic, and gendered oppression while writing themselves into the blues tradition. From Black classic blueswoman Bessie Smith's persona as a transgressive woman flouting white standards of female respectability—with her frank lyrics about sex, substance abuse, and domestic violence and her openly bisexual lifestyle—to contemporary white blues-rocker White's use of a highly stylized visual image for the White Stripes and a fabricated autobiographical backstory to sidestep the thorny issue of blues authenticity and whiteness, *Fictional Blues* is the story of how a varied group of blues makers invent and reinvent themselves through fictional autobiographical and biographical storytelling.[9]

WHAT IS THE BLUES?

In *Fictional Blues,* I define blues music not in strict formal terms but as a musical style encompassing elements of the blues as a musical form and as a narrative autobiographical aesthetic. In *The Blues: A Very Short Introduction,* Elijah Wald grapples with how to define this musical form and style. Wald stresses the difficulty in trying to nail down one definition, as there are myriad perspectives on the blues. Moreover, in the United States, the blues has long been associated with a state of mind or emotion. When having the blues is equated with sadness or depression, the music becomes a reflection of pain and heartache.[10] Scholars such as Wald, Albert Murray, and Ralph Ellison have resisted this limited perspective, especially given the significant number of blues songs classified as comical or dance-oriented. Some scholars contend that the blues is simply a musical form, usually with a standardized twelve-bar chord structure. Wald points out the flaw in that definition, as several other types of blues do not follow the twelve-bar pattern. As Wald states, "There are at least two other common blues chord patterns, the eight- and sixteen-bar blues." The AAB (with a lyrical structure of "two repeated lines followed by a rhyming third") has been a feature of numerous blues (and nonblues) songs, but all blues songs do not follow this pattern.[11] In *Fictional Blues,* I engage artists whose works fall within, as well as exist outside of, the normative twelve-bar AAB blues structure.

The blues is often defined as a cultural practice, with only a select few able to render an "authentic" performance. Wald asserts, "Many people consider the blues tradition to be primarily a matter of ethnicity and culture, the musical heritage of the African American South, which can rarely if ever be fully understood by northern, or foreign, or white artists."[12] This particular definition is the site of contentious debates. Many scholars, including Amiri Baraka, Eileen Southern, and Samuel A. Floyd Jr. argue for blues music as a strictly Black American art form, evolving out of African musical and cultural practices.[13] Alternatively, Wald, Murray, and Ellison offer a more culturally and racially inclusive definition of blues music. For those scholars, blues music, and Black American music more generally, is a cross-cultural and cross-racial project.[14] The blues exists due to the cross-pollination between African American and European American musical elements and is strengthened by the involvement of Black and nonblack artists and audiences. *Fictional Blues* engages the blues as a music, and a cultural tradition, that is defined by its Black origins but continues to be engaged by Black and nonblack musicians and fans in the twenty-first century. As such, my book features Black and nonblack literary and real-life blues musicians.

In *Fictional Blues,* the narrators and characters in the contemporary literary and musical texts may work in one of the canonical blues forms (twelve-, eight-, or sixteen-bar blues) or may simply feature blues facets "based on a pentatonic or five-note 'blues scale' that is frequently used by West African performers," including blue notes ("flatted third and seventh notes") and African-derived rhythms. In *Fictional Blues*, a western singer who "uses a broad range of microtones and moves between them with . . . freedom and subtlety" can also be deemed a blues or bluesy vocalist.[15] In other words, an artist does not have to use strict blues forms exclusively, or play only in a blues style, to be included in *Fictional Blues*. Rather, my approach allows for the inclusion of a broader range of artists and literary characters.

In the methodology I deploy here, vernacular definitions of blues music as first an emotional state, and second a cultural practice, are continually in conversation. Articulations of feeling in blues are in dialectical relationship with blues as a cultural practice. Although traces of sadness, for example, can be read in blues texts, I argue that expressions of sadness or depression can be found in many styles of music, including folk, rock, country, hip-hop, and so on. Blues music does not have proprietary rights to expressions of grief, longing, pain, or heartache. And the existence of upbeat, party blues songs is well documented.[16] As for the cultural practice argument, it is clear that early twentieth-century American blues music was able to flourish due to regional and sociological factors, including Black Americans' proximity to the legacy of slavery, relentless racial oppression expressed through repressive Jim Crow laws, economic hardship, and political and social limitations. However, blues music need not rely on these factors, nor is the experience of these conditions necessary, for an artist to produce "authentic" blues. Such requirements collapse the importance of racial and cultural interchange in the growth and development of blues music. Moreover, projections of authenticity directed at Black blues musicians, in particular, tend to overshadow their accomplishments as professionals in control of their work and their personas who are striving for commercial success. Also lost in the purely cultural argument is the blues musicians' personal agency through narrative self-invention.

THE CULT OF AUTHENTICITY: "A THICKET OF EXPECTATIONS AND VALUATIONS"

Notions of racialized blues authenticity began in the 1950s, when young white American folk revivalists became enamored with acoustic country blues music to the exclusion of electric blues.[17] For these largely middle-class collectors, rural bluesmen Son House, Charley Patton, and Robert

Johnson were more authentic than amplified blues players such as B. B. King and Bobby "Blue" Bland. Here I am defining "rural bluesmen" as men who perform in a Delta blues style, though the term "bluesmen," more generally, includes men who perform in a blues style (Delta or not) or form of music, and/or participate in a narrative autobiographical blues aesthetic. Most of these fans tended to conflate the *real blues* with particular class, regional, temporal, and, of course, racial experiences. For them, a so-called authentic blues musician was Black, poor, rural, and, most importantly, unsullied by modernity. As Wald suggests, "White urbanites, for obvious reasons, are fascinated by a creation myth in which genius blossomed, wild and untamed, from the Delta mud, and are less interested in the unromantic picture of Muddy Waters sitting by the radio and listening to Fats Waller, or a sharecropper singing Broadway show tunes as he followed his mule along the levee."[18] The concept of blues authenticity is also gendered, with many predominantly white and male blues scholars, critics, and fans viewing the mostly male country blues artists as prototypes of the authentic blues figure, while determining the women, as a result of both their popularity and their financial remuneration, to be inauthentic. While blueswomen—women who perform in a blues style or form of music and/or participate in a narrative autobiographical blues aesthetic—with southern performance roots such as Ma Rainey and Bessie Smith were considered to be legitimate blueswomen, others such as Mamie Smith were not. It is important to note that there was a sizable Black audience for urban blues—rural blues transported to the city with the aid of amplification—during the 1940s and into the 1950s.[19] While Black feminist scholars such as Angela Davis and Hazel Carby have long championed female classic blues artists, since the 1960s they have been comparatively marginalized even though they recorded records for race labels such as Paramount and OKeh before the Delta blues artists did, and enjoyed significant commercial success. *Fictional Blues* will build on the work of Davis, Carby, and others to help recenter Black women's blues as robust sites of narrative self-creation.

A majority of the seminal early blues studies affirm ideas about blues authenticity rooted in race. LeRoi Jones's *Blues People* (1963) claims blues music as Black when he states that blues music "is a native American music, the product of the black man in this country."[20] In *Blues, Ideology, and Afro-American Literature* (1984), Houston Baker also argues for Black people's sociological experience creating a distinct cultural expression.

According to Baker, "Black folk expression is a product of impoverishment of blacks in America."[21] Robert Palmer's *Deep Blues* (1981) similarly privileges particular racial and geographical experiences in the development of authentic Delta blues expression. According to Palmer, "Delta blues is a refined, extremely subtle, and ingeniously systematic musical language. Playing and especially singing it right involve some exceptionally fine points that only a few white guitarists, virtually no white singers, and not too many Black musicians who learned to play and sing anywhere other than the Delta have been able to grasp."[22] And, in the twenty-first century, *Living Blues* magazine continues to situate the blues within an exclusively Black American experience, articulating its mission as being to "document and preserve the *African American* [emphasis added] blues tradition."[23] There is also a twenty-first-century body of revisionist blues literature that moves beyond limiting ideas of authentic blues legitimacy. Elijah Wald, Patricia Schroeder, Paige McGinley, and Marybeth Hamilton are scholars from varied disciplines who interrogate the romance and mythology inherent in the blues tradition.[24] Despite these scholarly interventions, some contemporary critics, fans, and even American roots musicians themselves continue to perpetuate notions of authentic Black musical expression. *Fictional Blues* also contests outdated notions of blues authenticity in a general sense, determining that compelling blues storytellers can be found in varied races, genders, classes, geographical areas, and temporal spaces.

The concept of authenticity is foregrounded in certain genres of music more than others. Here I am borrowing musicologist Allan Moore's definition of "authenticity." Moore advances a tripartite system wherein a musical performance exhibits "first person authenticity," "third person authenticity, or "second person authenticity." As Moore states, "*authenticity of expression,* or what I also term 'first person authenticity', arises when an originator (composer, performer) succeeds in conveying the impression that his/her utterance is one of integrity, that it represents an attempt to communicate in an unmediated form with an audience." This is the type of authenticity that most music critics and fans seek in popular music artists. Within this model, critics and fans of rock music, for example, want to believe that the sentiments and stories expressed by the artists musically, as well as in performance and even offstage, are honest and true. Yet in rock there is some room for the idea that an artist might, from time to time, use a persona onstage, on a record, or even in an interview. Critics and fans of rock music yearn for "authenticity of expression" but are willing to sometimes accept performative artifice—the late David Bowie's early 1970s Ziggy Stardust character is one such example.[25] But musical styles situated within American roots traditions, particularly blues, attract fans, critics, and even practitioners, across races and generations, who hold tight to the idea that the blues is a racially naturalized style of music in which one has to have had a certain set of economic experiences, or be in a particular racialized body, in order to perform the music authentically.

When Roger Gatchet, for example, conducted a series of oral histories in the 2000s with African American blues musicians in the Austin blues scene, he discovered that "all four musicians articulate[d] blues authenticity as a quality that one can only access through a combination of racial and class identification, in addition to the lived experiences that are common to those identity categories." Henry "Bluesboy" Hubbard, a blues pianist and guitarist from La Grange, Texas, who served as a master to white apprentice blues players such as Clifford Antone, owner of the legendary Austin blues club Antone's, and blues-rock multi-instrumentalist, singer, songwriter, and producer Johnny Winter, asserts that, "Black guys has more soul, more feeling, when they play and white guys don't automatically have that. . . . If a white guy's playing a guitar and a black guy's playing, and they can be in a room, and you say, 'Hubbard, this guy's going to run some notes, and this guy going to run them, now you tell me which one is white and which one is black.' And I can pretty much tell you, you know. It's just that much difference."[26] This speaks directly to Jennifer Stoever's theorizing of the sonic color line that "enables listeners to construct and discern racial identities based on voices, sounds, and particular soundscapes."[27]

Not only does the race of the musician affect the quality of the blues performance, but racial difference can be transmitted through exclusively aural means. This idea echoes in E. Patrick Johnson's discussion about his interactions with an a capella gospel choir in Australia: "Although I thought they had a great sound and, to some extent, had mastered the gospel idiom, I nevertheless felt that something was missing. I realize now what I did not then: that I was waiting to *hear* [emphasis added] an 'authentic' voice in their music."[28] And Corey Harris, a contemporary African American blues performer who is more than a generation younger than Hubbard, also hears race in the music itself. In a provocative 2015 blog post titled "Can White People Play the Blues?" Harris answered the question this way: "Of course we are all free to play whatever styles we enjoy playing. Music is truly universal in the sense that all human beings respond to its language. But saying music is universal does not mean that all people feel the same piece of music in the same way. It doesn't mean that all music is the same. Neither does it mean that anyone can play it in the same way as those who have a blood connection to the culture."[29] The privileging of "first person authenticity" persists in the contemporary blues scene to such an extent that Moore's concept of "third person authenticity" is useful here. According to Moore, "*authenticity of execution, or* . . . 'third person authenticity.' . . . arises when a performer succeeds in conveying the impression of accurately representing the ideas of another, embedded within a tradition of performance." In this case, it is not the artist who is imbued with authenticity but the artist's appropriation of some other authentic music that provides the authentication. For contemporary blues fans and critics, as well as for other Americana enthusiasts, Moore's discussion of the "authenticity of execution" serves as the next best thing for American roots performers whose personal experiences might fall outside of the parameters of so-called first-person authenticity. While *Fictional Blues* contests essentialist notions of racialized blues authenticity, I recognize that the fictional and real-life blues musicians in this book enjoy or aspire to "first person authenticity," or instead rely on "third person authenticity," which allows them to convincingly appropriate a blues performance style.[30]

THE BLUES STORYTELLING TRADITION

Fictional Blues is primarily a book about storytelling. To be more precise, it is about the ways in which blues artists use fictionalized autobiographical narratives to create personas while effectively joining the long Black folk tradition in which dramatic real-life events come together with tall tales on the way to becoming folk ballads and blues songs—allowing these artists to write themselves into the blues storytelling tradition. *Fictional Blues* is interested in the ways in which blues musicians fictionalize their narratives about how their lives came to be. These fictions are disseminated through song lyrics; recorded musical performances; live stage performances, including onstage banter between the musician and the audience; interviews; and representational literary works about blues musicians. All of these media are vehicles for the dissemination of these autobiographical narratives. In *Fictional Blues*, these autobiographical fictions are expressed in myriad ways, including lies, telling tall tales, creating personas, and the idea that even in a story that purports to be objectively true, every good storyteller makes decisions about which moments to include and which to excise lest the listener become bored. In this way, even an autobiographical story that is based on objective verifiable truths is constructed and therefore fictional.

In *Fictional Blues* I demonstrate the centrality of storytelling as a means to both invent and reinvent a blues persona. When blues people tell stories through those mediums, and as they construct their autobiographical and biographical fictions, they create a self (or persona)—a different self from the singer or musician at the beginning of the tale. They create a new self through making decisions about which details of their life stories to include and which to leave out, deciding *how* to tell the story based on audience feedback—for Black blues people during the 1950–60s blues revival this sometimes hinged on white male audience expectations about blues authenticity. When I consider invention and reinvention, I look at them through an autobiographical lens—autobiography scholars Paul John Eakin, Timothy Dow Adams, Herbert Leibowitz, Sidonie Smith, and Julia Watson, who see autobiographical narrative as a necessarily "fictive structure," come to mind here.[31] I also see this invention arising through the African American folk tradition in which autobiographical and biographical stories exist in an indeterminate place between truth and fiction—a place where the objective facts of a tale are less important than the quality of the telling and the resonances the story has for an audience. This book focuses on blues people becoming so by telling their life stories and the life stories of other blues people, through fictional autobiographical and biographical narrative. Fictional autobiographical narratives exist in myriad forms, including oral autobiographical and biographical storytelling vis-à-vis "as told to" autobiographical works, interviews in publications, interviews in documentaries and television programs, and impromptu autobiographical storytelling onstage. They also occur in written autobiographical and biographical storytelling such as autobiographical narratives and letters, editorials, and articles in newspapers, and in performances such as live concerts, music videos, and participation in long-form music documentaries. And finally, they occur in musical forms through lyrics, musical call and response and repetition, and vocal performance, as well as in blues musicians' participation in record company/concert promoters' ideas about blues authenticity. All of these are featured in *Fictional Blues.*

Some of these stories contain fictions as a necessary corrective, while others contain fictions because doing so is an important part of the professionalizing process. Twentieth-century bluesman Tommy Johnson, for example, carried around a rabbit's foot at all times to increase his local celebrity, perhaps in the hope of giving people something to talk about or increasing the number of audience members for his country dances.[32] Similarly, Johnson's brother LeDell told David Evans that Tommy became an exceptional guitar player because he went to a Mississippi crossroads and sold his soul to the devil. Even though potential audience members likely did not believe this story, they just might have appreciated the extra work that went into the creation of Tommy's exciting blues persona. And, of course, as our twenty-first-century example Jack White reminds us, the intrigue of not knowing the true relationship between the two members of the White Stripes compelled music journalists and fans to want to know more about them. These fictions helped build audiences and sell records at the beginning of the twentieth century—and classic blues queens such as Bessie Smith, Ma Rainey, and Ethel Waters, with their reputations as transgressive bad women, were some of the biggest selling blues recording artists—as well as in our contemporary moment.

When I talk about narrative, specifically autobiographical narrative, I am not focused on formalized, generically marked autobiographical works. I am instead interested in blues artists who embody a persona to tell stories about their lives, and the lives of others, and to create characters through their lyrics such as Mamie Smith, Ethel Waters, and Jack White. These personas are extended through their live concert performances; their onstage banter with their audiences; their print, online, and television interviews; and their music videos and other visual cultural productions. These personas can be detected in generically marked autobiographical works as well. And, of course, blues characters in fictional literary works can also create and express themselves through personas.

Scholars across disciplinary fields have engaged the blues person's use of persona, and have made the argument that the "I" in blues lyrics is not necessarily the person singing the song but that instead the

"I" might be a constructed persona or a separate narrative character. In his article "Musical Personae," performance studies scholar Philip Auslander argues for this when he "posit[s] that in musical performance, this representation of self is the direct object of the verb *to perform*. What musicians perform first and foremost is not music, but their own identities as musicians, their musical personae."[33] Auslander, McGinley, Jeff Titon, and Dennis Jarrett engage this idea in different ways, but for the most part they pay attention to embodied versions of persona, focusing on the performance of blues music, and music more generally, and lyrics instead of on autobiographical narrative, as I do in *Fictional Blues*.[34] For these scholars, the "I" is unstable, echoing theories about autobiographical narratives by Sidonie Smith, Julia Watson, and others, who argue for distinctions between the "real" or historical "I"—"a flesh-and-blood person located in a particular time and place," the narrating "I"—"a persona of the historical person who wants to tell, or is coerced into telling, a story about the self," and the narrated "I"—"the version of the self that the narrating "I" chooses to constitute through recollection for the reader," demonstrating the ways in which the autobiographical "I" is fluid.[35] This unstable "I" allows the fictive characters and real-life blues musicians to work in a continual process of self-invention and reinvention through autobiographical storytelling. Finally, while *Fictional Blues* is focused on narrative concerns, these stories, particularly those of the Black blueswomen, are sometimes told through the body. As such, I am indebted to Daphne Brooks, Stephanie Batiste, and Uri McMillan for their work around Black women's reclamation of their cultural and political power through performance.[36]

BLUES: FROM THE POPULAR TO THE TRADITIONAL

Fictional Blues first looks to the early architects of blues myths—the Black men and women who used fictionalized autobiographical blues expression to take control of their own narratives and reclaim their subjectivity in the face of racism, patriarchy, and poverty. It demonstrates that throughout the twentieth century, and into the present, these authors use storytelling—focusing on a narrative that objectively happened while choosing what details to keep in or take out, or how fantastical to make the "truth" or the lie—to claim their own self-styled identities.

Black American bandleader, composer, and music publisher W. C. Handy is one such author. His 1941 autobiographical narrative *Father of the Blues*, in which he uses romantic mythmaking and self-promotion to put himself at the center of the story of the blues—a music that existed before he could "discover" it—would later inspire representational literary blues makers in the novels *RL's Dream* by Walter Mosley and *Reservation Blues* by Sherman Alexie.[37] Similarly, during a time when many middle-class Black women were trying to make their way into the white-conceived Cult of True Womanhood—where true women demonstrated "piety, purity, submissiveness and domesticity"—blueswomen such as Rainey used their lyrics to flout heteronormative women's roles imposed by the dominant culture.[38] In "Prove It On Me Blues," Rainey self-presents as a sexually confident woman with the freedom to enter into whatever sexual relationships she pleases, demanding,

> They said I do it, ain't nobody caught me
> Sure got to prove it on me
> Went out last night with a crowd of my friends
> They must've been women, 'cause I don't like no men.[39]

While Rainey was known to have sexual relationships with women, and in her self-penned song brags about her conquests, she dares the listener to "prove" her indiscretions. This sexual braggadocio, popular in men's blues songs, helped to create her legend as both fearless and sexually independent. That legacy echoes in the representation of Shug Avery, the blueswoman at the center of *The Color Purple.*

These myths also influence contemporary white musicians such as English singer-songwriter Amy Winehouse and blues rocker Jack White, who tell stories and construct personas that allow them to participate in the narrative blues tradition. For example, despite her privileged whiteness, Winehouse's unvarnished song lyrics, engaging sexual freedom and alcoholism, and her public struggles with domestic violence and substance abuse sparked a media backlash unmistakably tied to sexism and misogyny, reminiscent of the gendered mistreatment of transgressive real-life classic blueswomen like Rainey, as well as representational blues performers like Shug Avery.

As my book shows, Handy and Rainey are two examples of the many early African American music makers who worked within the blues tradition of fictional autobiographical self-fashioning and tall-tale telling. And it is in this spirit that contemporary literary blues characters and real-life blues makers engage the mythos fomented by these early artists. The following section serves as an example of the ways in which I will apply my theories about autobiographical blues self-creation to the rest of *Fictional Blues.*

A CASE STUDY: MISSISSIPPI HAM RIDER'S AUTOBIOGRAPHICAL SELF-INVENTION

Toni Cade Bambara's 1964 short story "Mississippi Ham Rider" is about a Black blues musician who refuses to be limited by stereotypical ideas about what a Black bluesman should be.[40] The fictional presentation of Ham foregrounds his autobiographical self-invention, using it to question, historicize, and critique the narratives of authenticity that emerge around the blues. "Mississippi Ham Rider" demonstrates the ways in which contemporary fictional musician characters participate in their own autobiographical self-fashioning while playfully destabilizing racialized myths.

Ham bears a resemblance to the real-life early twentieth-century country bluesman Son House, who enjoyed a successful second act during the 1960s transatlantic blues revival. According to Francis Davis, "By virtue of having survived most of his Delta contemporaries, he became a stand-in for all of them, a living link to the holiest blues tradition. Jesus and Lazarus and the twelve apostles all rolled into one."[41] While "Mississippi Ham Rider" does not include a character named Son House, Ham—due to his age—could have been his contemporary.

"Mississippi Ham Rider" features a young, Black, female, New York City–based record label representative named Inez Williams, who, with the help of her white male colleague Neil McLoughlin, attempts to convince Mississippi Ham Rider, an old Southern Black bluesman, to travel north to record new blues tracks. The titular character, with help from his family and friends, not only resists the duo's advances but also consciously asserts his right to create blues music on his own terms rather than conforming to romanticized notions of authentic blues expression. Inez, as the narrator, and Ham, in different ways, both reject the racialized tropes of the so-called authentic bluesman. Their intervention helps to make a pathway for the eventual emergence of Ham's individual blues identity.

Given her race and gender, Inez appears to be the correct choice for a label representative who might hold sway over Ham. Neil even teases Inez about her failure to seduce Ham into traveling north. He asks, "But wasn't he at least knocked out by your superior charms, not to mention your long, lean gams?" Although Neil's tone is more playful than sincere, it makes sense that the label representatives would expect that a pretty woman would soften Ham up. Except the opposite occurs. Inez's presence in the small Southern town highlights her generational and geographical distance from Ham. Inez is a liminal figure: She is an insider and an outsider; she is Black, but she is not quite Black enough. The story's references to sit-ins suggest that its time frame is more or less the same as the publishing date. In this context, Inez's first encounter with Ham is typically unsuccessful, as he is distrustful and uncommunicative with the young Northerner. Inez recounts, "We had talked for nearly an hour—or rather I had talked, he had merely rolled his eyes and stared into his cup as he swirled the watery coffee revealing the grounds." And when Inez leaves the coffee shop where she has spent the last hour with Ham, the waitress and cook eye her angrily as she walks out the door. Over her shoulder she hears, "So what's this high-yaller Northern bitch doin' hittin' on evil ole Ham?"[42] Inez's unforgivable sins of foreignness and light-skinnedness render her a target of scorn and prevent her from connecting with folks in the town.

Inez is as much of an outsider in the South due to her geographical background as Ham is a curiosity to Northern label executives, who, as Neil puts it, want "him in the flesh to allow the poor folkway-starved sophisticates to, through a outrageous process of osmosis, which in no way should suggest miscegenation, to absorb their native—."Given that the story takes place during the American country blues revival, it follows that Neil would reference white blues fans who are desperate for authentic Black blues expression yet resistant to experiencing proximity to everyday Black people. When Neil begins to reel off a list of so-called authentic, and cooperative, bluesmen he has encountered in the past, the descriptions feed into familiar bluesman stereotypes: "They were always pretty easy to find. Mobile, Auburn, just sitting there in a beat-up room in a beat-up town in a beat-up mood, just sitting there waiting for an angel of mercy—me. Doing nothing but a moaning and a hummin' and a strummin'—."[43] Neil, a white Northern man, represents these musicians as abject creatures who are waiting to be rescued.

At the end of Neil's reverie, Inez states, "Never mind, let's go find Mr. Ethnic-Authentic," revealing her cynicism about their roles as blues revivalists. She is aware that her white bosses in New York are looking for an image as much as a musical talent. Ham's saleable authenticity is why they are interested. What is compelling about Bambara's depiction of Inez, however, is that as conscious as she is about her label's cynical manipulation of the blues record–buying and –collecting public, she too at first falls into the authenticity trap. After Inez and Neil arrive at Mama Teddy's, a storefront soul food restaurant, to meet Ham, his wife Isabele tells Neil, "The man needs money, mister. He's been needing for a long time. Now what you gonna do for him?" Inez admits that she immediately sees Ham as a type rather than a person: "The image of the great old artist fallen on bad times, holding up in a stuffy rooming house, drinking bad home brew out of a jelly jar and howling blues out the window appealed to my Grade-B movie-ruined mind." Her movie reference suggests that she recognizes her own culpability in falling prey to a lazy stereotype, but it is as if she is helpless to resist popular characterizations of the blues figure since those are the ideas that circulate most widely. Inez is a product of her generation, so she is as inclined to see Ham as being "not of these times" as are the middle-class white folkies who push him into a confining bluesman box.[44]

When Ham finally arrives with his guitar, and Mama Teddy places "big bowls of things onto the table," he announces, "I don't sing no cotton songs, sister. . . . And I ain't never worked in the fields or shucked corn. And I don't sing no nappy-head church songs neither. And no sad numbers about losing my woman and losing my mind. I ain't never lost no woman and that's the truth." Ham asserts himself in this moment. He is cognizant of the mythology surrounding the Black bluesman, so much of it springing from the unjust political and socioeconomic status of Black people in the Jim Crow South. His monologue suggests that he recognizes that these experiences are real for some Black bluesman, but not for himself. And when Neil asks, "Well, what else is there? . . . I mean just what kind of songs do you sing?" and Ham responds, "My kind," he underscores his refusal to play the part of the old-timey, real bluesman for the profit of the white-owned Northern record labels that cater largely to white, middle-class youth. If he decides to go to New York, it will be on his terms. While Neil is confounded by Ham's monologue, Inez simply responds, "Good." In her narrator voice she claims she uttered the word for "no particular reason," but I argue that her utterance is a strong gesture in support of Ham's desire to be seen as a human being with subjectivity and the ability to craft his own blues identity, one that may not conform to the white record labels' desires, but one that will be personally and artistically fulfilling because it is his own.[45] Ham's moment of defiance helps Inez to see him as himself for the first time—instead of as the embodiment of a cultural myth. At the end of the story, Ham agrees to go to New York. His declaration of all the things he won't do affirms all the things he is, will become, and can create, including an alternative blues identity.

Ham is a fictional character who constructs his autobiographical narrative a little at a time as the story moves forward. In the beginning, Ham is largely silent, allowing Inez and Neil to fill in the gaps in his biography. However, by the end of the story, Ham reclaims his own autobiographical narrative. Echoes of this work will be found in the chapters outlined below.

FICTIONAL BLUES OVERVIEW

My opening chapter, "The Narrative Blues Tradition: Tall Tales, Myths, and Black American Folklore," tells the story of the architects of the blues and the ways in which they invented enduring mythological personas through autobiographical fictions. Beginning with a discussion of Stagolee, the early twentieth-century folk hero whose exploits were memorialized in ballads and blues songs throughout the twentieth-century and beyond, chapter 1 focuses on the ways in which the blurring of fact and fiction aided in the autobiographical invention and reinvention of American blues artists. These narratives helped to create mythical blues figures, such as the bad man, the transgressive (bad) blueswoman, and the bedeviled bluesman. Given that the contemporary writers and musicians in my book are in a conversation with an early to mid-twentieth-century version of American blues expression, a historical and cultural context is helpful. Through the discussion of important foundational cultural artifacts such as the multiple tellings and retellings of the Stagolee story; early interviews with Mamie Smith, whose 1920 "Crazy Blues" became the first recorded blues song by an African American woman;

a discussion about the myths about Ma Rainey and Bessie Smith's relationship; and the first-person accounts of Ethel Waters, David "Honeyboy" Edwards, and Mance Lipscomb, I explore the origins of the myths surrounding Black blues music that signal blues authenticity and continue to be beloved by fans and critics alike. Through an exploration of these texts, readers will have a better understanding of where these myths come from and how they continue to be shaped in American literature and popular music in the twenty-first century.

While the opening chapter introduces the women and men who created the blues and their enduring myths, chapter 2, "Shug, Big Mama, and Amy: Autobiographical Fictions and Addictions," focuses on contemporary fiction and popular cultural works featuring blueswomen in the mold of the classic blues queen. Building on my conversation in chapter 1 about Bessie Smith, Ma Rainey, and Mamie Smith, in this chapter I consider how the female blues persona is gendered. Many of the classic blueswomen subvert notions of acceptable feminine expression within a racist and patriarchal culture. This chapter examines the ways in which fictional and real-life blueswomen who have largely been erased from blues history—and if they are visible, they are deemed transgressive by their predominantly male critics—talk back to their limiting representations through autobiographical self-expression. I focus on blueswoman Shug Avery, and Squeak's unexpected transformation into a blues singer in Alice Walker's *The Color Purple.* I then turn to real-life blues singers Big Mama Thornton and Amy Winehouse. In Thornton's early years, she was dubbed the "New Bessie Smith." Thornton serves as a bridge between the classic blueswomen and contemporary reimaginings of the blues queen. Through unconventional autobiographical performances onstage and in interviews, she reclaimed ownership of her work as young white performers such as Elvis Presley and Janis Joplin garnered critical accolades and enjoyed tremendous commercial success covering her songs. The lyrics of Amy Winehouse, too, are part of a tradition of American classic blues expression. In songs such as "You Know I'm No Good" and "Wake Up Alone," Winehouse's vocals, lyrics, and performance style engage with music traditionally performed by Blacks in the United States, and create an alternative autobiographical narrative that contests her public persona largely derived from sexist and misogynistic mass-media representations of her life.

Chapter 3, "'I Was Astounded at What I Heard': Robert Johnson's Autobiographical and Biographical Afterlives," moves from representations of the classic blueswomen to a key country blues figure: Robert Johnson. A foundational blues musician, Johnson's mythical representation appears in a variety of contemporary cultural spaces. According to the crossroads legend, Johnson sold his soul to the devil in order to become a master guitar player. This obviously apocryphal tale, and Johnson's violent death, has given blues scholars and fans across generations much to talk about, and it has resulted in Johnson's commodification vis-à-vis biographies, fictional literary works, films, and ephemera. It has also, unfortunately, resulted in his often simplistic and one-dimensional rendering in fictional literary texts. His womanizing, restless spirit, and guitar are all relegated to mythical signs of an authentic bluesman, and in these works the fictional Johnson has no choice but to confront his limited (and limiting) representations. In sharp contrast to the classic blueswomen, who were all but forgotten by the latter part of the twentieth century, in the 1960s Johnson became the prototype of the authentic bluesman for young, white blues revivalists in the United States and England. In this chapter, I show the influence that the real-life Johnson had on the blues identities of Keith Richards of the Rolling Stones, Eric Clapton of Cream, and Bob Dylan, and the ways in which their romantic discussions about Johnson in their recent autobiographies read like a "memoir" of the 1960s blues revivalists' version of the blues. In the novels *Reservation Blues* by Sherman Alexie and *RL's Dream* by Walter Mosley, and in the short stories "Black Elvis" by Geoffrey Becker and "Stones in My Passway, Hellhound on My Trail" by T. C. Boyle, I discuss the ways in which Johnson's migrations and biographical legend serve as vehicles for the agentive autobiographical blues self-creation of other characters.

In chapter 4, "From John Anthony Gillis to Jack White: A Study in Blues Self-Invention," I turn to a white musician's autobiographical blues self-fashioning by focusing on blues-rock singer, songwriter, musician, and producer Jack White, a spiritual descendant of the early Delta blues players. This chapter engages White's ever-evolving identity: from John Anthony Gillis, a young, self-conscious, white blues disciple determined to stand apart from his contemporaries and the white bluesmen who preceded him, to "Jack White," a solo artist, producer, and businessman who takes an unapologetically postmodern approach to his work as a musician and as a music industry executive. In the first section of the chapter, I examine the visual presentation White constructed for himself and Meg White during the White Stripes era. In the second section, I analyze sonic aspects of White's blues self-fashioning through his vocal performance in "Ball and Biscuit" from the 2003 White Stripes album *Elephant.* And in the third section, I look at postmodern pastiche in White's solo work, specifically in his 2011 collaboration with Insane Clown Posse on W. A. Mozart's scatological 1782 vocal canon "Leck mich im Arsch" and in his video for *Blunderbuss*'s "Freedom at 21." All of these sections work together to demonstrate the ways in which White considers blues stereotypes and grapples with cultural appropriations in order to forge new approaches to engaging American music and Black American impacts on American culture writ large.

In chapter 5, "The Blues Apprenticeship: Racialized Conventions of the Acolyte," I explore the concept of the blues apprenticeship with origins dating back to Charley Patton's mentorship of numerous young, aspiring Delta bluesmen, including Chester Burnett, who would later be known as Howlin' Wolf. I argue that the subjects in this chapter engage the racialized authenticity paradigm that is built into the blues apprenticeship. All of the relationships I consider highlight the symbiotic connections between the young blues acolyte and the willing mentor, and show the ways that fictionalized autobiographical and biographical expression affects the various apprenticeships and vice versa. The chapter begins with a discussion about the racial dynamics in interracial short-term, institutionalized apprenticeships that are connected to state arts commissions and humanities foundations, such as the West Virginia Humanities Council West Virginia Folklife Apprenticeship Program and the Virginia Humanities Virginia Folklife Apprenticeship Program. The chapter will then turn to a discussion about white, Alabama-based blues performer Debbie Bond, who has apprenticed both formally and informally with a number of blues artists, including legendary Alabama-based guitarist and singer Johnny Shines. In the final section, I explore the concept of the conventional and unconventional blues apprenticeship as constructed around Ralph Ellison's essays about music; Gary Clark Jr., who began his career as the "Next Big Thing" in the blues; and classically trained vocalist and multi-instrumentalist Rhiannon Giddens, a solo artist and member of the Americana group Carolina Chocolate Drops. Ultimately, this chapter interrogates the ways in which blues artists invent and reinvent themselves within and through the apprenticeship paradigm.

Fictional Blues is the story of how a wide variety of blues artists—women and men, Black and nonblack—write themselves into existence through fictionalized autobiographical storytelling. These modes of autobiographical expression are not necessarily book-based or generically marked. Rather they are autobiographical utterances that sometimes reflect the main narrative, and, at other times, exist as embedded ones. No matter how the autobiographical works manifest, the fictive and real-life blues musicians in *Fictional Blues* demonstrate their agency and reclaim their power as they tell their own stories in their own ways.

1 The Narrative Blues Tradition

Tall Tales, Myths, and Black American Folklore

The earliest written-down version of the Stagolee ballad that San Angelo, Texas, art teacher Ella Scott Fisher sent to folklorist and teacher John Lomax on February 9, 1910 begins as follows:

'Twas a Christmas morning,
The hour was about ten,
When Stagalee shot Billy Lyons
And landed in the Jefferson pen.
O Lordy, po' Stagalee![1]

In her note Fisher states,

> This is all the verses I remember. The origin of this ballad, I have been told, was the shooting of Billy Lyons in a barroom on the Memphis levee, by Stack Lee. The song is sung by the Negroes on the

levee while they are loading and unloading the river freighters, the words being composed by the singers. The characters were prominently known in Memphis, I was told, the unfortunate Stagalee belonging to the family of the owners of the Lee line of steamers, which are known on the Mississippi from Cairo to the Gulf. I give all this to you as it was given to me. The effect of the song with its minor refrain is weird, and the spoken interpolations add to the realism. It becomes immensely personal as you hear it, like a recital of something known or experienced by the singer.

An incomplete record of the ballad—just ten stanzas—was later included in *American Ballads and Folk Songs,* published by John Lomax and his son Alan Lomax in 1934. The ballad tells the dramatic tale of an African American bad man named Stagalee who shot another Black man called Billy Lyons "Dead on the barroom floor" with his "forty-four gatlin' gun."[2] This early version was based on the real-life story of William Lyons's shooting death at the hands of Lee Shelton, a.k.a. Stack Lee, in a St. Louis, Missouri, saloon on Christmas night in 1895. However, it did not include details that would emerge in later published versions, and in earlier variants circulated orally, reflecting the true events of that evening. One missing detail in particular stands out: the fact that Shelton killed Lyons, in part, because of a Stetson hat, and, according to a story on December 26, 1895, in the *St. Louis Globe-Democrat,* "When his victim fell to the floor, Sheldon [*sic*] took his hat from the hand of the wounded man and coolly walked away."[3]

Stagolee. Stacker Lee. Stagalee. Stackolee. Stack Lee. Stack-o-lee. These are just a few of the names for the folk hero whose story—the essence of which is unchanged from song to song—resonates for generations of Black people in general, and Black men in particular.[4] Cecil Brown, for instance, relays his experience hearing the story of Stagolee while growing up in the South during the late 1950s and early 1960s: "As chanted in the form of a 'toast' by my Uncle Lindsey, the narrative presented a young god of virility." And he later suggests that "Stagolee's influence persists in rap music in the use of the first-person narrator, the performers' adoption of nicknames, the social drama, the humor, and participation in the commodity culture," demonstrating how this African American folk narrative, told orally and in song, continues to leave its traces.[5]

This story about a Black man who killed another Black man over a hat, and then showed no remorse, has been told and retold in varied mediums, including poems, books, songs, ballads, graphic novels, and plays. The tale was turned into a lengthy ballad as early as 1903. As noted by Brown and D. Quentin Miller, this narrative eventually moved beyond ballads and the blues and into American literature, with writers such as Richard Wright in his novel *Native Son* (1940), Toni Morrison in her novel *Song of Solomon* (1977), and James Baldwin in his poem "Staggerlee Wonders" (1985) engaging the myth of the bad man.[6] As Miller notes, though, by the time we see Stagolee as rendered by Morrison and Baldwin, he is distinct from Wright's Bigger Thomas, who was rooted in the tradition of the protest novel: "Baldwin and Morrison appropriate Staggerlee not as a hero of a protest movement, but rather as a figure ancillary to the heroes of their works, one who can clarify the dangers of uncontrolled anger and at the same time provide a path to salvation for the actual heroes."[7] In other words, over time, Stagolee's literary depictions move away from romantic glorification to considering how his violent story might be instructive for young Black men and women. The bad man tale also evolves over time to include women tellers. Ma Rainey's 1926 recording of "Stack-o-Lee Blues" not only clears the ground for other contemporaneous blueswomen, but it allows Amy Winehouse to perform her own live version of "Stagger Lee," generations later in 2011, months before she died, demonstrating how the tale crosses boundaries of race, gender, and time.[8]

On the face of it, the story is not particularly noteworthy. It was not the only murder that occurred in St. Louis that night—according to the July 14, 1896, edition of the *St. Louis Globe-Democrat,* four other similar crimes were committed.[9] So what was it that made the story compelling enough for it to be the urtext for a wide range of twentieth-century songs across multiple genres, including blues, jazz, folk, rock and roll, R & B, and soul? It is my contention that what is left out of the story drives the legend rather than what is there. The gaps in the Stagolee tale allow the tellers to add to the narrative, serving not only as storytelling collaborators but also as cocreators and reinventors of the original event. The longevity of the Stagolee tale is reflective of the beloved nature of stories, especially of the fantastical variety. The Stagolee tale has been performed as songs and instrumentals in a jazz style by artists such as Duke Ellington and Cab Calloway; as a blues song by more than one hundred bluesmen and women, including Ma Rainey and Mississippi John Hurt; and as an R & B or soul song by Lloyd Price, James Brown, Wilson Pickett, Ike and Tina Turner, and the Isley Brothers. In the 1930s and 1940s, John and Alan Lomax recorded prisoners singing the songs as folk protest music. Numerous pop and rock artists, such as the Grateful Dead, Bob Dylan, Huey Lewis and the News, and the Clash, have performed versions of the Stagolee ballad.[10] And Greil Marcus might have been the first rock critic to recognize the Stagolee legend as a metaphor for the Black artists themselves, as he discusses Sly Stone's *There's a Riot Goin' On* through this lens.[11]

As Brown and Richard Bauman suggest, oral literature, and its power, is tied to its "individual, social, and cultural" context.[12] David C. Rubin also argues that "oral traditions are viewed as human behavior, not reified texts."[13] In other words, the resonances of this oral and then written-down folk tale outline the people who told and retold the stories. As Fisher says of the Stagalee ballad, "It becomes immensely personal as you hear it, like a recital of something known or experienced by the singer."[14] Here Fisher suggests that the singer of a ballad, though working with a version far removed from the original text, can still find a way into the narrative, effectively making it his or her own. Moving from person to person, and across time and space, the song retains the story. As Rubin notes, "Remembering a piece for an oral tradition does not require the recall of exact words: recall of the general meaning and form is sufficient." And, as Rubin suggests, "one specific variant of a song is not being transmitted at all. Rather, what is being transmitted is the theme of the song, its imagery, its poetics, and some specific details."[15]

In the case of Stagolee, the core of the story revolves around the aftermath of a senseless murder on a Christmas evening in St. Louis—but the various singers, tellers, and retellers of the story can add verses to the narrative. These additions may, as in the example of Stagolee, include details that will draw the listener deeper into the tale, motivating them to invest just a little bit more in the narrative. In the version that Fisher presented to John Lomax, Stagalee goes to jail, but he is ultimately released after his "old woman" posts "a ten-thousand-dollar bail."[16] This version hews somewhat closer to the real-life story, in which instead of being immediately caught, tried, and sentenced to hanging, as in the Stagolee tale published by Howard Odum in the *Journal of American Folklore* in 1911, Shelton's well-regarded white lawyer Nat Dryden argued that

Shelton killed in self-defense, resulting in a hung jury. Dryden died on August 26, 1897, before Shelton's second trial, where he was convicted of murder and began a twenty-five-year sentence at Missouri State Penitentiary in October 1897.[17] On Thanksgiving 1909, Shelton was paroled, only to be arrested on robbery and assault charges two years later.[18] He ultimately died in prison on March 11, 1912.[19]

In the version of the Stagolee ballad that circulated during the 1930s in Texas and Louisiana—one collected by John Lomax—after Stagolee goes to prison and he briefly runs away, he is recaptured and killed by Chief Maloney.[20] While in real life it appears that Shelton, who was involved with the Democratic Party, and Lyons, a member of an influential Republican family, had a deadly argument over politics, in this version, and in others, the two spar over a gambling disagreement.[21] In this variant, Stagolee has a reputation that precedes him—when the police chief comes looking for Stagolee in the bar, he finds him "drunk an' layin' on de barroom floor." When the chief asks the bartender who that is, the bartender replies, "Speak softly." . . . It's dat bad nigger Stagolee." In this iteration there is mention of the hat: "Slowly Stack walked from de table, he said, 'I can't let you go wid dat. You win all of my money an' my milk-white Stetson hat.'" He is no longer the "po' Stagalee" from the version Miss Fisher gifted to John Lomax. He is now a "bad nigger" who is feared by the teller, the local community, law enforcement, and even, ultimately, the devil:

> De hangman put de mask on, tied his han's behin' his back,
> Sprung de trap on Stagolee, but his neck refused to crack.
> Hangman, he got frightened, he said: "Chief, you see how it be,
> I cain' hang this man, you better let him go free."

Of course, Chief Maloney does not let Stagolee go free, opting instead to shoot him "six times in de side." Stagolee finds himself in hell, playfully fighting with a new friend:

> Stack he tol' de devil, "Come on, le's have a lil fun,
> You stick me wid yo' pitchfork an' I'll shoot you wid my 41."
> Stagolee say, "Now, now, Mister Devil, ef me an' you gonna have some fun,
> You play de cornet, Black Betty beat de drum."

In all of these versions, the teller presents the story as if he or she were there for all of the events. The narrative is immediate and filled with formal elements that improve any story: dialogue, description, and sensory details. It does not matter if the teller really was there, as he or she claims in the 1930s version: "It was early one mornin' when I heard my little dog bark, Stagolee and Billy Lyon was arg'in' in de dark."[22] Whether or not this is an objectively true autobiographical moment is irrelevant. The story becomes the storyteller's own, and the teller embraces all of it: both what is objectively true, as in the news and eyewitness accounts of Lyons's real-life murder, and what is constructed. These new elements can either serve as a correction of the record—that missing Stetson hat—or to disrupt the record—Stagolee's eventual decision to "rule Hell by [him]self."[23] The tellers have space to blur the line between fact and fiction because of the details that are left out of the original story. These gaps allow for new ballad and song variants. The 1930s' coda, in which Stagolee and the devil play music together, is a preview into not only how the Stagolee folk tale became part of blues lore but also how the bad man, more generally, became part of the blues tradition.

In this opening chapter, I will explore the ways in which the construction and reconstruction of autobiographical and biographical narratives that move between fact and fiction, while simultaneously inventing and reinventing the tellers, echo storytelling approaches in the blues tradition writ large. Although the mythical narratives—sometimes originating from nonfictional events that mark African American folklore and the blues at the early part of the twentieth century—are fluid and unstable, and are meant to be added to and reimagined by each new teller, later generations of transatlantic white blues critics, scholars, and fans were prone to take these myths as the unadorned truth. Some of these same white blues enthusiasts viewed the makers of blues themselves as "authentic" figures whose songs—and tales that they told about themselves and others—are a kind of reportage, rather than giving bluesmen and women credit for the fictional dynamic of autobiographical and biographical invention and reinvention.

This chapter's argument is twofold. First, that there are myths—for example, the bad man, and its close relation, the bedeviled bluesman, as well as the transgressive (bad) blueswoman—born in the early part of the twentieth century that resonate into the twenty-first century, affecting the subjects in the rest of this book quite directly. And second, that these early twentieth-century blues artists fight for their voices to be heard through storytelling. Though their stories, songs, and performances are taken as evidence of their natural essential selves by future generations of blues lovers, these tales show that blues personas are built through autobiographical and biographical fictions.

Chapter 1 will survey important foundational cultural artifacts such as the various early tales, songs, and ballads about Stagolee, and the ways in which the bad man archetype extends into engagement and conversation with the devil and its connection to the blues—another thread that circulates through twentieth- and twenty-first-century blues culture. I will show how pervasive these myths are in the twentieth and twenty-first centuries in novels, autobiographical narratives, and songs by Albert Murray, Ethel Waters, and the White Stripes.

I'll place this foundational set of blues myths in dialogue with Texas guitar player, bluesman, and songster Mance Lipscomb's 1993 oral autobiographical narrative. *I Say Me for a Parable: The Oral Autobiography of Mance Lipscomb Texas Bluesman* offers insights into how these myths of the bad (blues)man and transgressive (blues)woman continue to evolve in American literature and popular music in the twentieth and twenty-first centuries. Within his narrative are traces of each of the blues myths outlined above, and they transpire in the same ways that Stagolee works, as oral storytelling that becomes a ballad, a song, and then is eventually written down.

Finally, I will demonstrate that blueswomen similarly mythologized themselves. I will focus on early newspaper interviews with Mamie Smith, whose 1920 "Crazy Blues" became the first recorded blues song by an African American woman, and contains the outrageous lyrics

I'm gonna do like a Chinaman, go and get some hop.
Get myself a gun and shoot myself a cop.
I ain't had nothing but bad news,
Now I got the crazy blues.[24]

I will also discuss myths about blueswomen Bessie Smith and Ma Rainey, whose independence and transgressive, and sometimes nonheteronormative, gender and sexual expression resonate into the twenty-first century. In chapter 2, we will see this bear out in the representations of Shug Avery, the blueswoman at the center of *The Color Purple*, as well as in the music and lives of mid-twentieth-century blues legend Big Mama Thornton and the late English singer-songwriter Amy Winehouse.

Early on in the 1974 novel *Train Whistle Guitar* by Albert Murray, we learn about the hotshot guitar whiz Luzana Cholly, who, according to Scooter, the young and impressionable first-person narrator, was so named because the state of Louisiana was where his "reputation as a twelve-string guitar player second to none, including Leadbelly," was made. Scooter and his best friend, Little Buddy Marshall, idolize Cholly for his guitar sound, reminiscent of a train whistle, and for "that holler he was so notorious for." But more than that they are awed by his fearlessness in the face of Jim Crow, "because the idea of going to jail didn't scare him at all, and the idea of getting lynch-mobbed didn't faze him either. All I can remember him ever saying about that was: If they shoot at me they sure better not miss me they sure better get me that first time. Whitefolks used to say he was a crazy nigger, but what they really meant or should have meant was that he was confusing to them." Cholly mystifies the white people who encounter him, and causes some Black people, such as Scooter's mother, to "say he was don't-carified." His willingness to flout conventional social constrictions confounds the people around him. The idea that a Black man might resist the Jim Crow social structure in any way, let alone through physical violence, was one that delighted many Black folks, while "confusing" the white people who did not think this was possible.[25]

Myth, and specifically, the myth of the Black bluesman, plays a crucial role in Murray's book, with the young Black boys learning as much about life from the oral storytelling in their small town of Gasoline Point, Alabama, as they do in their school textbooks. Scooter and Little Buddy look to Cholly as a model for how to navigate the 1920s Jim Crow South as Black men. They also engage Stagolee, who makes an appearance in Murray's novel in a variant depicting him as a wild piano player instead of a gambler. Through Scooter's first-person narration, we not only learn about another musician bad man figure, but we also see how even though this Stagolee is a generation removed from the original Stagolee, he is represented in similar ways:

> Mister Stagolee Dupas (*fils*), or the Stagolee Kid was also called Stagolee the Son of Stagolee and Stagolee the Younger and Stagolee Junior and Son Stag and Kid Stag not because he was the son of

> the original Mister Bad Bad Stagolee (who was sometimes referred to as old Trigger Fingered Stagolee) but because he had followed in the footsteps of and probably even surpassed his father (who was a piano player famous for making up verses about the original Bad Man Stagolee, the notorious gambler who packed a stack barrel Forty-four). Sometimes when Stagolee the Son of Stagolee used to start adding some of his own new verses, he would keep on going until he had a verse for every key on the piano.

Stagolee Dupas is not the original murderous Stagolee, but he has seven different names, almost as many as the original "Bad Man Stagolee." He also takes an active role in the mythmaking, adding to the Stagolee narrative "until he had a verse for every key on the piano."[26] Instead of engendering renown as a remorseless murderer, this version of Stagolee is celebrated because of his creativity, his ability to keep the original Stagolee legend alive. This underscores the important role of the everyday people who tell and retell not only this particular narrative but others that circulate widely and become the basis for blues songs.

The bad man also resurfaces in Ethel Waters's 1951 autobiographical narrative *His Eye Is on the Sparrow,* in which she demonstrates the ability to tell tall tales that resonate on a deeper level as truth. While traveling during the early 1920s—the same timeframe as the story in *Train Whistle Guitar*—in a trio with her lover, dancer Ethel Williams, and her pianist, Pearl Wright, she colorfully describes a dangerous Nashville, Tennessee, where "the rats there were heavyweights. They were game as bulldogs and big enough to climb ladders. Going into a washroom one day, I saw one of these huge rats drinking at the washstand. He turned, looked at me indifferently, then continued drinking. I actually, on one occasion, saw another drinking from a Coca-Cola bottle which he held up in his two front paws. Their cockiness gave me chills." Later she mentions the black bottom dance that she says originated in Nashville, and ties the song to a very rough Black neighborhood called Black Bottom. This is a section of town so dangerous that even the police will not enter. As she states, "The Negroes who lived in the Black Bottom neighborhood in Nashville were so bad, aggressive, and hurly-burly that the bravest white coppers didn't dare invade their streets. If the coppers had a warrant for one of the criminals who lived in the Black Bottom they'd send word in for him to come out and report."[27] This notion of a Black neighborhood being so dangerous that even the white policemen were scared of tangling with its residents invokes the bad man trope as expressed through the characters Luzana Cholly and Stagolee.

If we fast-forward to the early aughts, we encounter this figure as voiced by Jack White in the White Stripes song "Ball and Biscuit"[28] on their 2000 record *Elephant.* In White's lyrics and vocal delivery, the bad man's power to be both seductive and frightening is on full display. The threat of violence looms, as White's narrator uses coercion to get a seemingly reluctant woman into bed by informing her that he is the "seventh son."[29] White's narrator is confident that he will change the woman's heart and mind. After all, as the folkloric seventh son (presumably born of a seventh son), he is endowed with special, perhaps even supernatural, powers. This middle ground, where the bad man is both a violent human and a quasimagical figure in league with the devil, plays out in different versions of the Stagolee tale.

During the 1930s, Stagolee was not only good friends with the devil—"Come on, le's have a lil fun"—but he also, in time, takes away his pitchfork, saying, "Stand back, Tom Devil, I'm gonna rule Hell by myself."[30] As John W. Roberts notes, in the late nineteenth century, "the behavior of black badmen was portrayed as having a supernatural source, not uncommonly in powers acquired from the Devil or his influence in the world."[31] A 1940s variant of Stagolee by Onah L. Spencer titled "Stackalee" not only takes place in St. Louis, the real birthplace of Lee Shelton, but it also suggests that Stackalee's hat is somehow imbued with otherworldly powers. In an answer to Lyons's pleas for Stackalee to spare his life after shooting him, "Stack says, God bless your children, damn your wife. / You stold my magic Stetson; I'm gonna steal your life." And later in this same version, while in jail, Stackalee has a dream during which the devil attempts to steal his soul. But even the devil proves to be no match for Stackalee, eventually, according to the teller, shouting, "Come and get this bad man before he puts my fire out." The teller continues, "The next time I seed the devil he was scramblin up the wall."[32] The mythical connection between the bad man and the devil—either as friendly compatriots or as fierce competitors—resonates throughout twentieth-century blues.

This is a deeply-rooted trope. Peetie Wheatstraw né William Bunch, a 1930s blues singer and guitarist, recorded under the names Peetie Wheatstraw (the Devil's Son-in-Law) and Peetie Wheatstraw (The High

Sheriff from Hell). His persona as a man somehow in league with the devil became so entrenched that when Paul Garon was researching his book about the blues artist, he "spoke to no one who recalled Peetie Wheatstraw without remembering him as the 'Devil's Son-In-Law' or the 'High Sheriff from Hell.' Many of the same people had never heard of William Bunch."[33] And even the most casual fans of blues music, and perhaps even those who are just fans of American roots music more generally, have likely heard one of the most enduring tales in the mythological canon of the blues: one dark night in the early part of the twentieth century, Robert Johnson went to a Mississippi Delta crossroads and agreed to allow the devil to retain the rights to his soul, asking only for guitar mastery in return. Honeyboy Edwards, who met Johnson in 1937 and became a friend, commented on the legend in 1997: "People say he wasn't any good playing guitar until he went out to the crossroads and sold his soul to the devil. They say after that Robert could play any kind of music. . . . It may be Robert could have sold himself to the devil. In the way he was, the way he played and the way he acted, he could have felt that he sold his soul. A special feeling could have hit him like he done that and that feeling come out in his music." Edwards is hedging as he assesses the veracity of Johnson's possession. He does not commit to the story's truth or fictionality, though he does suggest that the answer might lie somewhere in the middle. He keeps the myth alive by saying that "he [Robert] could have felt that he sold his soul."[34] The desire to perpetuate this legend in the 1990s underscores the enduring tradition of oral storytelling, and the mythmaking that grows out of it. These autobiographical and biographical fictions circulate in blues circles because Black and white people alike enjoy the romance inherent in them—it appears that Edwards understands this, and is willing to accommodate his audience.

In line with this romantic thinking, it was Johnson's supposed demonic possession that impelled him to write songs with titles such as "Hellhound on My Trail" (1937), "Cross Road Blues" (1936), and "Me and the Devil Blues" (1937). Robert Johnson was not the only blues musician to have purportedly sold his soul to the devil. According to his older brother, LeDell Johnson, Delta bluesman Tommy Johnson (no relation to Robert) also sold his soul sometime after he left their Crystal Springs, Mississippi, home in the second decade of the twentieth century. Sometime between 1912 and 1914, he lived near Boyle—close to Dockery's

Plantation, where famous country bluesmen Charley Patton and Willie Brown played regularly. According to Robert Palmer, Tommy "spent a year or two absorbing the music of the Patton-Brown juggernaut and of musicians like Dick Bankston and Ben Maree who played in a related style."[35] Later, according to LeDell, when he asked Tommy how he became such an accomplished guitar player in just a year or two,

> he [Tommy] said the reason he knowed so much, said he sold hisself to the Devil. I asked him how. He said, "If you want to learn how to play anything you want to play and learn how to make songs yourself, you take your guitar and you go to where a road crosses that way, where a crossroad is. Get there, be sure to get there just a little 'fore twelve o'clock that night so you'll know you'll be there. You have your guitar and be playing a piece sitting there by yourself. You have to go by yourself and be sitting there playing a piece. A big black man will walk up there and take your guitar, and he'll tune it. And then he'll play a piece and hand it back to you. That's the way I learned how to play anything I want." And he could.[36]

Whether Tommy actually narrated this second-person story, LeDell constructed it on his own, or it was a mixture of the two—after all, Palmer suggests that by the time the two brothers were reunited, Tommy had already "acquired a sinister reputation to go with his new persona, a reputation he assiduously cultivated"—it is a story that draws on the tales of the Yoruban trickster god Esu, as well as African American folk ballads such as Stagolee, in which the bad man and the devil play music together in hell.[37] Of course, as Elijah Wald reminds us about the white blues collectors who emerged in the 1950s and 1960s in search of romantic blues authenticity, "Popular entertainers were reborn as primitive voices from the dark and demonic Delta, and a music notable for its professionalism and humor was recast as the heart-cry of a suffering people. The poverty and oppression of the world that created blues is undeniable, but it was the music's up-to-date power and promise, not its folkloric melancholy, that attracted black record buyers."[38]

Let us agree that the Black men and women who bought Tommy and Robert Johnson's records in the early part of the twentieth century likely did *not* do so because they really believed the men were bedeviled, but it is possible that the Black record-buying public in that historical moment recognized the "dark and demonic" myths for what they were, accepted them as part of the blues package, and perhaps even embraced them.[39]

How well does the myth of the bad man survive into the second half of the twentieth century? One place it appears is in the as-told-to book *I Say Me for a Parable: The Oral Autobiography of Mance Lipscomb, Texas Bluesman* by Mance Lipscomb and Glyn Alyn. In this autobiographical narrative, published in 1993 in the midst of the 1990s blues revival kicked off by a much-hyped CD release of *Robert Johnson: The Complete Recordings,* the bad man finds his way into Lipscomb's story through his discussion of what he terms the "Life Story Song" and the "True Story Song."[40]

When Albert Murray reflects on Louis Armstrong's multiple book-length and short autobiographical narratives in a 1999 issue of the *New Republic,* he asserts, "If it is properly done, the 'as told to' autobiography represents how the subject wants his story told."[41] That is certainly true, but it is important to note that the process of making what G. Thomas Couser calls "collaborative life writing" work well for all parties poses a significant challenge. Life writing scholars such as Couser, Carole Boyce Davies, Sidonie Smith, Julia Watson, and Alison Ravenscroft have considered the ethics of the as-told-to autobiographical narrative, particularly when there is a power imbalance between the subject and the chronicler.[42] As Couser states, "Often, collaborations involve partners whose relation is hierarchized by some difference in race, culture, gender, class, age, or (in the case of narratives of illness or disability) somatic, intellectual, or emotional condition that renders them vulnerable to exploitation." Here the concern is that the subject's voice will be muted or silenced, with the scribe taking full control of the narrative, as so frequently happens—certainly in the case of collaborative autobiographical narratives about Americans from marginalized racial groups—when "one member supplies the 'life' while the other provides the 'writing.'"[43]

Alyn—the man who writes down Lipscomb's tales—appears very careful to avoid the mistakes that some white chroniclers make when working on as-told-to autobiographical narratives with people of color. As Sidonie Smith and Julia Watson state, "In as-told-to or ghostwritten narratives, multiple levels of coaxing take place, including those of the ghostwriter or cowriter, whose prompting questions, translations of the autobiographer's oral speech, and revisions are often invisible in the final text."[44] The invisibility of the editor's handiwork can be problematic, as it makes it difficult to judge the faithfulness with which the writer rendered the subject's stories and storytelling style. Alison Ravenscroft advocates for an approach where the "white reader/editor might no longer demand the clean, tidy, translated text, the text that conforms to the grammar of white textual forms." While all of these are important points to consider when analyzing Lipscomb's narrative, I am most interested in the problematic nature of Alyn's chapter introductions, where, in spite of his best efforts to not disrupt Lipscomb's voice or storytelling approach, he still includes "clean" and "tidy" translations that "conform to the grammar of white textual forms."[45] Rather than his editing efforts proving to be "invisible in the final text," he instead wields a heavy hand, ultimately missing his goal of leaving Lipscomb's words intact.[46] And, perhaps most disturbingly, although Alyn does not translate Lipscomb's oral speech into so-called Standard American English, the dialect that he assigns to his interview subject is often unnecessary and stereotypical, and sometimes distracting to read.

In Alyn's general introduction, he justifies his decision to not translate Lipscomb's Black Southern dialect into so-called standard English. He did this, he says, to ensure that the audience would not lose the distinctiveness and strength of Lipscomb's storytelling: "When I attempted to translate his speech into standard written English, so much of the humor, poetry, and musical quality of his voice was lost that it appeared barren."[47] However, while Alyn takes pains to evoke a strong sense of Lipscomb's speech patterns, and the effects of language on his storytelling, the interviewer includes lengthy introductions to each chapter translating Lipscomb's work back into terms that might be legible to an audience more comfortable with so-called standard English. In other words, instead of allowing Lipscomb's words—still mediated and reimagined but at least somewhat unfettered—to speak for themselves, Alyn makes it clear that he does not trust the audience to understand Lipscomb's stories, or the cultural contexts in which they originated.

This choice creates two running narratives. In the first narrative, a blues singer tells his own life story (autobiographical narrative) with a mixture of facts and fictions, including digressions into the stories of others (biographical narrative), in his own way. This multivoiced narrative conforms to Richard Bauman's description of the manner in which "oral literature" reflects the social lives of a people, while demonstrating how these tales are shaped by the teller's social, cultural, and individual contexts.[48] This insider's narrative is juxtaposed with another narrative relating the same information, that of an unreliable outsider attempting to make sense of the oral version, and who projects his own biographical fictions onto the stories. This second narrative, however unreliable, becomes part of the official record anyway, much like the stories the 1960s white blues collectors told. Of course, *I Say Me for a Parable* was published during the second wave of the transatlantic blues revival during the 1990s, and it is situated within the category of narrative of "discovery" that was forged during the first blues revival—in which "lost" blues artists such as Mississippi John Hurt, Son House, Skip James, Edwards, and Lipscomb were found by white blues collectors while busy living their lives out in "obscurity," and were then signed to recording contracts and tapped to play blues festivals in the United States and Europe. *I Say Me for a Parable* retreads a familiar narrative arc, spanning Lipscomb's childhood growing up in the Jim Crow South, his musical development, his "discovery," and the influence of fame and money on his life.

Lipscomb was born on April 9, 1895—just under nine months before the Stagolee mythology began—in Brazos County, a few miles north of Navasota, Texas.[49] He stayed close to Navasota until his death on January 30, 1976, having left only briefly for Houston from 1956 to 1958, and for tour dates outside of Texas from 1961 to 1973.[50] Born to a father, Charles Lipscomb, who had once been enslaved and a mother, Janie Pratt, of partial Choctaw Indian ancestry, he worked as a tenant farmer for most of his life. His father was a professional fiddler who introduced a very young Mance to music, having his son accompany him on bass at local live shows in Navasota—what Mance calls "Saturday Night Suppers." Two pivotal events occurred in Mance's life between the ages of fourteen and fifteen. First he found the guitar, and then he found God: "An I was tendin church, purdy briefly. I had jest learnt how ta play gittah. Three or foe good songs. I wouldn look at that gittah. I wouldn touch it. I went an joined church, an stayed in church." However, about six months later, at fifteen, he was cast out of the church because, as he laments, "a few people told it out that I wadn converted, because I was playin my gittah. See, I kin tell a tale on you, an it could stick. I wadn playin the gittah, cause I had done decided ta give it away or sell it. But they told the wrong repoat."[51] The key idea to consider here is the implied analogous relationship of the guitar, but more specifically the blues guitar of the Saturday Night Suppers, with evil. This line of thinking would suggest that it is not possible to be a Christian convert while playing a musical instrument used in the context of drinking, dancing, fighting, romantic and sexual courtship, and general—and perhaps literal—hell-raising. In other words, this music, according to the church folks in Albert Murray's novel *Train Whistle Guitar*, is "Good Time Music, by which they meant the kind of nightlong blues-dragging, blues-rocking, blues-bumping, blues-jumping, blues-swinging, blues-shouting music for Saturday night honky tonk dances during which, according to them, somebody was forever getting stabbed or cutup or shotup and ending up either in the hospital or the graveyard, with somebody else either skipping city or going to jail and then on to the County Farm or the chain gang."[52] Despite asking Lipscomb to leave the church, the church elders still wish him well with his music, requesting, "Play us some good music, inyhow."[53] This speaks to the complicated relationship between the church and Black secular music, specifically the very early blues at the beginning of the second decade of the twentieth century. While many Black people involved in Southern churches, as well as Black people who were either middle class or aspired to Black middle-class respectability, eschewed blues music, there were still "respectable" Black people who listened to the blues.

After leaving the church—though Lipscomb makes it clear that he did not leave of his own volition and he believes that "if you got a religion, its in yo hawt. Not in the church house"—he became a musician with a strong local following in what he calls his three-county "precinct," or area of influence—Washington, Grimes, and Brazos—with his reputation preceding him among other blues musicians outside of Texas. According to Alyn, Lipscomb played songs at the Saturday Night Suppers in styles that varied from "field shouts to blues, rags, ballads, Broadway tunes, spirituals, and children's songs." He was influenced by his face-to-face encounters with Blind Lemon Jefferson and Blind Willie Johnson, as well as his aural encounters with recordings by various blues artists such as Big Bill Broonzy and Bessie Smith. Sometime during the 1920s, country and western yodeling legend Jimmie Rodgers invited Lipscomb to join him on tour, but Lipscomb said no. Finally, in 1960, folklorist Mack McCormick and Chris Strachwitz, soon-to-be owner of Arhoolie Records, recorded Lipscomb as he sang and played guitar at his home.[54] In 1961, Lipscomb played the Berkeley Folk Festival.[55] Between 1961 and his death in 1976, he performed all over the United States and influenced a new generation of artists, including Taj Mahal, Janis Joplin, and Bob Dylan.[56]

■

In a chapter called "Saturday Night Suppers and Life Story Songs," Lipscomb presents his own key concept called the "Life Story Song," a close relation to the "True Story Song." Lipscomb introduces the tale that is the inspiration for his Life Story Song as follows: "All right, I give you some explaynation right now, bout this music. What you call a Life Story Song. I'm talkin bout a song was sung in Marlin jail. A man sung his way out a prison, like Leadbelly? It come ta my town, I blieve, in nineteen-nineteen or thereabouts. A boy come from Marlin, Texas. Thats a bad jail! Don't never go ta Marlin jail. They'll throw the key away an tie it on a rabbit's neck."[57] Lipscomb's explanation is fitting, as he begins his story by invoking one of the more famous musical myths of a murderous bluesman singing his way out of prison: Lead Belly's release from Angola State Prison in Louisiana in 1934 due to the efforts of John and Alan Lomax. This was apocryphal; the Lomaxes had nothing to do with it, though Lead Belly had, in fact, sung his way out of a prison in Texas in 1925. After leaving Angola, Lead Belly was marketed by the Lomaxes as an exemplar of a rural performer—an authentic, pure marvel of down-home honesty.[58] He may have possessed some of those qualities, but he was mostly a regular man with musical talent who wanted to find a way to earn a living playing music. Lipscomb gestures at Lead Belly's mythical narrative as he begins his song about a bad man named Freddie.

Lipscomb tells a riveting story about a rapidly deteriorating relationship between a man named Freddie and his woman: "So finely, she done im so bad: she went an put a man in his house, where he was livin with her. An put the man in Freddie's bed. An that was his home, an that was his wife an woman. She say, 'If I make you a pallet on the flow an git in the bed wit anothuh man, then I'll git rid a you cause you got ta leave here.'" The context of why this woman would treat her man this way is sketchy. According to the tale, the woman simply "didn care too much about im" and he "let her do him iny way she wanted ta do im." Whether she was once good to him but then found someone new or she was always this inconsiderate is unclear. But soon the other man wakes up in the middle of the night feeling "in the mood," "them sprangs got ta cryin," and next thing you know "Old Freddie got mad an he got bad." His woman begs for her life, but Freddie "throwed his pistol down an leveled it down on her an shot the woman. Kilt the woman!" The other man runs away, but Freddie chases after him and even the sheriff does not stop him because he empathizes with Freddie's situation: "It makes a bad man, wit his gun in his hand. I tell ya: I'll play like I aint seen ya. You go ahead on, an try ta find that man." Of course, Freddie eventually goes to the jailhouse, but a funny thing happens: he *sings* his "way outa jail."[59]

Here the bad man trope reemerges: "Old Freddie got mad an he got bad."[60] These words forecast exactly how Freddie's misdeeds will be not only accepted but celebrated. Freddie was not born a bad man—he was made one. His woman has the temerity not only to have an affair, or to cheat, or, perhaps most egregiously of all, to decide that she no longer wants to be with Freddie, but to also sleep with another man—literally and figuratively—in the same room as Freddie sleeps on a pallet on the cold, hard floor. Freddie is provided with all of the justification he needs for murdering her—and her boyfriend too, if he can find him. This puts a new twist on the bad man archetype. While many listeners, over generations, reveled in the notion of a bad man, Stagolee, killing another over nothing more than a hat, there are other versions of the song that run counter to that narrative, variants in which Stagolee's victim deserved to die. For some, clearly, the idea that Stagolee not only shot Lyons because he would not return Stagolee's hat—not because they were arguing over politics or something weightier—but then coldly took his hat out of Lyons's dying hands and walked off as if nothing happened, has led to the myth's popularity. But there is another story: one in which Lyons, not Stagolee, was the true bully. In a 1905 letter from the city jailor of St. Louis, James L. Dawson, to then Governor Folk, in an attempt to help Lee Shelton—Stagolee—receive a pardon, he "recalled an earlier experience in Curtis' Saloon in which Lyons terrorized the patrons with a 'long knife very sharp on both edges.'"[61] In the variant of the ballad published by Howard Odum, a verse suggests that Stagolee's victim was the real bully:

> Stagolee shot bully; fell down on de flo'
> Bully cry out: "Dat fohty-fo" it hurts me so'
> Stagolee done kill dat bully now.[62]

This version echoes Freddie's tale in that his homicide is justified because the transgressive (bad) woman he killed also deserved it. Her behaviors, which Freddie perceives as emasculating, have a bullying effect. This resonates with the police officer, who after hearing Freddie's story says, "It makes a bad man, wit his gun in his hand," and it ultimately sways the jailer who lets Freddie go after hearing his song, the song that Lipscomb refashions into his own tune, just as Stagolee was created and revised countless times.[63]

As Lipscomb continues his tale, he speaks directly to the audience, or perhaps his chronicler: "I'm showin you what the song sprung from. Don't thank now that wadn true. This fella sung his way outa jail. How he got out of it: the jaila was carryin food ta the jail. An Freddie was out in the jailhouse, playin his old gittah. The fella stood there on the outside, an it sound so good, he had the food in his hand waitin fur Freddie ta end that song." Lipscomb is trying to show the chronicler the ways in which the folk tradition is being used, "what the song sprung from," in his words.[64] It is not only important to show that the song had an original life somewhere else, it is necessary for the musician to pay homage in order to fully participate. It is also crucial to recognize that the way in which the song grows from an original source, as with Stagolee, is a critical part of the oral storytelling experience. The artist first acknowledges the historical source material, and then the musician takes it and expands it to fit what it is that he wishes to convey. This is what Lipscomb means by the True Story Song. This is a song that begins with an objectively verifiable event, and then others add their real-life stories to it, or at least they contribute their constructed/fictional versions of their, or other people's, real lives to it.

Why does Lipscomb raise the specter of his own deceit? Why does he assume that the chronicler or the reader will automatically dismiss his story? These are important questions that speak to why we tell stories in the first place. We largely tell stories to impart something meaningful to an audience in an engaging way, and relating tall tales is one way to accomplish this. We can think about it as does Bauman when he suggests that "the aesthetic considerations of artistic performance may demand the embellishment or manipulation—if not the sacrifice—of the literal truth in the interests of greater dynamic tension, formal elegance, surprise value, contrast, or other elements that contribute to excellence in performance."[65] In other words, listeners and readers like to hear stories that inspire them to lean in closer, even as they wonder about the veracity of the tale. The enduring interest in the crossroads fable, for instance, means that people enjoy the story even as they dismiss it. Honeyboy Edwards does just that when he talks about Robert Johnson. He suggests that the tale is very unlikely, yet he cannot help mentioning that Johnson's demeanor was indeed a bit off—"In the way he was, the way he played and the way he acted, he could have felt that he sold his soul."[66] So, perhaps, Johnson either did sell his soul, or he thought he sold his soul somehow. In his reluctance to admit that the crossroads tale is just a myth, Edwards allows the reader or listener the joy of his leaving the question of truth wide open.

The tall tale, in this case, is not meant to do any harm—it is deliberately used to help people understand the constructed nature of Black folk stories. Lipscomb knows that all of the details in "Freddie" might not be objectively true, but that does not mean that the tale is untrue. The story is true because it transmits a basic truth about the very nature of oral storytelling, about stories being passed down and along, and the truth of something that sounds right to the listener. This "sounding right" to the audience goes beyond lying or truth telling in an objective way—there is probably a liberal use of non–truth telling going on here—but the important question is, Does the story *feel* true to a potential listener, and do the origins make for a good groundwork for future iterations that will sound true enough? If so, then the work is fictional but also true.

In Lipscomb's parable, it is the unruly woman who causes all of the turmoil, but the music—presumably the lyrics and the music—is what moves the jailer to set Freddie free: "Now he sung his way outa the jailhouse. But when I learnt that song I hadn never heard Freddie sang it. How I got the words, an got em rhymed together: a boy brought it ta Navasota from Marlin. Thats near about Waco. He was whistlin that song an sangin it, but he couldn play a gittah one." The way that Lipscomb hears about the tale is important—it is transmitted by a young man whistling a tune. This means that, like Stagolee, "Freddie" is an outgrowth of a real-life event—even if elements have been embellished—and it became a ballad. And then a young man whistled and sang it, and brought it to Navasota. The young man did not play the guitar, so the movement from him to Lipscomb was only based on singing and whistling. This once again shows the folk process. It indicates that the version this young man was whistling was already, likely, many times removed from the original incident: "An this fella come ta me. He sung that song, maybe foe or five times, where I was playin at a Suppa. An I rearranged that song, an then I come ta playin from that night, until right now."[67] This is why it is important that the young person sang the song to Lipscomb. This is how the song gets passed along, and Freddie is no longer just an ordinary man who takes extreme measures after his relationship falls apart, but instead he becomes a legend. Taking retributive justice to an extreme allows him to become a folk hero, a bad man.

Through an alternative, retrograde sort of folk process, bluesmen and women go from being innovative artists who perform their music to appreciative audiences in order to make a living and share their work (and eventually to record their music for a larger audience) to inhabiting a reimagined, romanticized version of themselves created by white folk revivalists and record collectors. An example of this occurred in May 1972, when after hearing Lipscomb play at the Kerrville Folk Festival 120 miles outside of Austin, Alyn says that he spent the rest of the day talking to Lipscomb backstage. He describes his impressions of Lipscomb as follows: "His authenticity flowed out of him like water from an artesian spring. He was *naturally* [emphasis in original] authentic because he made no effort to be so. I decided that day to read the book that had no doubt been written about such a fascinating character and influential music figure." Alyn strikes an essentialist tone here, and later, just before the autobiographical narrative begins in chapter 1, he invites the reader, "Imagine you've just driven up to Mance's home. You've gotten mud all over your clean car right after you turned into the driveway past the Navasota City Limit sign and bounced through the first big puddle."[68] Lipscomb is read here as a primitive blues figure who lives in simple but romantic surroundings—perfect ones for a Black bluesman. For Alyn, the mud on his clean car is something not to be lamented but cherished because it plays into the myth of discovery predicated on the "native's" life being somehow half-lived until the discoverer comes along and makes sense of it. He is authentic because he has spent so much of his life cordoned off from the outside world. That is to say, Alyn sees him as someone who is an exemplar of blues authenticity because he seems so "natural," without a trace of the persona one might have encountered in a rock star circa 1972. The idea that during the years before his "discovery" Lipscomb was living a full life as a performer in Navasota, and likely had the same desire as any rock star to give the audience a good show through a mix of art and artifice, eludes Alyn.

Allan Moore's definition of authenticity as predicated on the listener's subjectivity is helpful here. The way that Alyn experiences Lipscomb correlates with Moore's "first person authenticity," where "an originator (composer, performer) succeeds in conveying the impression that his/her utterance is one of integrity, that it represents an attempt to communicate in an unmediated form with an audience."[69] Yet that so-called naturalness and authenticity is itself constructed on its own layer of blues performativity. Is Lipscomb showing the white music industry people and interviewers what he thinks they expect from him whether objectively true or not? Is he simply a performer who tells rich and compelling stories for a living, and blurring the lines between fact and fiction is par for the course? In this case, his interactions in the 1960s and early 1970s, as well as his exchanges with his ghostwriter from 1972 until his passing four years later, provide moments of Lipscomb's autobiographical blues self-invention and reinvention. Telling stories about himself and others allows Lipscomb to participate in the narrative blues tradition in which autobiographical and biographical fictions are used for blues self-mythologization and, sometimes, to resist the misapprehensions of outsiders who do not understand the Black folk underpinnings of the blues.

As an example of this fundamental misunderstanding of Lipscomb's storytelling approach, Alyn simultaneously reads Lipscomb as an authentic bluesman while also suggesting that Lipscomb is not always honest—as Alyn explains Lipscomb's storytelling style: "Telling more than a few jokes, and sometimes seeing how credulous your face can contort before you realize he's caught you in a hooraw." This perspective misses the fact that a hallmark of the blues is its fluid narrative engagement with "the truth." While it is possible that Lipscomb sometimes told Alyn tall tales, it does not mean that he was being dishonest. The Freddie tale—from potential real-world event to ballad to song—is an example of how tall tales can also be honest: "I'm the only man played 'Freddie,' but the man was in the jailhouse. An he wadn on record. But see, I made a record outa it, on my numba one issue: 'Freddie.' Its jest as true as I'm talkin ta you. That's a True Story Song. Nearly ever song I sang about somebody's life. Even it might be by *my* life. An everbody show liked that song cause its sech a straight, straight song."[70]

Whether or not Freddie was a real person, or all of the details in the tale actually happened, the story is true because it resonates for the teller and the listener. In this case, Lipscomb feels enough of a connection to the Freddie tale that he reinforces its truthfulness. Lipscomb affirms that he appropriated a true story, but it is also "his" story because he was the only one to make a record out of it. Freddie himself experienced the actual events in the ballad—or perhaps some of them—but he was in jail, so he could not put them down on record. This incident was said to have happened in 1919, so it is not just jail that would have stopped him from recording the tale. Blues performers were not captured on shellac until the 1920s, so it is disingenuous to say that he was not recorded only because of jail. At any rate, Lipscomb is staking a claim to the work even though the tale is not his own, and the song itself was initially whistled and sung to him by a boy he did not know well. He took existing words and sounds and put new music to them. This allows Lipscomb to take ownership of the song. This is a True Story Song about a man named Freddie, but it also belongs to Lipscomb. And when Lipscomb asserts, "Nearly ever song I sang about somebody's life. Even it might be by *my* life," he suggests that he might see a little bit of Freddie in himself.[71] After all, this is what makes the Stagolee narrative so attractive to generations of storytellers—through picking up the thread, they are able to imagine themselves coldly stepping over Billy Lyons as they walk out the door with that white Stetson hat.

In thinking about the constructed fictions in the Freddie tale—beyond the questions of whether Freddie existed in real life or not, or if there were substantive differences between the version of the Freddie tale that the young man whistled and what Lipscomb shared with Alyn—an important consideration is the way in which Lipscomb transports his interpretation of the Freddie ballad into his song "Freddie." Strikingly, in many ways the tale is faithfully rendered. It is not just the events that occur in the story that are replicated. The language itself—some if it curious—remains intact. After relating the story of Freddie's woman cheating on him with another man while Freddie slept on a pallet on the floor, the lyric, as documented by Alyn, engages the bad man trope, gesturing at the tragic Stagolee/Billy Lyons interaction:

> He got mad. He got bad. Went for his gun, in his hand. . . .
> I kin hear her cryin, "Now, Freddie, spare my life if you please.
> I know ya mad. You got bad. Oh, wit ya gun in ya hand.[72]

The brief statement "He got mad. He got bad" is repeated in varied forms no less than ten times. Sometimes Freddie's badness, resulting from his anger, is recounted by the third-person narrator: "He got mad. He got bad." Sometimes, it is his wayward woman who directly faces his rage: "I know ya mad. You got bad."[73] Again, a man becomes bad because of the outrageous behavior of his woman. And sometimes he acknowledges his own newfound badness using the first-person point of view. But whether the badness resulting from his madness is expressed in the first, second, or third person, there is the strong suggestion that Freddie is driven by a woman—his woman—to do his bad deeds. There is only one inversion in one of the verses where he says, "It makes her bad. You bein mad," showing again that she is deemed bad or transgressive not only by her actions but by his narrative within the narrative about his woman.[74] His anger makes him kill his woman. She is the cause of that anger.

When considering the ways in which language is used in the story about a man named Freddie, and Lipscomb's song called "Freddie," the overlap is striking. In the story about Freddie, Lipscomb tells the audience that "Old Freddie got mad an he got bad." These words in the story match his lyrics: "He got mad. He got bad." There are other moments like this. The story has artful moments, such as the dialogue from the wife: "She saw him comin. An fell down on her knees. 'Freddie, I know ya mad, but spare my life if you please." And in the song Freddie's wife says, "Now, Freddie, spare my life if you please. I know ya mad. You got bad. Oh, wit ya gun in ya hand." This rhyme feels intentional in a way that suggests that Lipscomb's story about Freddie and his song "Freddie" are both equally constructed—what that young man whistled to Lipscomb as he was passing through Navasota and what Lipscomb shared with Alyn years later were likely demonstrably different. For instance, the formal language in which Freddie's wife pleads for her life, "spare my life if you please," feels a little too courteous given the urgent circumstances.[75]

All of this shows the power of narrative to make or unmake a person. The original incident—if it did, in fact, happen—is not particularly compelling. Just like the real-life Stagolee tale in which the murder itself is rather quotidian, the story of a man being cuckolded by his girlfriend or wife is not all that noteworthy. His pulling out a gun and murdering her is drastic, but there are plenty of other murders that do not become folk tales that turn into blues songs. It is the subsequent retelling of the story, with storytelling elements that pull the listener in, that makes the difference. I would argue that it is not only the narrative form and structure that first attracts the audience and then inspires a spirited retelling—the poetic and colloquial language, the rhythm and rhyme, the invented or reimagined dialogue—but it is what is left out, allowing the reteller to add more details, that make the narrative worth telling again and again.

For Stagolee it was the missing detail of the Stetson hat and the notion that Lyons was killed because he would not let it go, that gave future tellers the space to add to the story—to correct or distort the record.

For Lipscomb, "Freddie" is a True Story Song because it is based on events that happened to a real person in real life. But there is another element to consider: True Story Songs don't have to be about one specific story that happened to one person in a fixed time in history. A True Story Song can be a collective tale about, or it can resonate with, a particular group of people. As Lipscomb offers, after playing his version of his song "Out an Down" for Alyn: "Everthang I says in there, why, its compairin with whats happenin in people's minds an in what they were feelin an what they were doin an tryin ta do in them times. It'll make you feel sorry an sad. About yo past life an all like that. Thats the blues: nothin but a feelin. . . . People stay woke behind what I'm doin, because some a them thangs done hapmd ta them or somebody they knowed. See, all these songs come up ta me when I was settin down thankin bout somebody's mind, the future a their life." The notion that people can connect to a song that might not have anything to do with them directly yet will trigger a memory demonstrates the power of collective stories. And after telling a brief story about being introduced to the song "Spanish Flang Dang" by Mexican migrants who came to Navasota to pick cotton and playing it, he says, "What I'm doin, I'm brangin back remembers. Sich as these songs as what ya call True Story Songs." So it is unnecessary that the original source material for the story be sensational or something that can be sensationalized. Lipscomb takes the quiet, smaller stories and retells them so others can see themselves. The True Story Song is honest despite whatever embellishment tellers add along the way. While the act of writing and deciding what to keep and what to discard involves construction, hence rendering the work a fiction, at the same time, there is an essence of truth. It is that truth that the audience connects with. That is what Lipscomb anticipates as he retells the tales through his True Story Songs. Even though he takes the tales and puts his own stamp on them, he knows that they connect to an audience through familiar details that help stoke their imaginations by "brangin back remembers." They are true even though they are constructed and reconstructed numerous times. As he admits, between the ages of fourteen and twenty, Lipscomb had a small repertoire of three songs that he knew how to play: "Sugarbabe," "Out an Down," and "Take

Me Back." Lipscomb learned new songs from people in his hometown. It was through the transmission of fresh material by local musicians that he began to expand his range:

> Jest like that song "You Gonna Quit Me Baby—good as I been ta you, doggone." I done wrote that way back in nineteen-eighteen. That song jest come in ta Navasota in a cawnival. I got three or foe words outa it. See, people didn have but foe or five verses to a song, in them days. A lot a these verses I added to it myself, ta make the song go alonger. All my songs got addition to em. I thank about somebody's troubles, somebody's life story, an then I add the verses to em so it'll fit they mind.

The idea of a song written by Lipscomb about someone else's life fitting that person's mind is compelling. How does Lipscomb get in their mind? This is classic blues autobiographical fiction. The blues maker acts as medium taking control of other people's narratives. For all of the ways in which Alyn's mediation of Lipscomb's narrative is intrusive and discomforting, it is helpful for understanding his book's approach to disseminating Lipscomb's stories in light of Lipscomb's own willingness to be the voice for the stories of his friends and neighbors. This here is an argument for Lipscomb and the other blues people's intellectual autonomy and professionalism. An example is when Lipscomb sings that he "kin hear her [Freddie's lady] cryin." How does he hear this? Is it through empathy? Is it because he, at least partially, composed her so he can hear the cries? If so, it also translates into Lipscomb's performance:

> Well now peoples, they git me on the stage, they look in my face an say, "Thats a man looks like he sincerely in the way he's doin.' I'm is!" . . . See, all my songs are what you call True Story Songs. Life Story Songs. That music was jest in my mind ta learn it, cause I like it. If you like a thang, it'll folla ya. If you jest pick up sumpm as a habit, you kin soon furgit about it. Thats how most music oughta be workt up: if you play sumpm the way you like it, somebody else gonna like it, cause its comin direckly from you. Then its gonna run through ya, see. It means sumpm to ya, an you kin hand it ta the individual.

They are True Story Songs, but not for the reasons Alyn might think. In the introduction to the chapter "Frank Hamer, Alias Charlie Hayman," in which Lipscomb tells the stories of his adventures while working as an assistant to the white state trooper Frank Hamer—throughout the chapter Lipscomb refers to him as "Charlie Hayman" in order to protect Hamer and himself—Alyn suggests that here, and in other sections of the book, Lipscomb tells tall tales: "This leg of the journey requires a final set of directions. Mance places a couple of subtle road signs on the border between facts and stretching them into yarns. When lots of detail and facts accompany an incident, it is a true story. Boasting and exaggeration indicate a hooraw coming on, as does a continual attribution of the story to someone else."[76] Maybe there is no such thing as a hooraw, at least how Alyn means it. For Alyn, Lipscomb's stories are either true or not true. The line between fact and fiction is one that is easily demarcated. But in African American folkloric storytelling more generally, and in the blues tradition in particular, a story can be true in a way that resonates with the person telling the story as well as the audience, while also containing facts that are either objectively untrue or are embellished, and while having a constructed architecture that inherently renders a text fictional.

As John W. Blassingame, Gilbert Osofsky, Arna Bontemps, and others note, since the antebellum South, Black Americans have used folk tales to communicate anger or resistance to their oppression using coded language imperceptible to whites.[77] In John Russell David's "Tragedy in Ragtime: Black Folktales from St. Louis," when considering the interviews he conducted with St. Louis Blacks about the facts behind the Stagolee myth, he states, "Little evidence was found of blacks 'trying to put me on.'"[78] This is relevant because it engages a valid concern. Black Americans have a history, stretching back to the antebellum period, of being less than transparent in their communications with white people, and protesting their oppressive conditions through veiled language and storytelling. As such, there was the very real chance that—as some critics have argued about Ralph Ellison's bluesman character Jim Trueblood, whose story of having sex with his daughter while sound asleep becomes more colorful as he tells it repeatedly at the request of *Invisible Man*'s voyeuristic white listeners—David's interviewees might tell stories with the express purpose of entertaining the white interviewer and performing whatever it is they think the interviewer wants rather than telling a "true" story or sharing "real" facts. It is hard to tell if Alyn recognizes that this might be happening to him. He does, of course, raise the specter of Lipscomb occasionally telling a "hooraw," but Alyn does not insinuate that it is because he is white and Lipscomb is Black.[79] He suggests that Lipscomb just might be including tall tales every once in a while; however, he sees this as a potential obstacle to warn the reader about, not a feature of Lipscomb's storytelling.

Even though none of the "illiterate elderly" interviewees "put [David] on," as far as he can tell, they still, according to him, "blended myth and reality in their narratives." In response to David's declaration that he has discovered important objective facts behind the Stagolee story, Black folklorist and writer Nathan Ben Young retorts, "What are you going to do with all of those facts, don't you know that people are more interested in myths than facts?"[80] David mentions that Young shakes his head sadly when he says this. It is evident that he, like others, sees the narrative possibilities of the Stagolee tale as far more valuable than what *really* happened. Because, of course, those myths can *feel* like they really happened to the tellers and the listeners. Later generations of white blues fans took these folk/blues myths as reality. The tellers and their first listeners accepted them as "like reality," as "close to real," but they know the work that goes into the mythmaking—the labor, the agency, and the careful construction. Young might believe that "people" are more interested in myths than facts, but that does not mean that nobody knows the difference. Surely Lipscomb did.

The myth of the bad man and lively tales about humans' engagement with the devil have long been integral parts of African American oral storytelling. While these stories about violent men and malevolent beasts infuse the rural blues with a sense of danger, the classic blueswomen who emerged in the first two decades of the twentieth century were deemed transgressive for simply performing the blues at all. If one considers their determination to express themselves creatively in a white and male American culture that was not made for them, the controversial topics that they covered in their songs, and the ways they embodied a "don't-carified" sexual stance in their personal lives, they were truly ahead of their time.[81] In fact, in 1926, classic blues legend Ma Rainey recorded her own version of the Stagolee legend called "Stack-o-Lee Blues," melding the bad man and transgressive (bad) woman's experiences:

Stack O'Lee was a bad man, everybody know
And when they seed Stack O'Lee comin', they'd give him the road
He was my man, but he done me wrong . . .
He'd take everything his women would bring and everything they
had.[82]

As Brown notes, Rainey's version brings together lyrics from the Stagolee and "Frankie and Johnny" ballads.[83] In this song, Stagolee is a bad man, but he is also the narrator's (bad) man. According to Brown, the real-life Stagolee was known to be a mack or a pimp, and his girlfriend was one of his prostitutes. So in Rainey's song, we have the bad man, Stagolee, a man so fearsome that when people see him coming, "they'd give him the road," and we have the transgressive woman—perhaps one of his prostitutes—from which "he'd take everything."[84] This variant demonstrates the ways in which the classic blueswomen both participated in and advanced these Black oral histories while also creating new myths along the way.

Rainey was born Gertrude Pridgett in September 1882 in Alabama, but she was raised in Columbus, GA.[85] As a teenager, Pridgett performed in a local talent show called *Bunch of Blackberries*. Will Rainey, a minstrel comedy singer, met and fell in love with Pridgett, and he married her in 1904.[86] According to Daphne Duval Harrison, "The couple did a song-and-dance act for many years billed as 'Ma' and 'Pa' Rainey, 'Assassinators of the Blues,' with the Rabbit Foot Minstrels, but her [Ma's] blues singing soon became the drawing card of the performances." Rainey started recording for Paramount Records, a prototypical "race" label, in 1923. Prior to this, she was virtually unknown outside of the South, though she had a faithful audience who followed her as she performed in rural, small-town tent shows. Rainey joined the Theatre Owners Booking Association (TOBA) touring route around 1924.[87] The TOBA (known sardonically by some of their Black artists as "Tough on Black Asses") "organized and scheduled appearances of black vaudeville and tent acts in sixty-seven theaters across the South and Midwest." Because of her connection to the TOBA, in addition to performing for her Southern fans, Rainey was able to play shows for audiences in Chicago, Detroit, and Pittsburgh.[88] Known alternatively as the Mother of the Blues and Madame Rainey, Rainey was successful as both a recording artist and a live concert performer throughout the 1920s. She, along with her contemporary, possible protégé, and eventual rival, Bessie Smith, were two of the most important classic blueswomen who transgressed prescribed boundaries for women in the first half of the twentieth century. When professor and poet Sterling Brown and composer and ethnomusicologist John Work III visited Rainey backstage after one of her shows, according to Brown, she made sexual advances toward them: "That night when we saw her, she was having boy trouble. You see, she liked these young musicians, and in comes John Work and I—we were young to her. We were something sent down, and she didn't know which one to choose. Each of us knew we were not choosing her! We just wanted to talk, but she was interested in other things. She was that direct."[89]

Bessie Smith, born on April 15, 1894, in Chattanooga, Tennessee, inhabited, like Rainey, the stage persona of a transgressive woman flouting white, middle-class standards of female respectability—with her frank lyrics about sex, substance abuse, and domestic violence and her openly bisexual lifestyle.[90] In 1912, when Smith was eighteen, her older brother Clarence, a comedian with Moses Stokes's traveling minstrel troupe, secured an audition for her. She was hired as a dancer, and shortly began touring with the group. Ma Rainey was part of Stokes's troupe, and it was here that Rainey and Smith began what would become a long friendship.[91] After leaving the troupe in 1913, and after a brief interlude as a chorus girl for theatrical producer Irvin C. Miller, beginning around 1915, Smith spent the next several years working as a blues performer in theaters throughout the South, and as far north as Baltimore, with many appearances at the "81" Theater in Atlanta, a venue that was part of the TOBA circuit. She eventually headlined her own shows in the South and on the East Coast.[92] Known for her powerful and gritty vocals—in the early 1920s, during the blues race recording boom, Smith's voice was deemed "too rough" by Fred Hager at OKeh Records and too Black by Harry Pace at Black Swan Records—in 1923 she released "Down Hearted Blues" and "Gulf Coast Blues" on Columbia Records, selling approximately 780,000 copies by the end of the year.[93] Songs such as Porter Grainger and Everett Robbins's "Tain't Nobody's Biz-ness If I Do" (1922), and Clarence Williams, Danny C. Small, and Tim Brymn's "I Need a Little Sugar in My Bowl" (1931) reflect her audacious persona, with lyrics such as

If I go to church on Sunday,
Then just shimmy down on Monday,
Tain't nobody's business if I do do do do,

and

I need a little sugar in my bowl
I need a little hot dog on my roll
I can stand a bit of lovin' oh so bad
I feel so funny, I feel so sad.[94]

Smith also enunciates her transgressive (bad) woman persona in songs such as "Send Me to the 'Lectric Chair," written by Fletcher Henderson a.k.a. George Brooks (1927), in which a woman pleads with the judge to mete out a just punishment after she murders her lover:

I caught him with a trifling Jane
I warned him 'bout before
I had my knife and went insane
And the rest you ought to know.

and "Hateful Blues," composed by E. Johnson (1924), in which the narrator imagines the violence she will inflict on her cheating lover if she crosses his path again:

If I find that man while hurt is on my mind
If I see him, I'm gonna beat him
Gonna kick and bite him too
Gonna take my Wade & Butcher, gonna cut him through and
through.[95]

Shortly after Smith's first Columbia release in June 1923, she encountered record-breaking, sold-out crowds in the South. Fans flocked to the shows of the "Exclusive Columbia Artist," and by August 1923 she was earning $350 per week.[96] Throughout Smith's recording career—1923 to 1931—her records sold extremely well and kept Columbia in the black. During the peak of her popularity, her records routinely sold one hundred thousand copies within a week of issue, with Harrison suggesting that by the end of Smith's career her records "had sold an estimated six to ten million copies."[97]

Rainey and Smith are both artists whose works are important from both the perspective of both their musical contributions and their witting and unwitting participation in blues mythology. Rainey, like W. C. Handy, given her early arrival on the blues stage, found herself in the position of claiming initial credit if not for discovering the blues then at the very least for naming the idiom. John Work interviewed Rainey in a Nashville hotel where she and her band were playing somewhere in the 1920s or 1930s. It is important to note that Work mostly serves as the mediator for Rainey's words rather than allowing her to speak for herself, but even so, his description of their interaction is instructive. According to Work, he says that Rainey

> heard them [the blues] in 1902 in a small town in Missouri where she was appearing with a show under a tent. She tells of a girl from the town who came to the tent one morning and began to sing about the "man" who had left her. The song was so strange and poignant that it attracted much attention. "Ma" Rainey became so interested that she learned the song from the visitor, and used it soon afterwards in her "act" as an encore. The song elicited such response from the audience that it won a special place in her act. Many times she was asked what kind of song it was, and one day she replied, in a moment of inspiration, "It's the Blues." She added, however, that after she began to sing blues, although they were not so named then, she frequently heard similar songs in the course of her travels.[98]

This early myth is made all the more complicated by the fact that Rainey is not directly quoted—the words "man" and "act" and the phrase "It's the Blues" are the only parts that are in her own words. While I do not doubt the veracity of the details that Work includes, the decision to keep only certain elements of Rainey's first-person account shows his hand as the constructor of this narrative. Deciding what parts of the interview he conducted to include, as well as whatever parts he excised from Rainey's tale of naming the blues, are all in service to his construction of Rainey's mythos.

Figure 1. Bessie Smith with feathers. Photo by Carl Van Vechten. Library of Congress, Prints and Photographs Division, Carl Van Vechten Collection, [LC-DIG-ppmsca-09571].

Later researchers, such as Sandra Lieb in her definitive work *Mother of the Blues: A Study of Ma Rainey,* suggest that "this appealing story is likely a distortion." Lieb believes that because the word "blues" had existed as a term for depression or despondency as far back as the end of the eighteenth century, and that the blues as a form and style of music existed throughout the Deep South as early as the turn of the twentieth century, Rainey's/Work's claims are hard to believe.[99] Scholars such as Lieb, Harrison, and Chris Albertson are also rightfully skeptical about the origins of Rainey's moniker (Mother of the Blues)—though they concede that it is probably historically true—as it was Paramount Records who created the marketing campaign in the February 2, 1924, issue of the *Chicago Defender* for her first release, "Moonshine Blues," with the headline: "Discovered at Last—'Ma' Rainey Mother of the Blues!" Positioning Rainey as an artist "Discovered at Last," while simultaneously dubbing her the "Mother of the Blues," speaks to Rainey's status as a foundational and influential blues singer. Having already been performing at that point for close to twenty-five years—twenty years longer than Paramount suggests—her "discovery" would have likely raised eyebrows among the *Defender*'s Black readership who knew better.[100] The ad, complete with an illustration of Rainey wearing her signature necklace made of gold coins, and matching golden coin earrings, introduced her as such: "'Moonshine Blues'—The first record by Madame 'Ma' Rainey, the wonderful gold neck woman who starred for five years in three theaters in Pensacola, Atlanta, and Jacksonville! If it's Blues you want, here they are. 'Ma' sings 'Moonshine Blues' like she meant 'em ('I Ain't Never Goin' to Drink No More!')—it's the last word in Blues. 'Ma' Rainey is the only blues singer in the world elevated to the heights of 'Madame.' Now she sings *exclusively for Paramount.*"[101] Here is an example of a record company creating a mythic fictionalized narrative about their artist through visual culture—Paramount and other "race" labels did this frequently, creating illustrated ads with hyperbolic copy, trying to make their Black artists appear as "authentically" blues as possible. But there are other myths about Rainey with more mysterious origins.

Because of Rainey's position as a very early, if not the earliest, female blues singer, and the close association she had with Bessie Smith, there are a host of myths that pertain to the two of them, and keep them forever tied to each other. One of the more outrageous myths is that Smith was not only mentored and taught to sing, by Rainey, but that she was literally kidnapped by her and forced to be part of the Rabbit Foot Minstrels. This myth was discounted as early as 1972 with the original publication of Chris Albertson's book about Smith. In it, Smith's sister-in-law recalled how "Bessie and Ma Rainey sat down and had a good laugh about how people was making up stories of Ma taking Bessie from her home, and Ma's mother used to get the biggest laugh out of the kidnapping story whenever we visited her in Macon. Actually, Ma and Bessie got along fine, but Ma never taught Bessie how to sing. She was more like a mother to her." It is easy, though, to see why this myth persisted throughout much of the twentieth century. If Rainey *is* the Mother of the Blues, and as Maud Smith suggests, she was "like a mother to her [Bessie Smith]," raising her like a mother might, would she not do her best to teach her the skills that she herself had mastered? Perhaps even going so far as to hold Smith captive to impart her wisdom?[102] Or, at the very least, is this not how oral narratives work? People take an exciting story that they hear, and add to it without worrying about its truthfulness or fictionality, all the while creating new myths.

Although transatlantic scholars in the 1970s and 1980s, such as Lieb, Albertson, and Derrick Stewart-Baxter, resisted the romance of these stories, and opted instead to work hard to piece together objectively true stories on their way to establishing the historical record, it is human nature to revel in tall tales, to fill in the gaps of the verifiably true with the fanciful.[103] Blues fans during the 1950s and 1960s did this, as did some early blues scholars and critics. And, of course, so did the artists themselves. While there are no accounts that suggest that Smith and Rainey participated in these myths about Smith's kidnapping or their sexual relationship—there is lore suggesting that Rainey and Smith were lovers, and Lieb supports this as a viable possibility—in Smith's early recording days with Columbia Records, she did participate in some mythmaking with her label-mate Clara Smith: "Surprisingly, a good relationship developed between the two singers, who occasionally confused people by pretending to be sisters."[104] This is echoed in Jack and Meg White's contention, throughout the existence of the White Stripes, that they were siblings rather than a divorced couple.

During the 1950s folk revival and 1960s blues revival, the classic blueswomen were berated for not being authentic due to their professional demeanor and their glamour. As Wald, Marybeth Hamilton, Ted Gioia and others note, the 1960s blues revival did two things: captured blues for a new generation, and entrenched beliefs about blues authenticity that linger into the twenty-first century.[105] These blues collectors, scholars, and critics focused their positive attention on the folk/country blues performers. Artists such as Charley Patton, Robert Johnson, Son House, James Honeyboy Edwards, and Mance Lipscomb were deemed authentic and worthy of fandom and critical inquiry, while the vaudeville/classic blues players' contributions were overlooked. Ultimately, neither the country blues artists nor the vaudeville/classic blues players were given credit as being professionals in charge of their own images.

Classic blues singer Mamie Smith's 1920 hit "Crazy Blues," written by Black composer-publisher Perry Bradford, and released by OKeh Records, is the first blues song recorded by a Black woman.[106] The degree of success that the record found—as Wald puts it, "To the industry's astonishment, it became one of the biggest-selling discs of the year, and the blues recording boom was on"—paved the way for other Black women singers who came from the vaudeville and Southern tent show traditions, such as Bessie Smith, Ma Rainey, and Ethel Waters.[107] During the 1920s, these classic blueswomen were critically and commercially successful recording and touring artists. Despite their groundbreaking contributions, and vast commercial success, later generations of blues enthusiasts focused on the work of the predominantly male country blues performers.

It is not surprising that the country blues artists enjoyed a mythic revival during the 1950s and 1960s, given the scarcity of recorded Delta blues music, particularly at that time, and the dearth of information available about the lives of some of the rural blues artists—such as Robert Johnson. When there is less known about an artist and his or her body of work, it is easier to project fantastic ideas about the context and meaning behind those efforts. While the main criticism that blueswomen faced was inauthenticity, I would argue that it is precisely their measured consideration of their audience and their work's positive reception that shows their professionalism and their agency with respect to the mythic blues narrative. Their careers, much like those of the men, are self-consciously constructed through narrative storytelling in lyrics, during interviews, and in the creation of personas. As with Stagolee and the devil-haunted men of the Delta, these narratives take the form of autobiographical and biographical fictions—stories they tell about

Figure 2. Mamie Smith—"Crazy Blues" sheet music cover. From the New York Public Library, https://digitalcollections.nypl.org/items/510d47e2-cef8-a3d9-e040-e00a18064a99.

themselves and others, and biographical fictions about them, crafted by others, that they then amplify and advance.

In Mamie Smith's case, the press interview was a key locus of self-invention. By the early 1920s, Smith had long been a mainstay of the Vaudeville scene, touring as a dancer with the Four Dancing Mitchells from the age of ten, and later traveling with them as part of Salem Tutt Whitney and Homer Tutt's "The Smart Set." After moving to New York in 1913, she performed as a vocalist in various Harlem clubs.[108] "Crazy Blues" made her a huge star whose allure came, in part, from her glamorous stage persona. In an interview with the *Savannah Tribune* published on February 5, 1921, she candidly discusses her newfound fame, and the expectations of her new audience:

> I realize that these thousands of people who come to hear me at my concerts, expect much, and I do not intend that they shall be disappointed. They have heard my phonograph records and they want to hear me sing these songs the same as I do in my studio in New York. For that reason, I am taking with me my original jazz hounds, who are, in my opinion, the finest players of syncopated music in the world today. Another thing, I feel that my audiences want to see me becomingly gowned, and I have spared no expense or pains in frequenting the shops of the most fashionable modists in America, with the result that I believe my audience will like my gowns as much as I do, for I feel that the best is none too good for the public that pays to hear a singer.[109]

On its face, Smith's commitment to ensuring that her audiences receive her live music in a similar manner to how they experience it on record shows her professionalism. But it also demonstrates a crafting of an image that is not reliant on race label advertising or the management and dissemination of white people's notions and fantasies about Black performers and Black performance styles. She takes responsibility for gauging her audience's needs and what it takes to meet them. When she mentions that her fans have her records, and want that same sound reproduced live, she does not simply say that she is bringing a great band with her. She takes full ownership of it: "I am taking with me *my* [emphasis added] original jazz hounds." While scholars have suggested that the blues queens have historically been seen as less musically pure because of the classic blues' polish and the blues queens' glamour, Smith demonstrates that the gown is more than just a stage costume. It instead represents a contract, of sorts, between the singer and her public. When she says, "I feel that my audiences want to see me becomingly gowned," she is participating in a classic exchange between performer and audience, just as Lead Belly dressed in a nice suit when not performing in tattered clothes onstage in order to appease white stereotypes about Black blues performers, and Robert Johnson, though an itinerant musician, dressed in a natty pinstriped suit and hat. The crowd expects Smith to be glamourous, so she has "spared no expense or pains in frequenting the shops of the most fashionable modists in America." What is striking is that she does not simply show up wearing the gown onstage, leaving the audience to believe that procuring the gown reflects little effort. Here she lets her audience know that she takes great care in finding and choosing the right gown. Smith signals her commitment to wearing the most stylish gowns possible by following the lead of America's fashion icons—again, not merely because she enjoys glamour, or because she is trying to be "respectable," but because her audience expects it of her. As she says, "The best is none too good for the public that pays to hear a singer." She is an artist who cares about the quality of her phonograph records, as well as her live show, and she is also a famous blues singer on whom her fans can project their own celebrity fantasies.

In a story titled "From $20.00 per Week to $1,000 ptr [*sic*] Night: This Is What Happened to Mamie Smith in the Short Space of Three Years," published on October 14, 1921, in the *Topeka Plain Dealer*, Wm. E. Ready spends time with Smith after the first of her three performances in Baltimore's newly renovated Regent Theatre. Referring to Smith alternately as a "jazz artist," a "jazz singer," and the "Queen of Jazz Music," Ready focuses on her popularity and resultant commercial success, while trying to articulate what it is about Smith that allows her to enjoy more acclaim and financial rewards than many of her female jazz—and blues—contemporaries. While he allows that Smith does not possess "superior voice equipment," he maintains that she does have one thing over the other women jazz singers that have come before: "Soul." It is difficult to decipher exactly how the writer is defining the word soul here. Ready admits that these other performers lack what others might call "the human appeal" or "racial affinity," but he attempts to characterize Smith's gifts as something different, less tangible. Even without presenting a stable definition of soul, it is evident that the writer is impressed by what he views as Smith's down-to-earth nature. In this rare glimpse into Smith's off-stage personality, the writer, who speaks of himself in the third person, describes their interaction as such: "But the famous jazz singer has not been spoiled by her meteoric rise to her present commanding position. When the writer sought her out after her first performance on Tuesday evening, he was welcomed into her small dressing room up among the 'flies' of the Regent stage with the unaffected graciousness that might have been expected only in the quiet confines of the reception room of her own home."[110] This excerpt is telling, as it offers an early example of the Black newspapers' role in the development of Black jazz, and Black singers' celebrity. Ready communicates with an audience who, one year post–"Crazy Blues," was comprised of fans, or at the very least people who had likely heard of Smith but might not know her music. In framing her as an extremely popular and financially successful singer who also happens to be a nice woman who would make an elegant and magnanimous hostess while entertaining at home, the writer advances her glamorous reputation while also making her appear approachable. Perhaps, even, he is attempting to situate her within the Cult of True Womanhood, making her palatable to middle-class readers who might find the blues otherwise unappealing. It is notable that throughout the article Ready either describes his interactions with Smith or paraphrases her own words. Of course, Smith has the ability to speak very clearly for herself, as she demonstrates her control over her own image through her selection of what costumes to wear and the importance they hold. She clearly articulates this about her gowns in the *Savannah Tribune* article from a few months earlier.

In the *Plain Dealer* article, Ready offers a hint of innocuous gossip, referring to "Miss Smith, who in private life is Mrs. Ossey Wilson," and mentioning that "during the interview, a stalwart bronzed gentleman wearing kahki [*sic*] overalls, came in and was introduced as Mr. Wilson, the Madam's husband and business manager." He also focuses on the material markers of wealth that Smith possesses. He states, "He [the writer] also was introduced to another of the singer's constant companions, 'Jazz Baby,' a cunning tiny snow white poodle. She admitted that her chief recreation is driving her $11,000 car." The small dog has long been a status symbol among the very wealthy, and the $11,000 car, adjusted for inflation, would cost approximately $145,706.91 today. It is well known that Smith died without financial means, and this article supports the view that she might have spent her fortune indiscriminately. But it also shows that a Black woman musical performer with fame and money knew how to create a persona that would draw considerable interest from the Black press and the public.

While Ready mostly speaks for Smith in his article, there is one moment where he provides a direct quotation. With the interview taking place in Baltimore, Ready states that, "contrary to reports," Smith "is not a Baltimorian, but a native of St. Louis." Ready then provides Smith's reaction: "Every city in the country had laid claim to being her birthplace." This sentence is in quotations even though the pronoun does not make sense—the third-person "her" is used instead of the first-person "my." Whether through incompetence or a need for discursive control, even Ready's direct quotation of Smith reads like paraphrase. In any event, according to Ready, Smith is from St. Louis, yet according to her birth certificate, recently unearthed by John Jeremiah Sullivan, she was born in 1891, instead of the previously cited 1883, in Cincinnati, Ohio.[111] Smith's assertion that "every city in the country had laid claim to being her birthplace" is an example of the way biographical fictions emerge out of her autobiographical fictions. Smith's acknowledgement that she caters to audience desires when deciding what clothes to wear for her live performances correlates with the idea that it is best to let the fans believe whatever they wish about her geographical origins. While it is not clear whether there are interviews where she has denied being born in the cities of her various tour stops, it follows that given her investment in pleasing her audience, she might not have made much effort to correct the record as she traveled the country with her jazz hounds and her "cunning" white poodle.[112] While Mamie Smith participates in fictionalized autobiographical blues self-invention, in part, by allowing audiences to respond to her work as they please without interference, the blueswomen in chapter 2 use autobiographical self-fashioning to rewrite the false or incomplete narratives about their lives.

2 Shug, Big Mama, and Amy

Autobiographical Fictions and Addictions

It was the summer of 1971. Willie Mae "Big Mama" Thornton sat in the second to last row of a van headed toward a gig in Eugene, Oregon, with Muddy Waters to her right, and groundbreaking R & B performer Big Joe Turner in the row behind her. Her then manager, Link Wyler, sat next to Turner while peppering Thornton with questions. In Wyler's role as a crew member of the TV show *Gunsmoke*, he, along with others from the series, filmed the Pacific Northwest blues tour featuring Thornton, Waters, Turner, blues harpist George "Harmonica" Smith, singer-guitarist Bee Houston, and singer-guitarist J. B. Hutto.[1] In a clip from the resultant 2004 DVD *Gunsmoke Blues*, Thornton, wearing a black train engineer cap with white polka dots, a red oxford shirt, and a black leather coat, narrates the story of how she met Waters: "I've been knowing Muddy at least about fifteen years. I said from '52. . . . Yeah, that's the time I was pulling microphones up like this with one hand [she demonstrates for the camera]. Muddy say, 'Who is that?' Somebody said, that's the lady put out the 'Hound Dog.'" Even though Waters is sitting there, available to tell his own story from his point of view, Thornton recounts the day that she and Waters met from his perspective. Autobiographical storytelling, more specifically correcting the record, was an act Thornton performed regularly later in her career. She was disappointed that the two songs she was best known for—one she did not compose but made her own, "Hound Dog," and one she wrote but someone else made *her* own, "Ball and Chain"—did not provide the financial remuneration or the sustained commercial success to which she felt entitled. As such, many of Thornton's stage performances and interviews during the 1970s feature a moment when she reclaims her power through telling her story on her own terms.

After telling the tale of how she and Waters met, Thornton rehearses a variation of what was her recent live concert introduction for her song "Ball and Chain": "Here I am today with another big smash with a young lady called Janis Joplin which I wrote. Which it made a hit that I did myself: 'Ball and Chain.'"[2] In the video, Thornton places a subtle emphasis on those three words: "which I wrote," betraying her exasperation with audiences who are likely unaware of that fact, especially those who discovered her through the Janis Joplin and Big Brother and the Holding Company cover of the song.[3] There is also pride in her voice, with these lines prompting a spontaneous call and response between Thornton, Turner, and Wyler:

> "Who wrote 'Ball and Chain'?" Asks Wyler.
> "I did."
> "Willie Mae Thornton write Ball and Chain?" Wyler asks again.
> "Right On. I gets a check off of it once a while from BMI."
> "I know you do." Wyler agrees, patting her shoulder affectionately.
> "Right on." Turner chimes in.
> "I know you do," Wyler affirms once more.
> "I gets a check off a 'Ball and Chain' from Janis. I get a 'Ball and Chain' off of me."[4]

Although it is certainly fair to interpret her words here as suggesting that she receives royalties from her version of the tune, her words allow for a double meaning. Thornton does indeed "get a 'Ball and Chain' off of [her]," as she not only retakes ownership of her creative expression but also hears her words affirmed and echoed back to her by her audience in the van. Shortly after that, Thornton, leaning into Muddy Waters, says, "Let's go on down there to Eugene and tear up the joint." In this brief opening example, we see that using one's voice to correct the record, and assert one's power, are vital functions of autobiographical storytelling. Through autobiographical fictions—tall-tale telling, constructed narratives that contain subjective but no less honest truths, and self-mythologization—blueswomen create themselves.

As I have argued in the previous chapter, blueswomen have participated in multiple forms of fictionalized autobiographical blues self-invention from the early days of vaudeville to the twenty-first century. This impulse to resist racist, patriarchal, and classist categorizations and limitations through a retelling of their stories in their own voices is reflected in the words and sounds of fictional and real-life blues makers alike. These women, who dare to transgress heavily policed boundaries of what counts as acceptable feminine expression, use autobiographical storytelling to invent and reinvent themselves.

In this chapter, I argue that due to racism, patriarchy, and classism some blueswomen in contemporary American literary texts, and in popular culture, must combat negative biographical representations, in both public and private spaces, by detractors of different races, classes, and, perhaps most crucially, genders. These women deploy autobiographical agency in response to patriarchal representations, showing the full scope and multidimensionality of their stories. I bring autobiographical and biographical expression into dialogue to show how blueswomen self-fashion within multiple narratives: *The Color Purple* by Alice Walker; an oral history project with legendary blues singer Willie Mae "Big Mama" Thornton and R & B great Esther Phillips; and "You Know I'm No Good," "Rehab," "Tears Dry on Their Own," and "Wake Up Alone," contemporary popular songs with classic blues lyrical themes by the late English singer-songwriter Amy Winehouse. Combining literary criticism, blues music criticism, performance theory, and Black feminist theory, this chapter examines narratives generated by authors, composers, lyricists, and musicians. I use these multiple approaches to analyze the stories that the fictional narrators and characters—and real-life blueswomen—tell within the novel, the various songs, and the interviews.

The literary and real-life female blues characters in this book consistently subvert traditional gender roles. Their willingness to perform songs that portray heterosexual and lesbian sexuality, drug and alcohol abuse, domestic violence, and the rejection of marriage and a conventional domestic lifestyle reflects their feminist spirit.[5] The simple presence of Black blueswomen as performers onstage in a fictional juke joint or club demonstrates personal agency, but it also can put them at narrative risk for physical harm or social ostracism. In lyrics and vocal performances, blueswomen, fictional and real-life alike, express the full spectrum of their lived experiences. The content of their lyrics, and their approaches to their autobiographical self-fashioning, reflect the profound challenges they face due to their race, class, and gender. As Daphne Duval Harrison offers in her introduction to *Black Pearls: Blues Queens of the 1920s*, "The grief of a broken love affair is always poignant; it is more so when cast within a racist system. Black women's quest for independence is constrained by racial and sexual barriers and sometimes leads to types of behaviors that appear to be arrogant, promiscuous, or violent, but are in fact manifestations of a large repertoire of defense mechanisms employed to gain or defend respect in a hostile environment."[6] Given that *The Color Purple* is set in the first half of the twentieth-century; Thornton's career began in 1939, when she was just thirteen years old; and Winehouse's songs from the 2000s consciously evoke classic women's blues lyrics, these women's refusal to play the role of pious, prim, respectable ladies allows others—Black, white, male, female, and middle- and working-class—to label them as dirty and sinful. And in Winehouse's case, some members of the press reveled in her self-destructive behaviors. While Winehouse undoubtedly enjoyed multiple privileges as a white, twenty-first-century, commercially successful, and internationally known singer-songwriter, her drug and alcohol abuse, as well as the public incidents of domestic violence that occurred between her and husband Blake Fielder-Civil, made her fodder for narratives in the tabloid press with a strangely pre–civil rights tinge.

The beginning of this chapter focuses on literary blueswomen. The power of fictionalized autobiographical and biographical storytelling is demonstrated in *The Color Purple*, through Shug Avery, the fictional classic blues singer, in her telling of the story about the role that Albert's father played in the dissolution of her relationship with Albert; Squeak's startling transformation into Mary Agnes as she tells the story of her rape at the hands of her white warden uncle; and Celie's unlicensed telling of both of their stories—and her own—through which she finds her own voice. In the fictive world of *The Color Purple,* Shug Avery and Squeak are introduced in the 1910s and 1920s, and represent the early female vaudeville/classic blues performers.[7]

The next section, about Big Mama Thornton, fits chronologically, as Thornton was born in 1926. She is a blueswoman from the next generation who maintains ties to her predecessors: at the beginning of Thornton's career, she was called the "New Bessie Smith." When Thornton uses silence to protect herself from outsiders' fictions about her biography, and then spins her own yarns about her life story, radically recasting her autobiography in interviews and onstage in a new form of oral history, she reflects the narrative, folk roots of the blues tradition.

As a foil to my selection of literary and music texts featuring twentieth-century Black blueswomen, I include Amy Winehouse, an artist from the twenty-first century who was English of Jewish extraction. Her experiences with the tabloid and music press, who fictionalized her already-fictive autobiography and biography—her highly stylized visual image, her public interviews, and her confessional lyrics—through a salacious telling and retelling of the most private details of her life, helped motivate her alternative autobiography that contests her public persona largely derived from sexist and misogynistic mass-media representations of her life.

While Winehouse shared in the distinctive "whiteness of our own" ascribed to Jewish people in Anglo-American society, in her musical performance Winehouse enunciated a Black American musical identity and strived for Black musical "authenticity" rooted in the past.[8] This observation does not imply an endorsement of racially essentialist notions of musical production or musical authenticity, so when I suggest that Winehouse articulates a Black American musical identity, I am outlining Winehouse's desire—based on circulating cultural ideas about race—to participate in an American tradition of music making featuring Black artists, including twentieth-century pop music styles such as R & B, jazz, blues, and "girl group" soul. Winehouse, on her suggestively titled *Back to Black* CD, strives to perform an amalgam of soul, blues, jazz, and pop music that works as so-called authentically Black. In her visual presentation—tall beehive hairstyle and Cleopatra-style eye makeup—and song structure, she seems more aligned with 1960s girl groups Martha and the Vandellas or the Ronettes, while her voice, lyrics, and transgressive public persona seem just as deeply indebted to stereotypical images of the 1920s Black blues queen. Including Winehouse here demonstrates that blues traditions hinge, to a large degree, on autobiographical narratives told by the artists themselves, as well as biographical narratives told by others about the artists. Winehouse is an example of how autobiographical and biographical fictions can sometimes carve out spaces for musical artists to fit within the blues tradition regardless of race or class, or even the form or style of their music.

In the twenty-first century, while the bluesmen are celebrated figures, critics and scholars either erase female blues singers from the tradition—when blues critics and fans do talk about the women, they tend to focus on two or three names: Ma Rainey, Bessie Smith, perhaps Ethel Waters—or devalue their contributions. Even though country blues artists such as Robert Johnson, Son House, and Charley Patton did not, in their time, enjoy the same level of commercial success as their female counterparts, many contemporary blues scholars and fans take male country and urban blues artists—such as Johnson, House, Muddy Waters, John Lee Hooker, and Howlin' Wolf—as prototypical. Blueswomen—the real-life blues singers and the contemporary fictional and pop culture characters—must overcome significant race, class, and gender barriers to enter the canon of authentic blues. After all, in the romantic blues imaginary, approaching the music as a lucrative business opportunity is crass and decidedly inauthentic. As LeRoi Jones argues in *Blues People,* "Classic blues attempts a universality that earlier blues forms could not even envision. But with the attainment of such broad human meaning, the meanings which existed in blues *only for Negroes* grew less pointed. The professionalism of classic blues moved it to a certain extent out of the lives of Negroes. It became the stylized response, even though a great many of the social and emotional preoccupations of primitive blues remained." While Jones does not completely dismiss the blueswomen's contributions, his praise is mixed. He concedes the blueswomen's ability to reach a larger audience, but he also laments the inclusion of the white mainstream, necessitating a watering down of what he sees as authentic Black musical expression.[9] The idea that Delta blues icon Charley Patton, for instance, might have also seen himself as a professional when he drove to the 1930 Paramount recording session with Son House, Louise Johnson, and Willie Brown gets lost in such romantic blues idealization.[10] In this paradigm, the lone country bluesman, performing original songs with nothing but an acoustic guitar, exemplifies the singer-songwriter as folk hero. Bluesmen are celebrated as authentic, *real* artists, while the pioneering Black women who achieved fame and financial success despite *both* race and gender barriers are derided—almost entirely by men—as commercial sellouts. Critics such as Elijah Wald and Hazel Carby contest the notion that so-called authentic blues performers were "rural," "wandering" artistic geniuses unconcerned with monetary rewards.[11] And it is important to note that Ethel Waters, Bessie Smith, Ma Rainey, Mamie Smith, and Ida Cox have had a considerable impact on generations of popular singers, yet their stories remain largely untold. Janis Joplin, Bonnie Raitt, and Melissa Etheridge are just a few of the later blues-rock artists influenced by the earlier blueswomen. Countless other jazz, soul, gospel, and R & B artists such as Mahalia Jackson, Billie Holiday, Aretha Franklin, and Sarah Vaughan have benefitted from the groundwork laid by the singers of the classic blues.

In the early years of the twentieth century, large numbers of young, Southern, working-class Black women migrated to Northern cities in search of better job and economic prospects. There were many young Black girls and women who yearned for freedom from a life of domestic servitude *and* a chance to express their talent. These young women were already in precarious situations due to their race, class, and gender. As Harrison notes, "The typical black woman emigrant left home at age fifteen or sixteen, around 1915–1920, seeking the better life that itinerant laborers and songsters described in their stories and songs about the city." At home, field and domestic work were their only career prospects, while the North promised more freedom and diverse job options, including work in the entertainment industry. As Harrison states, "Young black women were often so dazzled by the opportunity for freedom, fortunes, and fame offered by the stage that they were willing to accept questionable living and working conditions to achieve them." Voices from various Black communities quickly chimed in with concern for both the physical safety and the moral direction of these young Black girls.[12] In a 1910 *Chicago Defender* article titled "Mothers Taking Innocent Daughters to Houses of Ill Fame to Play Piano Still Our Christians' Cry of White Slave Is Heard in the Community—What about the Black Ones?," the writer asserts that Black girls, aged fourteen through nineteen, can be found on any given night playing piano in Chicago's red-light district.

The author invokes the Cult of True Womanhood, asking plaintively, "Are our women societies like the Phyllis [*sic*] Wheatley Club, going to sit idly by and let womanhood be trampled under foot, or are they going to join hands in the holy war of the protection of the 'unknown' Black slave?"[13] Despite the disapproval of the Black middle class and the Black church, the pull of the North, with its chance for a better life, was too strong to deter these young women.

Black women have always been part of the American labor force. Most could not be housewives, as they were not allowed into the Cult of True Womanhood. In the eyes of the white ruling class, their sexual exploitation during slavery and Jim Crow resulted from their subhumanity and questionable moral fiber. Black women who aspired to respectability would never gain full entry to (white) American citizenship and the privileges that status endows, even those in the middle-class women's societies, such as the Phillis Wheatley Club, so an opportunity for more freedom and better job prospects on the stage, even at the risk of one's reputation, was attractive to women who made the long trek to the North. As Carby notes, "The behavior of black female migrants was characterized as sexually degenerate and, therefore, socially dangerous." They were not deemed "sexually degenerate" by whites alone: "The need to police and discipline the behavior of black women in cities, however, was not only a premise of white agencies and institutions but also a perception of black institutions and organizations, and the black middle class."[14] The judgment and policing of these young, single, freedom-seeking Black women's bodies, as well as their artistic expression, forced these women to find their own way economically, socially, and creatively.

It was against this historical backdrop that Rainey, Smith, Cox, and other first-generation, teenaged blueswomen emerged. While segments of both Black and white communities saw these women as dangerous and unruly, later Black women writers recognized their feminist contributions. Civil rights activist and academic Angela Davis was one of the first to make the argument for classic blues as feminist: "The female figures evoked in women's blues are independent women free of the domestic orthodoxy of the prevailing representations of womanhood through which female subjects of the era were constructed."[15] Carby ultimately takes a heroic view of their struggle: "The blues women did not passively reflect the vast social changes of their time; they provided new ways of thinking about these changes, alternative conceptions of the physical and social world for their audience of migrating and urban women and men, and social models for women who aspired to escape from and improve their conditions of existence."[16] Davis and Carby demonstrate the strength, resilience, and creativity of those iconic, historical, female blues makers, and this chapter builds on this important foundational work by showing the impact that storytelling has on these and future blueswomen's lives. The blueswomen in the following narratives take an active role in their own mythologization through autobiographical self-invention and reinvention, with their stories serving to counter the negative representations with which they have to struggle.

An epistolary novel set in rural Georgia during the 1930s, *The Color Purple* is written as a series of diary entries to God (and later to the narrator's sister Nettie) by Celie, a young, uneducated, Black woman who endures racial and patriarchal oppression. Celie writes about the physical, mental, and verbal abuse she suffers at her husband Albert's hands, yet she never writes Albert's first name, or even utters it in conversations with others, referring to him instead as "Mr. ——." Through the act of calling Albert "Mr. ——," not only does Celie highlight the emotional distance and age difference between Albert and herself—Celie is fourteen, while Albert is an older widower with four children—but she also obscures his identity in an attempt to erase him from her narrative. As portrayed in her diaries, Albert participates in Celie's oppression and has a great deal of power over her daily life and survival; but in that narrative space Celie controls his, and every other character's, representation. By refusing to name Albert, or his father—another oppressive figure—she undermines male power within her narrative world. This early signal clears the ground for Celie and the blueswomen around her to reclaim their power through unlicensed autobiographical narrative. Much in the way Leigh Gilmore's theory of "autobiographics" offers a feminist critique of the hegemonic autobiographical tradition, and positions women's autobiographies as political acts and expressions of personal agency, these women heed the call, using their stories to invent and reinvent themselves. Gilmore notes, "Erupting in texts where it is not licensed, women's self-representation has frequently been silenced or marginalized because it has not been interpreted/named/authorized as such." Since the autobiographical genre has been traditionally gendered as male, Celie's acts of self-representation, her "autobiographics," as well as her renderings of other characters' biographical details in her diary entries, are nothing short of subversive. Gilmore asserts, "Autobiographics, as a description of self-representation and as a reading practice, is concerned with interruptions and eruptions, with resistance and contradiction as strategies of self-representation."[17] Celie's simultaneous victimization in marriage and empowerment on the page is exactly this kind of contradiction. And the process of journaling, with its necessary starts and stops, leads to both interruptions in the narrative and eruptions of self-representation.

"Autobiographics" is focused exclusively on self-representation, on autobiography; however, the term is useful in a discussion about biography as well. In this text, as well as others in my book, fictional blues characters and real-life blues musicians not only tell their own stories but also act as unlicensed biographers. Esther Phillips's (tall, or at least exaggerated) tales about Big Mama Thornton is one such example.[18] Celie gives her version of events in *The Color Purple* and tells the life stories of herself and others the way she sees fit, yet she cannot find her voice in real time when interacting with Albert or his insolent children. Ultimately, her growth outside of her narrative space catches up to her strength within the confines of her journal. Celie is not a blueswoman in a traditional musical sense, so she is not the main character I am examining in this section; however, the structure of the novel is important, as Celie's highly subjective, first-person narrative necessitates the reader's skepticism regarding the portrayals of all of the characters and herself. Celie's narrative point of view calls into question the moments of dialogue she re-creates. For instance, she does not include quotation marks for any of the conversations she includes. Some of this might be explained as a function of Celie's lack of formal education; however, the missing quotation marks are also an indication of her authorial control. Perhaps Celie leaves out the quotation marks in order to guide and subtly craft each character's autobiographical expression. In this way, she serves as a biographer of sorts, who carefully constructs and reconstructs each subject's life story. This is not unlike a conventional biographer who conducts interviews with, and quietly observes, his or her subject and other key characters in the story, with the goal of creating a life in print.

Celie's world is altered significantly when Albert's girlfriend, blues singer Shug Avery, comes to town. Shug is sick with an undisclosed illness, and Albert invites her to stay in his and Celie's home to recuperate.

Celie is immediately intrigued by, and attracted to, Shug. When Celie first sees her, her description of the sick woman is rhapsodic: "And she dress to kill. She got on a red wool dress and chestful of black beads. A shiny black hat with what look like chickinhawk feathers curve down side one cheek, and she carrying a little snakeskin bag, match her shoes." Her representation of Shug is contradictory as well. She is fixated, at first, on Shug's outer appearance. Focusing initially on Shug's clothes, Celie takes a closer look, noticing Shug's short stumble as she gets out of the car, and seeing the truth of Shug's condition: "Close up I see all this yellow powder caked up on her face. Red rouge. She look like she ain't long for this world but dressed well for the next. . . . Under all that powder her face black as Harpo. She got a long pointed nose and big fleshy mouth. Lips look like black plum. Eyes big, glossy. Feverish. And mean. Like, sick as she is, if a snake cross her path, she kill it." From afar Shug looks better, healthier. Up close, Celie can see the physical toll of Shug's sickness, yet she continues to construct Shug's biography in wide-eyed, romantic terms, luxuriating in what she identifies as Shug's outlaw (blues) qualities. Shug's outlaw nature is stressed when Celie comments on her mean disposition while simultaneously bathing Shug and ogling her breasts. Celie writes, "What you staring at? she ast. Hateful. She weak as a kitten. But her mouth just pack with claws."[19] Even though Celie characterizes Shug as "hateful," her admiration for Shug's inner strength and potential for violence, even when incapacitated, and her desire for Shug's body, and to perhaps *become* Shug through absorption into her body, are barely concealed.

Later, when Shug feels well enough to play at Albert's son Harpo's new juke joint, Celie describes her: "Shug wearing a gold dress that show her titties near bout to the nipple. Everybody sorta hoping something break. But that dress strong." For Celie, Shug's clothing not only suggests economic advancement but also enunciates rebellion, as Shug has the agency and social mobility to earn a lucrative salary despite being a Black woman in the Jim Crow South. Shug is also comfortable with her sexuality, encouraging others to confront their own sexual feelings toward her. After Shug's set, Celie describes the following scene: "Shug come over and she and Sofia hug. Shug say, Girl, you look like a good time, you do. That when I notice how Shug talk and act sometimes like a man. Men say stuff like that to women, Girl, you look like a good time. Women always talk bout hair and health. How many babies living or dead, or got teef. Not bout how some woman they hugging on look like a good time." Given the time frame in which this story takes place, it is not surprising that Celie would view such sexual innuendo as the purview of men. When Shug talks about sex in public spaces with men and women present, Celie sees her as communicating "like a man."[20] And since Celie is used to men having all of the power in her community, she gravitates toward Shug and hopes for some of Shug's enunciated maleness to rub off on her.

Shug's rebellious nature becomes the site of much of the tension in the story and is fuel for Celie's eventual self-empowerment, and even Albert's shift from Celie's abusive oppressor to her compassionate friend by the end of the novel. Shug's audacious finery, as well as her sexuality, puts her in league with such larger-than-life characters as Ma Rainey or Bessie Smith. As Carby states,

> The women blues singers occupied a privileged space; they had broken out of the boundaries of the home and taken their sensuality and sexuality out of the private into the public sphere. For these singers were gorgeous, and their physical presence elevated them to being referred to as Goddesses, as the high priestesses of the blues, or like Bessie Smith, as the Empress of the blues. Their physical presence was a crucial aspect of their power; the visual display of spangled dresses, of furs, of gold teeth, of diamonds, of all the sumptuous and desirable aspects of their body reclaimed female sexuality from being an objectification of male desire to a representation of female desire.[21]

Throughout the novel, female sexual desire is foregrounded mainly through the relationship between Celie and Shug. As Celie describes, "First time I got the full sight of Shug Avery long black body with it black plum nipples, look like her mouth, I thought I had turned into a man. . . . I wash her body, it feel like I'm praying. My hands tremble and my breath short."[22] Here Celie's sexual feelings toward Shug are conflated with maleness. Only men feel such intense sexual feelings toward women. Sexual desire, in general, is meant to be the exclusive domain of men, with women having sex with their husbands for the express purpose of procreation. This notion is, of course, rooted in the heteropatriarchy that Celie has internalized. But Shug, like the blueswomen Carby invokes, transgresses these boundaries, engaging in recreational sex and reveling in her sexual desire for men and women alike. Shug's ability to assert her sexual agency is what makes her more "like a man," and Celie's sexualized response puts her in the same category. The romantic and sexual relationship that develops between Celie and Shug would not have been possible without Shug's easy relationship with her own sexuality. And as unsettling as these feelings are for Celie, they are crucial, as they create the opening for Celie's personal development and eventual emancipation from her abusive marriage.

While Celie depicts Shug in romantic terms, she renders others' representations of Shug in much harsher and disdainful language. Many of the Black people in Celie's community, including the local preacher and members of his congregation, view Shug as a whore and unrepentant sinner: "A woman at church say she dying—maybe two berkulosis or some kind of nasty woman disease. . . . Even the preacher got his mouth on Shug Avery, now she down. He take her condition for his text. He don't call no name, but he don't have to. Everybody know who he mean. He talk bout a strumpet in short skirts, smoking cigarettes, drinking gin. Singing for money and taking other women mens. Talk bout slut, hussy, heifer and streetcleaner." Albert's father, Old Mr. ——, attempts to erase Shug entirely. He is, after all, responsible for Albert marrying his first wife, Annie Julia, instead of Shug. Albert's father sees Shug as a danger to his son and to their family's way of life, as she is a transgressive figure who refuses to adhere to normative gender behavior. Shug's biography comes into play here, as her lack of respectability is tied to her unclear lineage. Albert's father cannot understand his son's fixation on Shug and states, "Nobody even sure exactly who her daddy is." From Albert's father's perspective, a woman must know where she comes from to be good, clean, and respectable, so he deems Shug a whore. "Just what is it bout this Shug Avery anyway, he say. She black as tar, she nappy headed. She got legs like baseball bats. . . . Why, say Old Mr. ——, she ain't even clean. I hear she got the nasty woman disease."[23] This suggests there is just one "nasty woman disease." In Albert's father's world, being a transgressive woman is its own disease. Judith Butler's discussion of gender performativity is helpful here. Specifically, the idea that gender itself is "performative" and "real only to the extent that it is performed," speaks directly to the price that women pay when they do not adhere to the performance of particular "acts, postures, and gestures" that uphold patriarchal structures. Women who transgress traditional gender roles are severely punished in the public and private spheres, but despite the dangers, these transgressions can be self-empowering.[24] There is an argument to be made for blueswomen as powerful figures precisely *because* of their transgressive actions. Shug Avery is one example of a blueswoman who stands as a figure of powerful feminist rebellion instead of abject oppression. Shug's status as a sexually dominant woman indicts her in polite society but helps boost her cachet as a blueswoman among the audiences who turn out to see her perform live. As Celie recounts, after Shug is once again in good physical health and begins singing at Harpo's juke joint, "The first Saturday night so many folks come they couldn't git in."[25] And her intimates, Celie and Albert, also respect her personal and sexual independence. From Celie's perspective as the second—really, third-choice—wife who must adhere to Albert's heavily policed domestic boundaries, it seems that it is precisely because Albert cannot control Shug's behaviors, or restrict her mobility—she is free to enter and leave his life as often as she pleases—that he feels unwavering desire for her.

But of course, Albert's feelings about Shug are mediated through Celie's diary entries, which serve as vehicles for her autobiographical expression. Similarly, the ideas about Shug held by Albert's father and the local preacher are rendered by Celie alone. She has the power to shape the narrative around who Shug is: how Albert and others, and even Celie herself, view Shug. Through Celie's decisions about what details about Shug's life to write about—the parts that include Celie, and the events that Celie learns about from Shug, dating back from before she knew her—she acts like an autobiographical storyteller who self-consciously constructs her narrative. Its constructedness points to its fictionality, with Celie deciding who gets to speak and when. So while Albert's father may condemn Shug for not having a "respectable" biography, Celie gives Shug the opportunity to tell her own story, recasting her biography in autobiographical form. As Celie washes and combs Shug's hair, Shug lets her guard down, reaches for a cigarette, and hums a tune.[26] Celie writes, "First she say, hurry up and git finish. Then she melt down a little and lean back gainst my knees. That feel just right, she say. That feel like mama used to do. Or maybe not mama. Maybe grandma. She reach for another cigarette. Start hum a little tune. What that song? I ast. Sound low down dirty to me. Like what the preacher tell you its sin to hear. Not to mention sing. She hum a little more. Something come to me, she say. Something I made up. Something you help scratch out my head." Here Shug uses music and memory to mine her own autobiography. The memory comes into focus as she tells her story. What is true is not immediately clear, as Shug corrects her backstory as she goes along. At first, it is her mother combing her hair, and then it is her grandmother. This detail is important, as she is describing an intimate moment where she is feeling peaceful and vulnerable. If it is her grandmother, does that mean she could not feel as connected to her mother? Her intimacy with Celie grows as she tells her story. It is as if remembering these autobiographical details helps Shug to become more comfortable sharing her blues expression. The song—and Shug—are not "low down dirty."[27] Being a blueswoman is part of her identity, so she can create blues music only when she is at peace with herself, even if she is not safe in the world around her. As Celie nurtures her, combing her hair as a (grand)mother might, Shug allows the music that is inside of her to come out. She sings the blues as she remembers pieces of her backstory, as doing so is part of her life narrative. Telling her story allows her to continue adding threads to her life that will then become more autobiographical backstory.

Celie also allows the reader to hear Shug's voice for an extended period of time, as Shug reflects on her difficult relationship with her mother and ruminates about what her life with Albert might have been. In a long letter to God, Celie discloses her anger at Shug's and Albert's renewed closeness and then learns that Shug used that relationship to discover that Albert has been keeping her sister's letters from Celie. Celie is devastated to find out that Albert is capable of such cruelty, and Shug does everything she can to comfort the two of them. Shug sets out to reframe her and Albert's backstories, perhaps hoping to show Celie that circumstances made Albert the way he is, and to justify choosing him as her mate and father of her children so long ago. Shug talks about the cold relationship between her and her mother, and how that motivated her desire for Albert:

> One thing my mama hated me for was how much I love to fuck, she say. She never love to do nothing had anything to do with touching nobody, she say. I try to kiss her, she turn her mouth away. . . . My daddy love me to kiss and hug him, but she didn't like the looks of that. So when I met Albert, and once I got in his arms, nothing could

> git me out. . . . Shug say, the last baby did it. They turned me out. I went to stay with my mama wild sister in Memphis. She just like me, Mama say. She drink, she fight, she love mens to death. She work in a roadhouse. Cook. Feed fifty men, screw fifty-five.

Shug is unapologetic about her sexuality, though she acknowledges that it created a wedge between her mother and herself. No matter what others may think of her—and in this text the most negative responses come from men—she embraces her desire for sex and male companionship and celebrates those drives in her aunt. What is also striking about this diary entry is that Celie admits to being numb to what Shug is saying to her: "I don't even want to say nothing. Where I'm at it peaceful. It calm. No Albert there. No Shug. Nothing."[28] Her Zen-like reaction to Shug's autobiographical expression most certainly affects the way that Celie constructs Shug in this entry, though it is difficult to say whether her calm causes her to represent Shug's words inaccurately, or if Celie's distance allows her to record Shug's dialogue faithfully *because,* in that moment, she has no vested interest in advancing a romantic view of Shug.

As Shug talks, she becomes more despondent and even cries. "Nobody dance like Albert when he was young. Sometime us did the moochie for an hour. After that, nothing to do but go somewhere and lay down. And funny. Albert was so *funny.* He kept me laughing. How come he ain't funny no more? she ast. How come he never hardly laugh? How come he don't dance? she say. Good God, Celie, she say, What happen to the man I love?" In this moment of autobiographical expression, Shug recuperates Albert's image in an effort to convince Celie, and herself, of his inherent goodness while demonstrating why, despite her love for him, she cannot be with Albert in the long term. Not only is his spirit dead in the present, but in the past he was unable to protect Shug from his father. As Celie writes about Shug's relationship with Albert, "I was so surprise when I heard he was going to marry Annie Julia, she say. Too surprise to be hurt. . . . His daddy told him I'm trash, my mama trash before me. His brother say the same. Albert try to stand up for us, git knock down. One reason they give him for not marrying me is cause I have children. But they *his,* I told old Mr. ——. How us know? He ast." This goes back to the question of birth and patrilineage. According to Old Mr. ——, Shug is "trash" because Old Mr. ——does not know for certain the identity of the father (or fathers) of her children.[29] For Old Mr. ——, and the others who condemn Shug for her nonfeminine behaviors, the fact that Shug and Albert never married is proof of her children's illegitimacy, even though she and Albert attest to Albert's paternity. Shug's gender renders her powerless in the face of Old Mr. ——'s judgments, leaving her no choice but to tell her *own* story through autobiographical acts. The old trope of "mama's baby, papa's maybe" works to undermine women's authority to legitimize their own families. For Shug and Celie, storytelling creates a pathway to powerful self-representation and offers the opportunity for healing after years of patriarchal oppression.

In many ways Shug Avery is a perfect blueswoman character. She reads as any one of the classic blueswomen—Ma Rainey, Bessie Smith, or Ethel Waters. As described by Celie, she is of a large stature—both physically and in the manner of her presence. She is bold, audacious, "mean" with a mouth "pack with claws," even in a weakened physical state, and she is comfortable with both the concept and expression of sex, as well as her fluid sexual identity.[30] Celie's depiction of her aligns with most people's ideas of what a woman who sings the blues in the 1920s and 1930s Jim Crow South might be like, or how her reception might be. Shug's story, then, offers an example of how autobiographical blues narrative works within a fictional, written-down framework. In the novel, Shug's self-referential expression is embedded within the larger narrative—occurring in shorter utterances rather than through a longer, sustained story—and is told by Celie rather than directly expressed by Shug. Her words are rooted in nonfiction—her version of the truth—versus tall tales, but still her stories are constructed. And it is Shug's careful revision of Albert's father's "story" about her that allows her to reclaim her own narrative effectively.

The emergence of Mary Agnes as a reluctant blues queen who exists outside of representational blues norms is unexpected and intriguing. And even more so, the mentoring relationship between Shug and Mary Agnes speaks to the Black sisterhood or womanist ideology that Walker's novel espouses.[31] But most importantly, Squeak's blues development demonstrates how a woman who defies the usual expectations for a blues singer can be fashioned into one through autobiographical and biographical fictions.

With Shug performing one night at Harpo's juke joint as a backdrop, Celie introduces Squeak as Harpo's "little yellowish girlfriend."

Speaking about Squeak in the diminutive, she is a perfect foil to Shug. Squeak is short, slight, and light-skinned. Shug is tall and dark-skinned. Celie also immediately claims Squeak as one of her own. Squeak capitulates to conventional gender roles, or as Celie puts it, "She like me. She do anything Harpo say." Squeak is also set up in contrast to Sophia—Harpo's estranged wife—who was her own person in her marriage to Harpo, refusing to obey her husband and physically powerful enough to defend herself against his domestic violence, even to the degree of, as Celie marvels, having just a "little cut all blue and red under her eye" after one of their most vicious physical altercations. Sophia may not be a blueswoman in a conventional sense, as she does not sing or write songs, but she shares some key qualities with other female blues singers. Most notably, she and Shug both flout gender roles and dare the men around them to tell them what to do. Celie even comments on Shug's male behavior when Shug hugs Sophia and tells her she "look[s] like a good time."[32]

So the showdown between Squeak and Sophia, when she walks into Harpo's juke joint with her prizefighter boyfriend, leaves Squeak at a grave disadvantage. After Squeak stakes her claim to Harpo, cussing at and slapping Sophia while Sophia and Harpo dance in a tight embrace, Sophia's reflex is to punch Squeak with a closed fist.[33] Squeak's physical wounds are great—she loses two teeth—but it is evident that she is tougher than she may appear to be on the surface. Squeak proves to be resilient. In fact, she shows strength over time just as Celie does, though Squeak's character arc from doormat to independent woman is faster. Celie's rendering of Squeak as a blueswoman begins long before Squeak, née Mary Agnes, sings her first blues song. Celie tells her story before Squeak tells her own through song lyrics later in the novel. And Celie's description of Squeak as a naïve and weak little girl, alongside the brief but graphic nature of the violence—the aftermath of Sophia's punch resulting in one of Squeak's teeth hanging loosely outside of her mouth, while the other clanks off of Celie's drink glass—sets up the expectation that Squeak will, like her nickname suggests, be quiet, or even silenced, in the face of serious physical violence.[34]

But it is Squeak who initiates the altercation with Sophia. She slaps her first, so it might make sense to read her defense of her relationship with Harpo as a paradigm that might reflect a blues lyric about a woman who loves her man so much she is willing to fight another woman to keep him. She is also able to take a punch. Even though she is missing two teeth, according to Celie, she "start banging on Harpo leg with her shoe. You git that bitch out a here, she cry, blood and slobber running down her chin." She cries, and she does not continue swinging, but she does not collapse in a heap either. She keeps hitting Harpo with her shoe—she keeps staking a claim to her man.[35] She is not the brawling, hell-raising, loud-talking blueswoman of blues legend—the kind whose scariest manifestations existed in the imaginations of Black church preachers, the Black middle class and aspirational Blacks who hoped to reach the middle class, and whites who already held a general disdain for Black people, and for Black women specifically. She is a "nice girl, friendly and everything," but she has been done wrong, and that wrongdoing plants a seed that will flower after she is raped by her white prison warden uncle later in the novel as she tries to help facilitate Sophia's release from jail after Sophia's physical altercation with the mayor.[36]

Squeak/Mary Agnes is a blueswoman in varied dimensions. She makes the decision to sing later in the novel, and she even eventually joins Celie and Shug in Memphis, embarking on a singing career and beginning a romantic relationship with Shug's man. But I would argue that she is every bit the blueswoman in a narrative sense as well. Her story, specifically the autobiographical story that she tells about her life in the first blues song that she sings, and her name change situate her within the narrative blues tradition. Celie can clearly be read as a woman whose life could be a blues song. And Celie, as both the narrator and the narrative shaper, suggests that one can be a blueswoman by singing it or living it. Someone can be part of the tradition by telling their own story of pain, resilience, and transcendence absent a stage. And in this way, all four of the main women in *The Color Purple*—Celie, Shug, Sophia, and Squeak—are blueswomen.

When Squeak comes back from the jail in the aftermath of her rape, she tells a story, on her own terms, about her life. Whereas earlier she has to be coaxed, red-faced, to admit that she is related to the warden, after her rape, she tells what happened in a strong, clear voice. "He saw the Hodges in me. . . . And he didn't like it one bit." When Harpo interrupts and suggests that he wants to exact revenge on the white people who are responsible for this, Squeak, for the first time, stands up for herself, finding her voice in the process. "Shut up, Harpo . . . I'm telling it."[37]

And it is in the telling that we learn more about Squeak. Not necessarily because what she tells us is the truth, but because what she tells us is a version of the truth that is important to her. This is both an example of Gilmore's autobiographics—Squeak is not licensed to speak, but she asserts her voice, for the first time, anyway—and her vocalization of her constructed autobiography. When talking about her rape, she is in charge of what parts of her narrative—which creates her autobiography—she wants to share and which parts she wants to obscure. She willingly and openly recounts her conversation with the Warden that follows the script that Harpo and Mr. ——wanted her to follow—"I say what yall told me to say," but then her demeanor changes when she discusses her rape. She reflects on her uncle's leering gaze—as he listens to her testimony, he scans her body. Squeak recounts that as she speaks, "he come from behind his desk, lean over my chair." As he moves closer to Squeak and closer to enacting sexual violence, her voice grows quieter, muted. As Celie puts it, her strong and clear speech becomes a "mumble."[38]

As she finally tells the story of her rape, it quickly becomes clear that the sexual violence is tied up in how she looks. The warden asks her, "Who your daddy? . . . Where you git them eyes?" The warden is attracted to the white parts of her, but he simultaneously denies where those features come from so he can rape her without sin: "He took my hat off, say Squeak. Told me to undo my dress. She drop her head, put her face in her hands. My God, say Odessa, and he your uncle. He say if he was my uncle he wouldn't do it to me. That be a sin. But this just little fornication. Everybody guilty of that."[39] He is unafraid of man's laws because they do not apply to him in this context, but he tells himself what he needs to believe: that he has not flouted God's laws.

After telling her story, Squeak asks Harpo if the reason he is with her—has sex with her—is because of her color: "She turn her face up to Harpo. Harpo, she say, do you really love me, or just my color?" It is striking here that she doesn't ask if it is her complexion. Given that they dressed her up as a "white woman" earlier in the hope that she might yet convince the warden—her white uncle—to release Sophia from jail, there is a conversation going on here about her race and racial identity. She is a light-skinned, biracial woman who, if you dress her up the right way—in this case, this simply means costuming her in a way that transcends her actual class position: her "starch and iron dress, high heel shoes with scuffs, and an old hat somebody give Shug"—she won't be able to pass phenotypically as white but she will look at the very least like a respectable Black middle-class woman imitating white middle-class values. In answer to Squeak's question, "Harpo say, I love you, Squeak. He kneel down and try to put his arms round her waist. She stand up. My name Mary Agnes, she say."[40] When Squeak asserts that her name is Mary Agnes, not Squeak, she is also making it clear that she wants a sense of belonging, that she is Black too. No matter how white she may appear, or how dressed up she is, and no matter that her father and uncle are prominent white men in the town, she cannot ever be a white woman. Her uncle reminds her of this as he rapes her. He sees that she is biracial, and he admits that he remembers seeing her in the past, but he will not admit that he is related to her. The fact that Black and white strands of the same family live in the same town acts as a reverberation of chattel slavery, when enslaved Black women were routinely raped by their white masters to replenish the slave labor, while simultaneously the masters created families with their wives, leading to siblings participating in opposite sides of the chattel slavery paradigm. And the blues song that Squeak eventually writes centers around this.

Celie's description is particularly striking when describing the moment when, six months after her rape, Mary Agnes finds her singing voice. The idea that Mary Agnes's voice is not like Shug's—"It little, it high, it sort of meowing"—helps to restructure our expectations of what a blueswoman is.[41] A blueswoman does not have to conform to a fixed aural construct. Nor does she necessarily become a blueswoman because she does or does not sing a song. She becomes a blueswoman because she takes control of telling her story, and she reclaims her name.

There is a long history of African Americans renaming themselves. In the postbellum South, newly freed slaves claimed new names—Frederick Douglass discusses his renaming process after escaping bondage in his *Narrative of the Life of Frederick Douglass, an American Slave*.[42] And more than a century later, against the backdrops of the Black power and Black arts movements, Black artists, intellectuals, activists, and everyday folks chose new names to reflect their African lineages. There is also, of course, a rich tradition of blues musicians claiming new monikers for themselves.

In Mary Agnes's case, she rejects a nickname that might be a fitting blues nickname in order to reclaim her birth name. This appears to be in part because her nickname is a diminutive. It speaks to her small stature, her small voice, and mixed up in there is her "yellow" complexion. Her color brings her closer to whiteness, which paired with her voice and height is what made it possible to consider dressing her "like she a white woman."[43] Squeak is a "yellow" woman who can never be white, while Mary Agnes is a Black woman who wants to be seen as such. In embracing her given name, bestowed on her by her Black family, Mary Agnes sees an opening to claim her Black ancestry.

In her letter to God, Celie states that Mary Agnes begins her blues career singing Shug's songs. This makes sense, given that Shug is a model for how to be an independent woman with a voice—a strong speaking and singing voice. She has certainly been a guide for Celie. But Mary Agnes eventually writes her own blues lyrics:

> They calls me yellow
> like yellow be my name
> They calls me yellow
> like yellow be my name
> But if yellow is a name
> Why ain't black the same
> Well, if I say Hey black girl
> Lord, she try to ruin my game.

Mary Agnes writes these lyrics while Sophia serves time in the local jail. The "black girl" in this song reads as Sophia. When Celie first introduces Sophia to God, she comments, "Harpo so black he think she bright, but she ain't that bright. Clear medium brown skin, gleam on it like on good furniture. Hair notty but a lot of it, tied up on her head in a mass of plaits. She not quite as tall as Harpo but much bigger, and strong and ruddy looking, like her mama brought her up on pork." Mary Agnes's complexion is described by Celie as "yellow," a characterization that might be used interchangeably with "bright." Both words are meant to depict light brown or near-white skin. On the night that Mary Agnes and Sophia first meet, it is important to remember that the smaller, lighter skinned, and quieter-voiced Mary Agnes provokes the violent altercation. She interrupts Sophia and Harpo as they dance, she tells Sophia to leave Harpo alone, calls Sophia a bitch, and then slaps her. Mary Agnes's physical appearance suggests Black middle-class respectability and a white, patriarchal version of femininity. Yet she is the aggressor in the fight. Mary Agnes's positioning as a Black woman means, though, that just as she really cannot be dressed up as a white woman, she also cannot really be part of the Cult of True Womanhood. She is Harpo's romantic partner, but she is not married to him. His wife is still his wife, and she is welcome to return any time she likes. So Mary Agnes is not a respectable woman in white people's eyes no matter how light-skinned she is. She knows this all too well, so she uses her song to undermine the idea that her color is all of who she is. The song is also a vehicle for Mary Agnes to talk to Sophia. Harpo tells Celie that Mary Agnes is still angry at Sophia for knocking out her teeth, even though she put herself in harm's way to help Sophia.[44] These lyrics retread the fight between Sophia and Mary Agnes.

While Mary Agnes's song highlights the central concerns undergirding her violent altercation with Sophia, her initial encounter with Sophia also reflects what Angela Davis calls the "songs of female competition."[45] Mary Agnes's willingness to engage in a physical fight with Sophia to protect her relationship with Harpo speaks to Davis's contentions that in the years after emancipation, "competition and rivalry in love may be seen as evidence of the historical construction of black working-class individuality" and that "through the blues, black women were able to autonomously work out—as audiences and performers—a working-class model of womanhood."[46] Mary Agnes's story, as it unfolds in Harpo's juke joint, is reminiscent of Gertrude "Ma" Rainey's original composition "Rough and Tumble Blues." In the opening stanza of Rainey's song, the lyric begins,

> I'm Going to the Western Union, type the news all down the line
> I'm Going to the Western Union, type the news all down the line
> 'Cause mama's on the warpath this mornin' and don't mind dyin'.

While it appears that Mary Agnes's decision to instigate a fight with Sophia is spontaneous, and in reaction to her dancing with Harpo, the sentiment in "Rough and Tumble Blues" mirrors Mary Agnes's actions that night. She responds with fury, and even though Sophia, at first, declines to fight for Harpo, literally or symbolically, Mary Agnes forces the confrontation and acts as though she is unafraid of death. Sophia is physically imposing, a true rival for Harpo's affections, yet Mary Agnes persists. In the Rainey song, the narrator states, "I got rough and killed three women 'fore the police got the news." Mary Agnes does not kill anyone, but she does begin the process of erasing an earlier version of herself: the almost-white woman who cannot be white by virtue of her race and class. In this spirit, the blues offered something to Mary Agnes that her previous life did not. As Davis suggests, "The blues provided a space where women could express themselves in new ways, a space in which they sometimes affirmed the dominant middle-class ideology but also could deviate from it."[47] As soon as Mary Agnes figures this out, she finds her voice, resists Harpo's patriarchal dominance, and eventually runs off with Celie, Shug, and later still, Shug's man. It is here that she fully reclaims Black womanhood, reinventing herself through a new narrative about her life, and a new autobiography all her own.

In the previous section, Mary Agnes finds herself as she escapes from Harpo to begin a new blues life with her sisters, Celie and Shug. In this part of the chapter, Big Mama Thornton finds herself as she uses her voice to claim and reclaim credit for her significant contributions to American popular music. As Big Mama Thornton sits in the back of the van in the summer of 1971, on the way to Eugene, Oregon, the conversation inevitably turns to Elvis Presley. The specter of Presley loomed large for Thornton, as she viewed him as someone who took ownership of something that belonged to her—her voice. While she did not compose "Hound Dog"—two young Jewish men from Brooklyn, Jerry Leiber and Mike Stoller, did the honors—the song was written for her with her vocal style and persona in mind. She also suggested in subsequent interviews that while Leiber and Stoller wrote the words to the song, she gave them her voice, making the song her own.[48]

This ongoing narrative of Presley's theft of "Hound Dog" persisted to such a degree that Alice Walker's 1981 two-character short story "1955" features Gracie Mae Still acting as a stand-in for Thornton—with a nod to classic blues icon Ma Rainey—and Traynor as a version of the young Presley. In the story, Traynor buys one of Gracie Mae's rhythm and blues songs—the tune is unnamed but bears a striking resemblance to the Leiber and Stoller song—and becomes a massively successful recording artist. However, according to Gracie Mae, he never finds true peace of mind and happiness because he plays Black music, and due to his whiteness he is unable to *feel* it. Although in real life Thornton did not write "Hound Dog," this version supports Thornton's perspective on artistic ownership: just because she did not receive writing credit does not mean it is not her song. This idea that blueswomen compose their songs through vocal interpretation and performance rather than conventional songwriting has long been echoed by Angela Davis (*Blues Legacies and Black Feminism*), Daphne Duval Harrison (*Black Pearls: Blues Queens of the 1920s*), and Sandra Lieb in her groundbreaking book *Mother of the Blues: A Study of Ma Rainey*.[49]

As the van rolled along, Thornton states about Presley:

> "Well, he refused to play with me when he first come out and got famous. They wanted a big thing for Big Mama Thornton and Elvis Presley. He refused, and I'm so glad I can tell the world about it."
>
> "Well, there's one thing we gonna do we gonna tell the truth," says Wyler.
>
> "Well, that *is* the truth."

The camera lingers on Thornton's face, allowing the audience to catch a glimpse of what appears to be the sad inevitability of the erasure of her vital artistic contributions.[50] Yet I would argue that it is precisely her determination to continually tell stories from her own perspective about her work, and her impact on both the blues and rock and roll, that shows the power of autobiographical self-creation. Her repeated claims of ownership of songs like "Hound Dog" and "Ball and Chain" shape the narrative around both her musical legacy and her autobiography.

Willie Mae Thornton was born on December 11, 1926, in Ariton, Alabama, and was raised in Montgomery. She left home at fourteen to perform as a member of Atlanta-based impresario Sammy Green's "Hot Harlem Revue," a traveling variety show for which Thornton sang, danced, and worked as a comedienne. She quit the troupe in 1948 because, according to her, they owed her "quite a bit of money."[51] In 1950, she signed a recording contract with Peacock Records in Houston, Texas. In 1952, Thornton joined bandleader Johnny Otis's troupe, and in that same year she recorded "Hound Dog," a twelve-bar blues song written for her by Leiber and Stoller, and featuring Otis on drums.[52] "Hound Dog," released in 1953, was a hit, selling approximately one million copies, though Leiber, Stoller, and Thornton saw little of the profits.[53] Elvis Presley's 1956 rock and roll version sold more than seven million copies worldwide, and helped earn the songwriters and Presley a nice paycheck.[54] Thornton's displeasure at watching Presley, a white man, receive accolades and ample financial remuneration for his version of a blues song that was written specifically for her has become part of a larger narrative of Thornton as a perpetual victim of cultural theft. In her article "Listening for Willie Mae 'Big Mama' Thornton's Voice: The Sound of Race and Gender Transgressions in Rock and Roll," Maureen Mahon notes, "In many popular music histories, Thornton has been reduced to a symbol: the ripped-off African American musician on whose unacknowledged shoulders subsequent generations of rock and rollers stand." While it might be fair to suggest that Thornton did not receive her rightful share of the fame stemming from her artistic output—"Ball and Chain," a song she wrote, helped make blues-rocker Janis Joplin a breakout star at the 1967 Monterey Pop Festival, but it is important to note than unlike other male rockers, such as Led Zeppelin and Elvis, Joplin was careful to ask for Thornton's permission to cover her work and made sure that Thornton received royalties—Thornton's limited representation as the mistreated and long-forgotten blueswoman overshadows her contributions to American popular music generally, and to rock and roll in particular. Thornton's unusual gender-bending visual presentation set her apart from her contemporaries, and paved the way for future women in rock to take a bold, individualistic approach to their performance styles: "These choices are evidence of an unconventional, transgressive, and liberated form of black femininity that rejects prevailing expectations of how women should comport themselves to secure respectability. Steeped in working-class, African American blues culture and possessing a powerful sense of self, Thornton followed her muse in terms of musical, interpersonal, and sartorial choices—a textbook example of rock-and-roll attitude and speaking clearly in one's own voice."[55] A 1970 live performance by Thornton with the Buddy Guy Blues Band demonstrates her self-possession and offbeat style. Not only does Thornton wear a suit in this performance, but she makes a point to remind the audience *twice* that she wrote "Ball and Chain": "This is a song I wrote, made famous by me and Janis Joplin. I wrote this tune called 'Ball and Chain.' I hope you like it." She also tells the crowd that the song was made famous first by her, and second by Joplin.[56] This is not exactly true, as Thornton's version was never released by Bay-Tone Records, so the song did not chart. Thornton played the song live, but it did not reach a large, mainstream, white audience until Joplin started performing it. However, Thornton's reclamation of the song as her own serves as a new kind of oral history, one that can be enacted in a staged performance, falling under the umbrella of Daphne Brooks's "Afro-alienation acts," in which "the condition of alterity converts into cultural expressiveness and a specific strategy of cultural performance."[57] In this case, that strategy involves Thornton's intentional correction of the historical record in order to ensure her inclusion in the blues and blues-rock scenes during the 1960s and 1970s. This allows her to tap into the cultural power that Stephanie Batiste suggests performers engage "as a means of exploring its dimensions, looking for spaces of manipulation and freedom in a manner far from binary."[58]

Between June 1973 and October 1974, journalists Robert Neff and Anthony Connor interviewed iconic blues men and women, including Thornton, Waters, and John Lee Hooker, as well as lesser-known blues artists such as Chess Records session keyboardist Lafayette Leake and pianist and singer Little Brother Montgomery, for their 1975 oral history *The Blues: In Images and Interviews.* Their goal was to "let musicians speak as the music itself speaks—directly to the listener."[59] In this section, I will discuss parts of the transcript of Neff and Connor's interview with Thornton, as well as excerpts from their raw interview with Esther Phillips.[60] It is fitting that these conversations appeared during the mid-1970s, a time when the oral history form had shifted from a celebration of the privileged to an activist enterprise. As oral historian Linda Shopes puts it, "oral history's scope widened in the 1960s and 1970s in response to both the social movements of the period and historians' growing interest in the experiences of 'nonelites.'"[61] Neff and Connor's loose, unfiltered, and wide-ranging dialogues gave voice to the groundbreaking and, in many cases, unheralded artists who have influenced generations of musicians worldwide. Neff and Connor interviewed R & B great Phillips, who toured with Thornton as a member of Johnny Otis's California Rhythm and Blues Caravan in the early 1950s. While Thornton was reticent about her past, Phillips was happy to share her recollections of Thornton's poor personal hygiene and subversive gender expression. Standing at nearly six feet tall, and weighing close to two hundred pounds, Thornton's "Big Mama" nickname was given to her by Apollo Theater manager Frank Schiffman—due to both her imposing physical presence and her powerful voice.[62] Thornton flouted gender norms by foregoing so-called feminine gowns and heels onstage and opting instead for plaid work shirts, slacks, and, occasionally, men's suits. Thornton's unwillingness to share details about her personal life creates the space for others to speak for her, disrupting the recuperative potential of the oral history form. Thornton's unruly and supposedly unfeminine behaviors are analogous to the transgressive interviews with, and about, her, with their blurring of the lines between interviewer and subject and the fluidity of the oral history form more generally.

While it is likely that in 1973 Neff and Connor set out to conduct a conventional oral history of Thornton, they instead transgressed the form. During the 1970s, the oral history interview was meant to add to the objective historical record, and give those who have been silenced due to their race, gender, and socioeconomic class the opportunity to speak for themselves. Even so, the process of creating an oral history had remained unchanged since the beginning of its modern existence in the 1940s as, according to Shopes, "the practice of history was understood—and is still largely understood—to consist of a careful reconstruction of 'what happened' based on a thorough and dispassionate investigation of the extant record."[63] However, Neff's and Connor's interviewing styles are anything but dispassionate, as the men reveal their biases toward prevailing notions of normative gender performance, and demonstrate a stalker-like interest in Thornton's private life. So they, as well as Phillips, fill in the gaps left by Thornton's silences, another expression of "Afro-alienation."[64] Due to Thornton's physical absence, we must rely on Phillips's subjective memories when she talks about events that transpired between the two of them twenty-five years earlier. Instead of succeeding at the traditional, objective approach to the oral history interview that was more common during the 1970s, Neff and Connor's work supports the current view of oral history as a "kissing cousin" to memoir. Just as the first-person narrator in a memoir must do, the oral history subject mines his or her past experiences for key details, and makes decisions about which ones to share and which ones to excise, affecting both the narrative itself as well as its reception. As Sharon O'Brien notes, "Both are forms of narrative in which ordinary people claim the authority to tell their own stories; both are forms tinged by imagination as well as memory (since the oral history narrative, like memoir, is shaped by selection and omission, as well as by the length of the interview and the interaction between interviewer and storyteller). And memoir, like oral history, arises from the interconnection of two or more sensibilities, since memoirists commonly write of relationship to others, as well as to the self in the past."[65] Phillips, Neff, and Connor each took a memoiristic approach when engaging Thornton's work and legacy. Given that Thornton was an independent woman who lived her life on her own terms, perhaps it should not come as much of a surprise that she set the terms for the interviews.

During their conversation with Thornton, Connor and Neff try to persuade her to reveal intimate details about her negative music industry experiences. Thornton's strong will shines through when she shoots back with: "Everybody comes asking me the same thing, man, it sounds like a record stuck. Yackity, yackity, yackity, yack. . . . I like to talk about the future, not the past, because the past is done and over." Later the interviewers try again to get Thornton to tell *their* version of her story. Rather than allowing Thornton to speak for herself on her own terms—what the oral history form is meant to accomplish—the interviewers reinforce the same tired narrative: "Earlier this evening you told us you have a memory like an elephant. You know, somebody does you wrong you don't forget it. But in this interview tonight, you're telling us mostly about things that have worked out well. We know, everybody knows, that you have been messed over by basically white people, but also black people have messed you over. You haven't told us anything about that. Now don't you hold any bitterness towards those people?" At first, Thornton simply replies, "No." But then she elaborates: "I still got a memory. I don't forget. But I don't hold no grudge. Why should I hold a grudge? It don't make any difference. I still don't get what belongs to me, so that don't make no sense."[66] Thornton's unwillingness to provide more information prompts the interviewers to ask other musicians who know Thornton to speak for her, including Phillips and Muddy Waters. Rather than merely asking the artists about Thornton's experiences in the music industry, they also seek confirmation about her difficult nature. While Waters keeps his comments about Thornton professional, and even diplomatic, Phillips tells a riveting tale that satisfies the interviewers' curiosities. Her performance harks back to the Black folkloric tradition, in which the teller is spurred on by the positive reactions of the listener to continue his or her tale, like Ralph Ellison's *Invisible Man* character, Jim Trueblood, who gets what he wants by telling white people what they want to hear. In this case, Phillips offers an increasingly unflattering portrait of Thornton—her own autobiographical and biographical fictions—that clearly entertains the two white interviewers.

Phillips was born Esther Mae Jones on December 23, 1935, in Galveston, Texas. In 1949, at fourteen years old, Phillips won an amateur talent contest at Johnny Otis's Barrelhouse Club in the Watts neighborhood of Los Angeles, California. Soon after, Phillips—renamed Little Esther Phillips—joined Otis's traveling revue, where she shared the bill with Thornton.[67] During her interview with Neff and Connor, Phillips states that due to Thornton's poor hygiene, when she would leave the tour bus their male band mates would put soap and other cleansing products on Thornton's empty seat. Each time Thornton returned to her seat, she would notice the items and immediately blame Phillips.

> Phillips: "She would always put it on me, and then the guys wouldn't defend the fact that I didn't do it, which made her dislike for me more intense."[68]

This caused a serious rift between the two women, with Thornton harboring anger toward the young singer. Here's a section of the interview—in Phillips's own words and with the occasional interjection by one of the interviewers—in which Phillips talks about one night while on tour in Ohio when a drunken Thornton threatened to beat her up:

> Phillips: I remember we were somewhere in Ohio, and she drank a fifth of J. W. Dant straight, and she decided that she wanted to jump on me. I've never—I mean of course I fought in school, but I wasn't about to fight her. I don't think I've ever really been dumb, because I could see that I was gonna have a problem with her. And some hustler in Chicago sold me a .22. A little .22 automatic pistol that my mother didn't even know I had. When we got to Ohio—and where we were playing there was the one way in, the one way out. And the dressing room was behind the bandstand. Like when you come on the bandstand, you'll have to walk up two or three steps and then you're right on the bandstand. So we were in the dressing room, and she told me she was gonna kick my ass. And the band was playing, and I'm back there by myself with her. But I had my piece with me though. I had to have it because she would drink and, man, go out . . . She was sitting on the radiator. I'll never forget it 'cause I was so scared. I didn't know what to do, and the band was playing and she had me cornered 'till I couldn't even get to the door. And she was sitting there drinking this straight 100 proof J. W. Dant. A whole fifth. And she said,

"You know what bitch, I'm gonna kick your ass." I said, "You are?"
Neff/Connor: "No. No. No. You're not six feet tall."
Phillips: I was so scared. I said, "Oh my God."

Phillips goes on to describe in great detail how she not only pulled a gun on Thornton, but also how it accidentally went off, causing Otis to stop his set early to rush backstage. No one was hurt, and the incident prompted the band members to tell Thornton the truth; however, by then, the relationship between Phillips and Thornton was damaged beyond repair. Neff and Connor continue to insert themselves into the narrative by commenting on Thornton's so-called freakish behaviors. After Phillips mentions that Thornton would wear ball gowns with combat boots onstage, one of the interviewers interjects, "What a strange woman."[69]

And then after listening patiently for a few minutes as Phillips steers the conversation back to her upbringing, one of the interviewers asks her what she thinks of Thornton's singing ability. It is evident that Neff and Connor want Phillips to tell Thornton's story if Thornton will not, even if that means they will get a distorted version of the truth.

Phillips: "When somebody's laying on the floor kicking their legs up, man, with a mic. I couldn't even hear what she was saying half the time."
Neff/Connor: "Did it ever strike you as strange that such a big, rough and a masculine woman could sing songs like 'Sweet Little Angel?'"

Phillips suggests that Thornton's performance aesthetic was so off-putting that it prevented her from hearing Thornton's voice. And when the interviewer asks, "Did it ever strike you as strange that such a big, rough and a masculine woman could sing songs like "Sweet Little Angel?," it is clear that, the interviewers, along with Phillips, see Thornton as unfeminine, and therefore transgressive.[70]

Neff and Connor did not include any of the sections of the interviews with Thornton or Phillips that I cite here in the published version of *The Blues*. It is striking that in the published version, the authors placed Thornton's and Phillips's comparatively benign musings about their relationships to drugs and alcohol side by side on the same page. This positioning on the page negates the actual physical and emotional distance between the two singers in 1975, while reflecting their proximity to each other on the road in the early 1950s. So the sordid, perhaps realer, history is the sprawling, messy version—the one hidden in the archives—while the mass-produced, published version is neater, with the rough edges smoothed over. So in the end, the transgressive version of Thornton's oral history remains obscured, just like the transgressive Thornton herself. Through her attempts to reclaim her power from Neff and Connor—two stand-ins for other white men in the music industry who exploited her—Thornton mirrors Shug Avery in *The Color Purple*, who powerfully resists Albert's father's limited and inaccurate version of who she is. Thornton's persistent reminders—to anyone who would listen—about the popularity and importance of her music was her way of revising the biography written by outsiders about her life. She uses oral autobiographical narrative to retell her own story, as many times as necessary, making sure her voice is finally heard.

Amy Jade Winehouse was born on September 14, 1983, in Southgate, London, and died of alcohol poisoning at twenty-seven on July 23, 2011, in Camden, London. During Amy's childhood, her father, Mitch, was a taxi driver, and her mother, Janis, was a pharmacist. She grew up with music, as some of her maternal uncles were jazz musicians. At twelve, Winehouse was accepted into the prestigious Sylvia Young Theatre School, an independent performing arts school in North London. At sixteen, a schoolmate passed her demo tape to an A & R executive at Island/Universal Records. In 2003, Winehouse released her debut album, *Frank*, a mixture of jazz, soul, pop, and hip-hop, to critical acclaim and commercial success (*Frank* went double platinum). In 2006, she released her second, and last, album, *Back to Black*, an international critical and commercial success that has sold more than twenty million copies worldwide to date.[71]

Two days after Winehouse's death—a tragic culmination of her years of substance abuse and other self-destructive behaviors—Steve Kandell reflected in an article for *Spin:*

> It's inevitable, really, that we'd eventually choke a bit on the rock mythology that's been crammed down our collective throats for most of our lives. The tortured genius, the hellion libertine, the martyr dying for the noble cause of nihilism—this is what we usu-

> ally mean when we say "rock star," and we're always on the hunt for fresh blood. And truth be told, that sort of bloodlust accounted for much of the initial, explosive response to Amy Winehouse in early 2007. The natural ability was never up for debate; combine that with an equally natural self-destructive bent, and the ensuing reception was predictably breathless. Not proud of this, but it's how your myth-making sausage gets made.[72]

Kandell's statement speaks indirectly to the question of musical authenticity. In some genres authenticity is foregrounded more than others, rock in particular being a genre in which, historically, critics and fans have wanted to believe that the sentiments and stories expressed by the artists musically, as well as in performance and even offstage, are honest and "true"—that is, their personas and art are somehow aligned with their factual autobiographies. Blues music also evokes the desire of some scholars, critics, and fans to believe that its makers express, in song and even through their actions, a true representation of their life stories. Accordingly, Winehouse's personal excess generated as much of the media's interest as her music. In a February 2007 concert review in the *London Evening Standard* for a London Astoria show in which Winehouse was sober and focused, John Aizlewood asserts:

> She may still be painfully thin and she'll always have the most naff tattoos this side of David Beckham, but there were no too-short skirts, no smoking, no swearing, no projectile vomiting and unless looking reasonably happy counts, no signs of insobriety. This might be the moment she has chosen to refocus on her day job rather than the bacchanalian debauchery which threatens to relegate her music to a sideshow, as it has for the walking cautionary tale that is Britney Spears. The inevitable irony of her understated professionalism was that it rendered the occasion less riveting than it might have been.[73]

In one brief review Aizlewood supports everything Kandell accuses the media (including himself) of having done. Besides suggesting that a professional, drama-free Winehouse performance is not as engaging as her shambolic ones, the male critic cannot help commenting on Winehouse's usual "too-short skirts"—the message being that on her worst days Winehouse's unacceptable brand of sexuality is at the forefront. Even though this particular Winehouse performance is *not* transgressive in any way, Aizlewood mentions past failures lest audiences forget that she *really* is a mess. Winehouse's reception by media and fans had everything to do with the belief that her public persona was not artifice but an authentic depiction of her personal, autobiographical narrative. Winehouse herself did define her work as autobiographical. In an April 2007 article for the *Lancaster New Era*, Judy Jarvis notes, "British singer-songwriter Amy Winehouse has decided to invert the equation. Her album 'Back to Black' has one primary anti-hero: Amy Winehouse herself. 'I only write about stuff that's happened to me—stuff I can't get past personally,' Winehouse told *Blender.com*. 'Luckily, I'm quite self-destructive.' Winehouse, as she admits freely on the saucy album, is her own worst enemy."[74] In a March 2007 *New York Times* article, Jon Pareles considered the impact of Winehouse's autobiographical approach on her music: "She claims her lyrics are autobiographical, which would make her a real handful: a drinking, pot-smoking, compulsive cheater whose main excuse is the title of her current single: 'You Know I'm No Good.' But she also has pangs of conscience and moments of loyalty and longing. As knowing as she is about her attitude and her musical references, she also gives her songs a heart."[75] Given that Winehouse viewed her own work in autobiographical terms, my goal is to explore the ways in which she expresses herself onstage and on record that resonate with classic blues tropes, and predictably reaped opprobrium from the media. She also subverted normative definitions of autobiographical expression, refashioning herself at times, to resist the media's narrow representations of her work and life. Since much of Winehouse's musical, visual, and performance styles owed a debt to so-called Black American culture, it will be useful to briefly situate Winehouse within a larger scholarly conversation about white-to-Black passing and blackface minstrelsy.

Winehouse's attempt to perform her version of Black American music has a long tradition. In *Near Black: White-to-Black Passing in American Culture*, Baz Dreisinger treats white-to-Black passing as a function of certain white Americans' proximity to Black Americans. As Dreisinger states, "Because 'blackness,' so to speak, is imagined as transmittable, proximity to blackness is invested with the power to turn whites black."[76]

Members of the late Sharon Jones's Dap-Kings played on six of the eleven *Back to Black* tracks, and Winehouse's stage act included two African-British backup singer-dancers dressed in retro 1960s-era suits. Even though most of the members of the Dap-Kings are white, given Sharon Jones's quasiblues queen persona of her own, the white members of the Dap-Kings are the conduit through which Jones's "blackness" flows to Winehouse. Winehouse's *Back to Black* producer, Mark Ronson, similarly used the horn sections from the Dap-Kings and Antibalas, an interracial Brooklyn-based funk and Afrobeat band for his hit "Uptown Funk." Dreisinger's text includes an examination of white musicians Johnny Otis and Mezz Mezzrow, who famously lived and worked among Black people and self-identified as Black. Both of these musicians wrote compelling autobiographies in which they sketch out their musical and personal transformations from white to Black men. Mezz Mezzrow's *Really the Blues* and Johnny Otis's *Upside Your Head* show white musicians' autobiographical self-invention as Black musicians.

In *Crossing the Line: Racial Passing in Twentieth-Century U.S. Literature and Culture,* Gayle Wald also examines Mezz Mezzrow. Her study focuses on the inherently gendered nature of the passing narrative. For Wald, while Black-to-white passing is feminized due to the disempowered position of Blacks in American society, white-to-Black passing is a "masculinized (and often masculinist) enterprise."[77] Both Wald and Dreisinger see a disparity in how overt white-to-Black passers are *versus* Black-to-white ones. Dreisinger states, "Black passing narratives are commonly, though not exclusively, fictional; white passing narratives, however, often merge the fictive with the factual and lean toward the autobiographical." Dreisinger believes this is due in part to passing whites' full embracing of the powerful feeling racial transgression affords them.[78] This is why Mezzrow and Otis proudly display their "blackness" through the vehicle of the autobiographical narrative. Winehouse does the same through her lyrics, visual presentation, and performance style. Since Winehouse is a woman, however, the white-to-Black passing narrative as a confident and celebrated "masculinist enterprise" is disrupted.[79] While her whiteness allows her the freedom to experiment with musical styles and voices, and to cross cultural and racial boundaries in ways that are not as easy for Black artists, her gender places her into a separate category of white-to-Black passers. Her appropriation of "black" musical performance styles earns her critical praise, while she is castigated by some music critics, and a sizable number of U.K. tabloid presses, for her unsanctioned gender expression.

Winehouse's song "Some Unholy War" contains the following lyric:

If my man was fighting
Some unholy war
I would be behind him.[80]

And in "Me & Mr. Jones" she declares, "Nobody stands in between me and my man / It's me and Mr. Jones," with the last part of that lyric an allusion to Billy Paul's 1972 soul hit about an extramarital affair, "Me and Mrs. Jones."[81] Winehouse's repeated use of the phrase "my man" to refer to her lover, or a man she respects, has its roots in Black American working-class lingo. As Angela Davis suggests, "African-American working-class argot refers to both husbands and male lovers—and even in some cases female lovers—as 'my man' or 'my daddy'"[82] Winehouse's sexually provocative lyrics, as well as her public battles with both substance abuse and her then husband Fielder-Civil, subverted ideas about how a young female artist should behave, even in 2007.[83] Like Shug Avery, and eventually Squeak, in *The Color Purple,* and Big Mama Thornton before her, Winehouse used "black" musical styles while regularly transgressing acceptable forms of gender performance. In fact, in an August 2007 article in the *Daily Mail,* Kathryn Knight states, "Such antics have occurred with such regularity that the celebrity magazine Heat has taken to running a regular feature called Where's Wino?" In the United States, a December 2007 issue of Florida's *St. Petersburg Times* ran this headline after Winehouse was arrested for interfering in Fielder-Civil's criminal case: "WINO ARRESTED; POP HATES ON DOHERTY."[84] In the article, the unnamed author referred to Winehouse as "Wino" and offered this comment: "Amy Winehouse was arrested Tuesday in connection with an investigation into 'perverting the course of justice,' British authorities said. (We'll pause a minute to let that one sink in.)" The joke here is that Winehouse is already so clearly perverse that the writer cannot understand why the authorities even need to investigate. In the article, Winehouse's father complains that his daughter is friends with Pete Doherty, formerly of the rock band The Libertines and another figure who at that time waged a public battle with substance abuse. Winehouse's father was worried that Doherty would be a negative influence on his daughter. Beyond Winehouse's transgressions of public propriety, she also tries on "blackness" through her lyrics in which she occasionally adopts a Black male persona. In this way, Winehouse transgresses her gender in two ways: she performs her gender wrong, à la Butler, and at times she goes so far as to simultaneously cross both gender and racial boundaries. The fact that she prospered commercially, and enjoyed critical accolades from serious music critics, while sometimes adopting a Black male voice speaks to all of her privileges. Even so, she ultimately paid a price for her gender misbehavior.

Furthering Wald's argument, due to Winehouse's white privilege, her transgression of racial roles certainly confers power. Because she is white, she can always fall back on her whiteness if it is more convenient. While the other blueswomen in this chapter—Shug, Squeak, and Thornton—are punished severely for their unruly gender expressions, they are unable to use whiteness as protection. This reality is reinforced when Squeak is sexually assaulted by her white uncle. Like Mezzrow and Otis, the lessened risk inherent in Winehouse's racial passing allows her a powerful freedom that most Blacks who pass for white do not enjoy. Her musical passing also does offer some masculinist elements, despite her being very clearly a woman. In fact, in "'This Voice Which Is Not One': Amy Winehouse Sings the Ballad of Sonic (Blues)face Culture," Daphne Brooks situates Winehouse within what she calls "sonic (blues)face culture, a vocal phenomenon pioneered by black and white female entertainers in early twentieth century popular culture." Brooks also states, "Listen to Amy Winehouse in critical hermeneutic stereo and one hears her conjuring a secret history of sonic Black feminist praxis first captured on wax in the voice of Mamie Smith in 1920." Yet she also suggests that Winehouse evokes a masculine sensibility through her lyrics:

> But perhaps, more than anything else, "blackness" on Winehouse's album is a sign of masculine musicality. Whether declaring to her man that she'd "rather be at home with Ray" (Charles) than in rehab, hatin' on a suitor for having gotten in the way of her and her "man, Mr. Jones" (aka rapper Nas, Nasir Jones), spitting remorse for having "missed the Slick Rick gig," or perhaps most cryptically, telling a confidant that, "Next to Sammy, you're my best black Jew," Winehouse may be musically invoking black female vocality, but her lyrical identifications, her performative posturings are so, so def, pop ya

collar, hip hop masculinist gestures, all the way down to her weirdly inverted "you my nigga" bonding reference to Sammy Davis Jr.

While Brooks finds Winehouse's masculine pose to be confounding, it is perhaps a way for Winehouse to reclaim the power taken away from her given the media's control over her image. By adopting a Black, male pose, she participates in the tradition of blues self-fashioning. She is a white woman, but she uses a Black, male persona in some of her work. Of course, given her white privilege, she easily appropriates a Black male narrative. A Black blues maker would not be able to transgress such a lyrical—or sonic—color line quite so easily. While Bessie Smith assuming the role of a gin peddler in 1928's "Pickpocket Blues" or Robert Johnson suggesting he is being pursued by hellhounds in 1937's "Hellhound on my Trail" is not a perfect comparison, Winehouse's Black, male pose is a version, however problematic, of blues self-fashioning—certainly as practiced by white transatlantic blues artists such as the Rolling Stones and Led Zeppelin. As Brooks's argument continues, she suggests that rather than Winehouse demonstrating in her music a desire to be sexually involved with Black men, she instead appears to be a white woman "longing to *be* [emphasis added] a black man." This theoretical Black man, however, is "stitched together from hip hop and bebop and juke joint mythologies."[85] Brooks's argument makes sense, as Winehouse's version of a Black man, as well as her take on the Black blues queen, is mired in stereotypes and snippets of fictional blues tropes.

However, I would argue that the concept of blues authenticity is rooted in narrative fictionality to begin with, so Winehouse is merely contributing to that tradition. It is her understanding that writing things down and telling one's autobiographical truths, however fictional—in this case, through song lyrics, onstage, and in interviews—is what proves a person's existence and shapes a self. And it is the pastiche that Brooks alludes to earlier that serves as an important element of the blues. Importing lyrics from different places and making them one's own, and creating and developing a persona for live performances, music videos, and interviews with the press, forged from varied musical styles and visual images circulating widely in American culture, are hallmarks of the blues tradition, from its earliest days at the end of the nineteenth century to today. Tommy Johnson's decision to prominently carry a large rabbit's foot, for example, tapped into African American folkloric ideas about its power to bring good luck to the wearer, situating him within the early twentieth-century, rural blues tradition.[86] Willie Dixon's 1960 composition "Spoonful," made famous by Howlin' Wolf, was influenced by Charley Patton's song "A Spoonful Blues," written more than thirty years earlier. "A Spoonful Blues" in 1929 was inspired by "All I Want Is a Spoonful" by Papa Charlie Jackson, recorded three years before that.[87] These are three different songs, with discrete lyrics and vocal performances that are unique to each version, yet they are related in theme: the dangers of overindulgence in illicit pleasures. These songs—their subject matter and their relationships to each other—are part of a larger blues narrative, as each composer constructs their blues personas through these works. And Winehouse continues this through her appropriation of diverse elements of "black maleness," culminating with a makeshift, fictional autobiographical performance that is somehow uniquely hers.

Through all of the sensationalistic media exposure, Winehouse's lyrics revealed her vulnerable side and acted as a counter to one-dimensional representations of her life and work. As Pareles suggests, Winehouse herself pushes her image as a sexually promiscuous woman in songs like "You Know I'm No Good," in which the narrator admits to being an untrustworthy sexual partner who cheats on her man while submitting to his demeaning sexual interrogation:

> You say, "What did you do with him today?"
> And sniffed me out like I was Tanqueray
> . . . .
> I told you, I was trouble
> You know that I'm no good.[88]

The narrator, a constructing and constructed version of Winehouse (her narrating and narrated "I"), plays the role of the immoral, debased woman with abandon and even seeks out and receives the punishment she feels she deserves.[89] Rather than telling her man to back off, she allows his attempt to smell the scent of another man on her body. In that moment, her body is no longer hers. She submits to him as if she is his property. But why not, since she is "no good?" In this case, both the narrator and her lover articulate a version of her personality. The boyfriend asserts that she is a lying whore who cannot be trusted (biography) and the narrator agrees (autobiography). This construction demonstrates that Winehouse, the artist, through her lyrical persona, wants her audience to recognize her full humanity. She is talented and internationally famous, yet she, like other people who experience feelings of low self-esteem, engages in a public, real-life version of this song's narrative. She is more than the sum of her media depictions—she is a multidimensional person who, perhaps, struggles to love herself. By writing a mini autobiographical narrative that serves to broaden ideas about who Winehouse really is, she takes control of her own story in much the same way that Thornton did when she championed her own successes in the back of that van headed to Eugene, Oregon.

In "Wake Up Alone," the narrator shows another, often overlooked, side to her personality, mourning the loss of her lover and focusing on the quotidian in the hope of forgetting her pain:

> I stay up, clean the house, at least I'm not drinking
> Run around just so I don't have to think about thinking
> That silent sense of content that everyone gets
> Just disappears soon as the sun sets.[90]

The narrator's focus in this song is on finding peace amid her heartbreak, and she attempts to quiet her restless mind through cleaning the house. What is striking is that she wants to feel better. She stays awake rather than collapsing into a depressive sleep. She avoids drinking, even though a drinking problem is inferred. This part of the narrator's autobiography shows what is at stake. Not only does her loss subject her to a possible deep depression, but it also puts her physical health at risk. Winehouse was known for her tough antirehab talk in her hit "Rehab." In this song, Winehouse brags, "They tried to make me go to rehab but I said, 'No, no, no.'" Yet in "Wake Up Alone" she avoids alcohol and engages in housework to shut her worried mind off. Digging deeper into "Rehab," it is also evident that the reason Winehouse's narrator does not want to go to rehab is not merely due to childish defiance; it is because she believes she engages toxic substances because her man is gone. If he would only return to her, she would stop drinking:

> I don't ever wanna drink again
> I just, ooh, I just need a friend.[91]

According to this narrative, it is Winehouse's narrator's broken heart that renders rehab ineffective, not her poor character or perverse nature. She drinks because she feels unloved, and she has the insight to recognize that perhaps she should love herself. In "Tears Dry on Their Own" Winehouse's narrator sings,

> I cannot play myself again
> I should just be my own best friend
> Not fuck myself in the head with stupid men.[92]

This verse demonstrates, through a narrating "I," Winehouse's genuine vulnerability as a counter to her unsympathetic media portrayal. Through her lyrical rendering of her autobiography, Winehouse successfully adds her voice to the record. She was more than simply a self-destructive mess. She was also a talented and sensitive singer-songwriter who attempted to assuage her unrelenting loneliness with drugs and alcohol. And she was a white, female performer who participated in the narrative blues tradition by utilizing, alternatively, Black female and Black male personas as an act of self-creation. In order to participate in so-called authentic Black American musical expression, she used blues tropes, personas, and vocal styles—with these devices ultimately allowing for her autobiographical self-expression. It is through her music, and most notably her lyrics, that Winehouse was able to revise the prevailing, flat, media narrative about her life, her music, and her impact on popular culture in the United Kingdom and the United States.

The transgressive fictional and real-life blueswomen—Celie, Shug, Squeak, Sophia, Big Mama, and Amy—in this chapter reclaim their power and use their personal agency through autobiographical acts. Their self-expression is not limited to book form, as in many cases they share details about their backgrounds through musical performance. What ties all of these narratives—literary and musical—together is the importance that voice plays in the women's movement toward self-realization. In all of these texts, the women's strengths are found in their words, and they use those words to effectively reject their limited and reductive representations in the larger culture.

3

"I Was Astounded at What I Heard"

Robert Johnson's Autobiographical and Biographical Afterlives

At the beginning of *The Search for Robert Johnson*, a 1992 documentary film narrated and hosted by John Paul Hammond—son of esteemed record producer John H. Hammond, and a respected blues singer and guitarist in his own right—legendary white blues rock guitarists Keith Richards and Eric Clapton declare their admiration and musical debt to iconic blues singer-songwriter-guitarist Robert Johnson. Richards enthuses, "You'd think you were getting a handle on playing the blues, and then to hear Johnson—whoa! There's a long way to go yet." Richards adds, "The voice is so eerie and compelling." For Clapton, Johnson is "the greatest singer, the greatest writer."[1]

"Mesmerized by the myths of his [Johnson's] life," Hammond retraces the bluesman's steps. Starting in Robinsonville, Mississippi, where Johnson's mom and stepfather moved around 1918, Hammond talks to his childhood friend Wink Clark and to Nat Richardson, the son of a local juke joint owner.[2] He also travels to Arkansas and, eventually, Austin,

Texas, "between HW 61 and the River" to see Johnson's ex-girlfriend, Willie Mae Powell, who listens to a recording of "Love in Vain," a song that Johnson reportedly wrote for her. Delta bluesmen Honeyboy Edwards and Johnny Shines also feature prominently in this film, but perhaps the most important—and in its time, groundbreaking—moment is the introduction of Claud Johnson, Robert Johnson's only heir. When the documentary was released in 1992, Claud's existence was a new discovery, and in June 2000 the younger Johnson's claim was ruled legitimate, with the Mississippi Supreme Court ruling in Claud's favor after a protracted legal battle with some of his father's more distant relatives.[3] The film ends in Southern Mississippi—Greenwood, to be exact—where Johnson died.

This narrative within the narrative, in which Hammond re-creates, in visual form, decades of blues research and scholarship by Gayle Dean Wardlow and Mack McCormick, reflects the ways in which storytelling and, particularly in the case of Johnson, mythmaking—in varied mediums, including literature, film, and popular culture more generally—has shaped, and continues to shape, his legend.[4] The ways in which Richards and Clapton speak about Johnson demonstrates a romantic approach to engaging his life and work. He is more than just an excellent blues musician. He is someone with an "eerie and compelling" voice. He is a figure whose unknowability, due to the spare available factual data about his life, makes him rife for romantic longings and projections. And these blank spaces in his objectively factual biography help to situate him in the African American folk tradition, in which ballads and songs develop precisely because of the room to invent and reinvent people and events through fictionalized autobiographical and biographical narratives.

From around 1931, until his death in 1938, Johnson toured regularly throughout the United States and Canada. He mostly traveled by himself, but sometimes he went on the road with blues singer and guitarist Johnny Shines, and crossed paths with blues musicians such as singer, guitarist, and piano player Henry Townsend and Robert Lockwood Jr., whom Johnson taught to pay guitar.[5] When Wardlow says, "To some extent, he seemed to become a slightly different person in these different communities. The way he'd present himself," and then he and McCormick proceed to list his various names—Robert Spencer, Robert Moore, Robert James, Robert Barstow, Robert Sacks, Robert Dusty, and, of course, Robert Johnson—echoes of Stagolee can be heard. This reminds the audience that the legend of Johnson is not just one of fictions and mythmaking but it is part of a long tradition of African American folk storytelling. And even though much of the romance was originated and disseminated by white blues collectors, critics, and scholars, the tradition of blues invention and self-invention was forged by the blues people themselves.

Robert Johnson was born in Hazelhurst, Mississippi, most likely on May 8, 1911.[6] Johnson emerged when country blues masters such as Charley Patton, Son House, and Skip James were performing and making records, though he was younger and far less successful during his lifetime. Patton was one of the most famous of the Delta bluesmen in the early part of the twentieth century—a "rock star" in his time whose stage antics included playing the guitar between his legs and behind his back.[7] Blues scholars such as Elijah Wald, Francis Davis, and John Fahey view Patton as a key Delta blues innovator who influenced numerous artists, including Booker White, Son House, Howlin' Wolf, and even Robert Johnson.[8] As Davis asserts about Patton, "Though he may not have been the first Delta guitarist to use a bottleneck, or the first singer from the area to bellow his lyrics in what we now characterize as a Delta growl, he may have been the first Delta *bluesman*—the performer who codified these and other elements into the blues, and established the blues as a vehicle for personal commentary."[9] Yet it is Robert Johnson's legend that looms larger in the minds of casual blues fans.

One reason for Johnson's sustained notoriety is Columbia Records' 1961 release *King of the Delta Blues Singers*, which introduced Johnson's work to a new generation of young, white, and largely middle-class American folkies. During the late-1950s and into the mid-1960s, white folk revivalists were enamored with acoustic country blues music largely to the exclusion of electric blues. Johnson's music found its way across the ocean, influencing English musicians such as Eric Clapton of Cream, Robert Plant of Led Zeppelin, and Keith Richards of the Rolling Stones.[10] Johnson's representation in a variety of contemporary cultural spaces has also played a role in his continued relevance. For instance, in 1994 the United States Postal Service put Johnson's image on a stamp. Numerous films take Johnson as subject, including the 1986 narrative film *Crossroads* and the documentaries *The Search for Robert Johnson* (1992) and *Can't You Hear the Wind Howl?* (1997).

At the heart of blues romanticism is the legend that Robert Johnson sold his soul to the devil in order to become an expert blues guitarist. The endurance of the crossroads narrative demonstrates the power of autobiographical self-creation. The core of this story advances the idea that Johnson was its originator (though there is certainly no proof of this) rather than it being a tale that was attributed to him much later during the 1960s transatlantic blues revival. This story, recycled ad infinitum, is predicated on people uncritically sharing it across time and distance. Similar to the Black folk tradition in which stories are told, shared, embellished, and retold, this story is one that can be found in fictional literary works; in visual culture, including film and television; in popular culture more generally; and, perhaps most surprising of all, in blues histories by scholars and music critics. In their book *Robert Johnson: Lost and Found*, about how the crossroads legend came to be, Barry Lee Pearson and Bill McCulloch note, "It is informative to study how misinformation about Johnson was recycled, how myth became accepted as fact, and most significantly, how Johnson's most respected chroniclers too often shaped or invented facts to serve their own needs."[11] I would argue that what this scholar and journalist, respectively, are actually interrogating is how the African American folk tradition that eventually morphs into the African American blues tradition is brought to bear on Johnson's legend. Essentially, Johnson's mythos is built on the fictional autobiographical and biographical narratives that continue to fuel the tellings and retellings of his life and legend in popular culture, and in expressive art of all kinds. Ultimately, Pearson's and McCulloch's findings—after reading through scholarly and journalistic works about Johnson by Stephen Calt and Gayle Dean Wardlow, Peter Guralnick, Mack McCormick, Samuel Charters, Paul Oliver, and others, and discovering that the likely origin of the crossroads tale is a single interview with Son House in a 1966 article in *DownBeat* by Pete Welding—confirm the importance of stories and storytelling in the blues tradition, whether those tales originate with the blues makers, fans, or scholars and journalists.[12]

In "Hell Hound on His Trail: Robert Johnson," after House talks about his surprise at how quickly Johnson learned to master the guitar, Welding states, "House suggested in all seriousness that Johnson, in his months away from home, had 'sold his soul to the devil in exchange for learning to play like that.'"[13] And, as Pearson and McCulloch attest, "From House's quote, the trail of incriminating references leads to a David Evans interview with the brother of the blues artist Tommy Johnson and then to a Greil Marcus commentary in the book *Mystery Train*, Peter Guralnick's short biography *Searching for Robert Johnson*, Robert Palmer's book *Deep Blues*, and the Hollywood feature film, *Crossroads*."[14] All of these texts engage the crossroads myth, embracing the version of Johnson that reflects notions of racialized blues authenticity. The literary texts in this chapter can easily be included in this list. And so can a conversation about the impact that the real-life Robert Johnson had on the blues identities of Keith Richards, Eric Clapton, and Bob Dylan.

In this chapter, I engage the 1995 novels *Reservation Blues* by Sherman Alexie and *RL's Dream* by Walter Mosley, and the short stories "Black Elvis" by Geoffrey Becker (1999) and "Stones in My Passway, Hellhound on My Trail" by T. C. Boyle (1979).[15] In each text, Johnson, the character, is in a dialogue with his historical, mythologized, biographical representation. Multiple versions of the real-life Johnson's crossroads tale and violent death have been documented in numerous fiction and nonfiction works, over several decades. In many of these projects, the creator takes an overly idealized approach, rendering Johnson in simplistic, one-dimensional terms. In these works, Johnson is mythologized in much the same way as Stagolee is in the various ballads and songs that have celebrated his *badness*. Johnson's womanizing, restless spirit, and guitar are all relegated to mythical signs of a racialized, gendered, and classed authentic bluesman. Fictional representations of Johnson frequently characterize him as a man disconnected from the places he calls home. If he is not actually haunted by Satan or demons, at the very least Johnson, the character, is distracted, disordered, and alienated from the conventional dictates of the community spaces he occupies. Whether or not supernatural forces are to blame, Johnson is frequently depicted as an ethereal character, one who appears to exist in a liminal space, somewhere between dreams and reality.

The literary works in this chapter engage these myths—sometimes overtly—and the fictional Johnson has no choice but to confront his simplistic representation. As this book's argument centers on the blues as a narrative tradition, and it was a specific moment of narrative—the tale of the crossroads—that helped to grow Johnson's legend, it is appropriate to focus on an examination of these fictional works featuring a character named Robert Johnson. Three of the four texts I examine in this chapter—*Reservation Blues*, *RL's Dream*, and "Stones in My Passway, Hellhound on My Trail"—include a recounting or reimagining of that iconic moment; all of the narratives, save “Stones in My Passway,” include characters other than Johnson who are compelled to tell stories about their lives, about the blues, or about how they somehow fit within the blues tradition whatever their race or regional identity.

Two of the novels offer geographical and temporal migration and autobiographical narrative as correctives for Johnson’s limited and uncritical representations. *RL’s Dream* features Soupspoon, an elderly and terminally ill New York City–based Black blues guitarist from Mississippi who uses his vivid memories of Johnson to tell the story of the Delta blues. And in *Reservation Blues,* Johnson wanders onto a Spokane Indian reservation and catalyzes the main character’s participation in the blues tradition through storytelling and mythmaking. Ultimately, in this chapter, I argue that while the fictional Johnson is frequently silenced, and his romantic, idealized, mythological image is placed in the foreground by the narrator or other characters, his migrations and narrative legend serve as vehicles for the agentive autobiographical blues self-fashioning of other characters. Moreover, when allowed to speak for himself in his new environments, the fictional Johnson undermines commonly held beliefs about his life, blues music, and his place within the American blues tradition. Narrative and embodied self-invention also occurs in the blues-rock memoirs I engage in this chapter, as musicians remake themselves in reaction to their introduction to the real-life Robert Johnson’s music.

My argument will proceed as follows. First I will examine the ways in which *Chronicles: Volume One* by Bob Dylan (2004); *Life* by Keith Richards, with James Fox (2010); and *Clapton: The Autobiography* by Eric Clapton (2007) serve as unofficial, minibiographies of the mythologization of Robert Johnson and the blues more generally. These memoirs all begin as bildungsromane about the early formation of white blues players, with each book detailing the moment when the young blues acolyte in question discovers Robert Johnson, a necessary rite of passage.

Then I will analyze “Stones in My Passway, Hellhound on My Trail,” a short story that embraces the mythology surrounding Johnson while attempting to re-create the last hours of Johnson’s life and traumatic death. T. C. Boyle’s romantic rendering of Johnson makes sense given his positionality as a white, male baby boomer—born in 1948—placing him within the demographic of the young blues enthusiasts who flourished during the 1960s. Next, I will have a conversation about *RL’s Dream,* in which Mississippi bluesman Soupspoon is determined to tell the story of the blues, as well as his own coming-of-age tale, before he dies. As Soupspoon talks about his life in the Delta, he details the ways in which Johnson served as a catalyst for his growth as a bluesman. Following that is a discussion about *Reservation Blues*, a novel recounting the adventures of Coyote Springs, a Spokane Indian rock band whose meteoric rise is aided by Robert Johnson's demonically possessed acoustic guitar. Finally, I will turn to "Black Elvis," a short story about an interaction between an African American Elvis impersonator and a Korean American Robert Johnson imitator. This story takes a postmodern approach, playfully disrupting Johnson's mythology, as well as idealized notions of blues authenticity. Ordered this way, the literary texts take us from a thoroughly romantic, authenticist approach to the blues tradition—in Boyle's narrative, Johnson exists in a sensual blues world of his own making where the only events of importance pertain to his own physical survival or to playing music—to a subversive undermining of the very notion of blues authenticity.

In *Chronicles: Volume One*, Bob Dylan describes the "stabbing sounds" emanating from Johnson's guitar: "From the first note the vibrations from the loudspeaker made my hair stand up. The stabbing sounds from the guitar could almost break a window. When Johnson started singing, he seemed like a guy who could have sprung from the head of Zeus in full armor. I immediately differentiated between him and anyone else I had ever heard."[16] Eric Clapton experiences a sense of revulsion during his first exposure to Johnson's music: "At first the music almost repelled me, it was so intense, and this man made no attempt to sugarcoat what he was trying to say, or play."[17] Keith Richards details his first exposure to Johnson's music this way: "I was astounded at what I heard. It took guitar playing, songwriting, delivery, to a totally different height. And at the same time it confused us, because it wasn't band music, it was one guy."[18] In these accounts, the musicians use words like "stabbing," "repelled," and "astounded" to describe their first engagements with Johnson's music. Clapton's, Richards's, and Dylan's autobiographical engagement with Robert Johnson mirror the stages of transatlantic engagement with the blues writ large. I argue that these contemporary autobiographical renderings not only show the enduring power of Johnson's mythos but also effectively tell the larger story—the biography—of transatlantic white engagement with the blues from the Southern United States.

Broadly speaking there were three key phases of engagement during the 1960s blues revival on both sides of the Atlantic—what I term "Discovery," "Encounter," and "Re-assessment," with movement in both directions between "Encounter" and "Re-assessment." During the process of Discovery, as with Clapton's, Richards's, and Dylan's emotional renderings of their initial listening experiences with Johnson's music, the blues revivalists engaged the works as if they were brand new, without cultural and historical contexts, or a long tradition. Since the music was new to *them,* it was quickly dehistoricized, and the voices on shellac were remade in their own imaginations. Just as Clapton, Richards, and Dylan subtly take ownership of the music, and very quickly endeavor to make it their own—as Clapton admits, "I tried to copy Johnson, but his style of simultaneously playing a disjointed bass line on the low strings, rhythm on the middle strings, and lead on the treble strings while singing at the same time was impossible to even imagine"—the blues revivalists, on Discovery, advance their own visions about the music and its makers that bear little resemblance to the blues musicians' real stories.[19] Like Dylan, who says that every time he listened to Johnson, "it felt like a ghost had come into the room, a fearsome apparition," the blues revivalists treated the Delta blues musicians as ethereal characters who appear to exist in an in-between space between the corporeal and spiritual planes.[20]

Given the subjective—and necessarily fictional—nature of reconstructing a life through the memoiristic form, it is particularly striking that the transatlantic musicians in a twenty-first-century context, as well as the transatlantic blues collectors, scholars, and critics at the forefront of the 1950s and 1960s blues revival, advance a static and racially naturalized biography of Robert Johnson and the blues. As Marybeth Hamilton puts it, "At the core of the idea of a Delta blues, of an undiluted and primal black music, is an emotional attachment to racial difference that extends back at least to the mid-nineteenth century, to abolitionists' enchantment with the peculiar power of black singers, their uncanny ability to allow their white listeners to experience an unimagined transcendence, a level of emotional intensity otherwise out of their reach." At the heart of the invention of the country, or more specifically the venerated Delta, blues musician is the lone Black male figure whose music exists in a pure realm, independent of professional or commercial concerns, mirroring the white (and predominantly male) collectors and critics who also saw themselves as authentic evangelists of the blues. American blues collector James McKune, who as the head of the so-called blues mafia helped catalyze the 1960s blues revival, and British blues historian Paul Oliver, whose influential *Blues Fell this Morning: The Meaning of the Blues* (1960) engaged blues lyrics as autobiographical renderings of Black suffering, were two such figures who disconnected Black blues makers from their cultural contexts, remaking them into what Hamilton suggests are "supposedly uncompromised voices . . . perceived as pristinely untouched by the modern world."[21]

Another American collector, Samuel Charters, who published his seminal work *The Country Blues* in 1959, notably attempted to situate blues musicians within a Black American cultural milieu, focusing on country blues artists such as Lonnie Johnson, Leroy Carr, and Big Bill Broonzy who were commercially popular with Black audiences during the 1930s instead of artists such as Son House, Skip James, and Charley Patton, whose records did not sell nearly as well.[22] While the book was a critical success, McKune loudly protested in print Charters's decisions about which country blues musicians to feature. In a column he wrote for a British record collectors' publication, *VJM Palaver*, titled "the Great Country Blues Singers," he began his rebuttal by stating, "This essay makes up for what Sam Charters did not say, or did not say fully enough, in his book *The Country Blues* . . ." For McKune, it was a grave mistake to rely on the masses'—in this case the African American record-buying public's—tastes. The greatest country blues figures were not to be confused with the most popular ones.[23] In 1961, McKune and his blues mafia, through their independent label, Origins Jazz Library, released the music of the great Delta blues performers, the ones, as Hamilton puts it, whose "very obscurity testament to their ferocious integrity, the rough, ragged intensity of the songs that they sang." These recordings featuring Charley Patton, Son House, Skip James, and Robert Johnson influenced important future blues enthusiasts and scholars such as John Fahey, Robert Palmer, Greil Marcus, and Jeff Todd Titon, and spurred the 1961 Columbia Records reissue of Johnson's recordings and a 1962 release by Library of Congress called *Negro Blues and Hollers*.[24] Soon McKune's version of blues authenticity gained prominence, and once the blues mafia discovered in 1964 that Son House was still alive, the blues revivalists were set to encounter the "living, breathing embodiments" of the Delta blues.[25]

It is here that phase two, the Encounter, occurs. This is the moment when the blues revivalists made assessments about the people making music, deeming them primitive, exotic, authentic, special, and ultimately imbued with particular attributes and sets of experiences that make then uniquely qualified to play blues music honestly. It is important to note, however, that the boundaries of blues authenticity are heavily policed, so the men, and yes they were predominantly men, who were "discovered" during the blues revival had to fall within the bounds of blues authenticity lest they be punished.

In his memoir, Keith Richards describes seeing Muddy Waters at a big blues show in the United Kingdom that included Sonny Terry, Brownie McGhee, and John Lee Hooker:

> And Muddy came on, acoustic guitar, Mississippi Delta stuff, and played a magnificent half an hour. And then there was an interval and he came back with an electric band. And they virtually booed him off the stage. He plowed through them like a tank, as Dylan did a year or so later at the Manchester Free Trade Hall. But it was hostile—and that's when I realized that people were not really listening to the music, they just wanted to be part of this wised-up enclave. Muddy and the band were playing great. It was a knockout band. He had Junior Wells with him; I think Hubert Sumlin was on there too. But for this audience, blues was only blues if somebody got up there in a pair of old blue dungarees and sang about how his old lady left him. None of these blues purists could play anything. But their Negroes had to be dressed in overalls and go "Yes'm, boss." And in actual fact they're city blokes who are so hip it's not true.[26]

After years of projecting their fantasies onto the "searing" but disembodied voices on their record players, the blues revivalists and "discovered" blues musicians found themselves in a complicated dynamic. As Hamilton puts it, "The men they rediscovered cooperated with the fantasy at least to the extent of appearing as old as the music was supposed to be. . . . [But] most of the resurrected heroes were well past their prime—Son House, in particular, was in an advanced stage of alcoholic deterioration—and none of them were prepared for this explosion of white interest in a music that African Americans had rejected long ago. Uneasy with the role they were allocated, they rarely played it as sincerely as their new audience imagined."[27] McKune also moved on from the blues in 1965, right after the blues became a business, just as it had been in the past despite the blues revivalists' romantic insistence on engaging Robert Johnson's recordings as if they exist outside of modernity.

Finally, in phase three, Re-assessment, the three musician memoirists and the blues revivalists, as well as those from the following era, attempt to move beyond the romance of blues mythology and authenticity in order to engage the music as connected to African American culture and history, as well as other musics and folk traditions that came before. The memoirists, in particular, eventually find that there is more to Johnson's story than a superficial encounter offers. Johnson, just like the other Delta Blues players, is a professional working within a tradition. As Richards allows,

> We realized that the guys we were playing, like Muddy Waters, had also grown up with Robert Johnson and had translated it into a band format. In other words, it was just a progression. Robert Johnson was like an orchestra all by himself. Some of his best stuff is almost Bach-like in its construction. Unfortunately, he screwed up with the chicks and had a short life. But a brilliant burst of inspiration. He gave you a platform to work on, no doubt as he did to Muddy and the other guys we were listening to. What I found about the blues and music, tracing things back, was that nothing came from itself. As great as it is, this is not one stroke of genius. This cat was listening to somebody and it's his variation on the theme.[28]

Dylan's friend, folk singer Dave Van Ronk, also understands that Johnson is not as original as Dylan at first suspects: "Johnson's voice and guitar were ringing the room and I was mixed up in it. Didn't see how anybody couldn't be. But Dave wasn't. He kept pointing out that this song comes from another song and that one song was an exact replica of a different song. . . . Dave thought Johnson was okay, that the guy was powerful but that it was all derivative."[29] Dylan recognizes that Johnson is engaging a tradition with layers, not just performing his "natural role," but he still deems him original. He also engages Johnson's crossroads tale—teasingly, of course, but he is careful to leave the tiniest hint of possibility that it might be true: "Johnson recorded in the '30s, and in the 1960s there were still some folks around in the Delta who had known about him. Some even, who knew him. There'd been a fast moving story going around that he had sold his soul to the devil at a four-way crossroads at midnight and that's how he got to be so good. Well, I don't know about that."[30]

Transatlantic blues scholars in the 1970s and 1980s, such as Sandra Lieb, Chris Albertson, and Derrick Stewart-Baxter, avoided romantic approaches to engaging the blues.[31] And in the twenty-first century, there are a number of critics and scholars who actively subvert notions of racialized blues authenticity. Even so, some contemporary blues critics, fans, and musicians persist in viewing blues music through a romantic and authenticist lens.

So why is this the case? Why does Richards dismantle the myth of blues authenticity through his story about Muddy Waters but then advance it again through Johnson?: "You would have no jazz without blues out of slavery—that most recent and particular version of slavery, not us poor Celts for example, under the Roman boot. They put those people through misery, not just in America. But there's something produced by its survivors that is very elemental. It's not something you take in in the head, it's something you take in the guts." And why does he suggest that the blues is born of experience, not professionalism?

> The drive in the band was amazing among Mick, Brian, and myself. It was incessant study. Not really in the academic sense of it, it was to get the feel of it. And then I think we realized, like any young guys, that blues are not learned in a monastery. You've got to go out there and get your heart broke and then come back and then you can sing the blues. Preferably several times. At that time, we were taking it on a purely musical level, forgetting that these guys were singing *about* shit. First you've got to get in the shit. And then you can maybe come back and sing it.[32]

Perhaps the blues memoirists and revivalists move between Reassessment and Encounter because for both it is difficult to resist the impulse to insert themselves into the blues narrative. After all, the blues tradition is a narrative one in which blues people are made through autobiographical fictionality.

T. C. Boyle's "Stones in My Passway, Hellhound on My Trail," which is overtly concerned with blues mythology and blues authenticity, is a useful place to begin a discussion about fictional renderings of Robert

Johnson's legend. Boyle's story was published before there was much information about Johnson's life. As Patricia Schroeder offers, "Sam Charters's sketchy *Robert Johnson* had appeared in 1972, Greil Marcus's highly romantic *Mystery Train* in 1975, and a few articles in music journals had tackled the elusive subject in the late 1960s and early 1970s, but Boyle's story was written before the groundbreaking research of Gayle Dean Wardlow or Peter Guralnick was published."[33] Given its publication date, it is not surprising that the narrator renders Johnson as an outsider who exults in his role as a rebellious bluesman, eschewing work in the cotton fields while accepting his low social status. Portrayed by Boyle, Johnson is happy as long as he can make a little money playing the music he loves, drink as much as he wants, and chase and bed multiple women.

This story takes care to include as much historical detail as was available at the time. For Boyle, telling a story about Johnson's life and death—providing a fictionalized biography, of sorts—is as important as celebrating Johnson's music. As Schroeder shares from her own virtual conversation with Boyle via an Internet message board, Boyle writes, "The story came from my love of the music and from my desire to tell the definitive story of his death (definitive in my universe, anyway)."[34] Boyle set out to tell the previously untold story of Johnson in a fictionalized work while also being faithful to historical details, though his caveat about his story's definitiveness highlights his ultimately subjective and highly romantic rendering of Johnson's life and death. Though the story is brief—just seven pages—it includes a fair amount of factual information about current events in the United States during the time that Johnson lived: "It is 1938, dust bowl, New Deal. FDR is on the radio, and somebody in Robinsonville is naming a baby after Jesse Owens. Once, on the road to Natchez, Robert saw a Pierce Arrow and talked about it for a week. Another time he spent six weeks in Chicago and didn't know the World's Fair was going on. Now he plays his guitar up and down the Mississippi, and in Louisiana, Texas, and Arkansas. He's never heard of Hitler and he hasn't eaten in two days." While this passage supports the predictable and well-worn concept of the primitive Black immune to technology and modern progress—how would it be possible for Johnson to spend six weeks in a major city like Chicago and not at least overhear talk about the World's Fair while busking on a city corner?—it also demonstrates how important the concept of the primitive is to blues mythology. Recounting Johnson's travels without providing a contrast with the goings-on in mainstream white culture would not have the same effect. It is necessary to show that there are multiple Americas occurring at once. A shared one ("It is 1938, dust bowl, New Deal"), a Black one ("Somebody in Robinsonville is naming a baby after Jesse Owens"), and a white one ("He's [Johnson's] never heard of Hitler").[35] As Schroeder suggests, Johnson is "a figure of romance, detached from the historical setting Boyle carefully constructs around him."[36] But more than that, given Johnson's race and class, the only way Boyle, a white baby boomer, and other American blues aficionados of that generation can label Johnson as authentic is to render him as a dream. He is in the real world, but he is not of it. Many writers represent Johnson as a sensitive artist who would crumble under the weight of a modernized world at war. Rather than drawing him as a professional American blues musician with an awareness of current events, and at least the same, perhaps superficial, understanding that the average white American citizen has about politics at home and abroad, Boyle portrays Johnson as an ethereal being alienated from everyday life. Therefore, it makes sense that the character named Robert Johnson would disengage himself from the reality of the depression and the growing fascism abroad. Most importantly though, it is Johnson's otherworldliness that cements his myth, making him worthy of narrative treatment.

Boyle attempts to put Johnson's story in its historical context, sticking to the factual events in Johnson's life that were known at that time, but he still fictionalizes key biographical details. For instance, in this story, as in real life, Johnson meets with a producer whom he calls twice and interrupts at dinner the night before a recording session. In the story, the producer's name is Walter Fagen and they meet in New Orleans, while in real life the producer's name is Don Law Sr. and they met in Dallas. In the story, and in real life, Johnson made the first call from the police station to let his producer know that he had been picked up on vagrancy charges and needed to be bailed out of jail. Johnson made the second call when he wished to solicit a prostitute and needed more money.[37] The narrator suggests after that incident that "Robert's dream is thick with the thighs of women."[38] According to the narrator, not only is Johnson childlike and irresponsible, but he is also a stereotypically oversexed young Black man. While the fictionalizing that occurs in this section is of minor historical details, it calls attention to the constructed nature of the work, and underscores its narrativity. What makes Johnson such an attractive subject are the various larger-than-life stories—the crossroads tale, his drinking and womanizing, and his violent death—that help situate him within the so-called authentic blues tradition. It is not the content of the various stories about Johnson, or their veracity, that make Johnson's legend. Rather it is the very *existence* of those compelling, half-believable stories that places Johnson within a rich and flexible narrative blues tradition.

The final scene of "Stones in My Passway" is an example of how a compelling blues story can be mythologized. There are conflicting accounts of Johnson's death, and the story of his demise has been told in multiple fictional and nonfictional contexts. As Schroeder states, "The white researchers focus on disease and illness—pneumonia, syphilis, liver damage—while the black Delta residents focus on violence—poison, stabbing, shooting."[39] In this sense, it is not surprising that Boyle would choose to re-create a violent version of Johnson's death, as a poisoning is in line with how some of Johnson's contemporaries believed he died, and it also reflects stereotypical ideas that conflate the Black bluesman and the bad man:

> Cramps. A spasm so violent it jerks his fingers from the strings. He begins again, his voice quavering, shivered: "Got to keep moving, got to keep moving, / Hellhound on my trail." And then suddenly the voice chokes off, gags, the guitar slips to the floor with a percussive shock. His bowels are on fire. He stands, clutches his abdomen, drops to his hands and knees. "Boy's had too much of that Mexican," someone says. He looks up, a sword run through him, panting, the shock waves pounding through his frame, looks up at the pine plank, the barrels, the cold, hard features of the girl with the silver necklace in her hand. Looks up, and snarls.[40]

The violent end—on all fours snarling like a dog—is fitting for a man who suggested through his lyrics that a hellhound was on his trail. Boyle, through his narrative voice, tells a story about Johnson that has elements of historical accuracy while simultaneously keeping Johnson outside of history. By focusing on Johnson's romantic qualities, Boyle advances Johnson's blues mythology in the name of fostering blues authenticity. However, this storytelling approach has an additional outcome: it demonstrates the ways in which the stories themselves make the blues tradition unique. What follows are alternative narratives that allow Johnson to have a greater role in the construction of the stories that feature him.

In *RL's Dream*, told mostly in close third-person point of view, Walter Mosley takes a similarly romantic view of Robert Johnson; but instead of a tale coalesced exclusively around rehashed historical facts about Johnson's life, this text uses Johnson as a vehicle for recounting the larger story of the Delta blues scene and as a model and backdrop for the tale of a fictional unknown Delta guitarist named Atwater "Soupspoon" Wise. Soupspoon is nearly seventy years old, and he has bone cancer that has metastasized into his lungs and pelvis. He lives with his young, white, female neighbor, Kiki, who takes him in after he is evicted from his apartment. As a teenager, Kiki was raped repeatedly by her father, and in adulthood she has become an angry and violent alcoholic who lashes out verbally and physically at Soupspoon and others in her home and work environments. Kiki is emotionally damaged, but she has great compassion for Soupspoon and she makes it her personal mission to save him.

Soupspoon believes that he is dying, so as soon as he starts to feel better after his initial cancer treatments, he begins to document his story as a young boy growing up in the Mississippi Delta by way of tape-recorded conversations with Kiki. The epigraph at the beginning of *RL's Dream* is an excerpt from a fictional book within the book called *Back Road to the Blues* by William Early in 1986—close to the time frame of the narrative of *RL's Dream*. Early, who was based in Chicago, contacted Soupspoon several years earlier. As Soupspoon remembers, "He wanted to interview me twenty years ago for a book about the blues. He called it *Back Road to the Blues*. I didn't want to at the time. That was a bad time in my life an' I didn't want to think about no blues."[41] But now, given the state of Soupspoon's health, he is ready to tell his story—his first-person autobiography. He is also interested in tying his own accounts into a larger narrative about the important Delta blues originators. This dual focus allows Soupspoon to simultaneously tell his story as an autobiographer and biographer, with his Delta blues biographical narrative including his precious memories of his friend, Robert Leroy Johnson.

Throughout the story, Soupspoon refers to Johnson as RL. In the epigraph of *RL's Dream*, Soupspoon describes Johnson to Early in a way that is reminiscent of Boyle's approach: "RL wasn't no real man. A real man gits born, does what li'l he can, and then he dies. . . . But RL fooled you. He played the guitar when he shouldn't'a been able to, an' nobody knows how he died. Maybe it was the pneumonia, maybe a jealous man. Satan coulda come an' made him bark like a dog 'for takin' him home." Soupspoon describes Johnson as a magical creature who managed to both exemplify Delta culture and somehow transcend it. He did not live by the same rules as the other Black men and women who suffered under Jim Crow and were too busy trying to survive to truly live. He played the guitar better than anyone Soupspoon had ever seen, he traveled outside of the Delta, and he possessed a hypnotic charm that drew audiences and women to him. As Soupspoon recounts,

> That's how it was with Robert Johnson.
>
> You looked up one day and there he was singing and acting crazy. He told you about far-off places in the world and played music that was stranger yet. He made songs that were deep down in you—and then you looked up again and he was gone. He took something of yours that you didn't even know you had; something your mother and your father never knew about. And taking it away he left you with something missing—and that something was better than anything else that ever you had.[42]

According to Soupspoon, Johnson's music is so powerful that it awakens something within the listener that needs to be fed, and when Johnson disappears—likely due to his frequent touring during the 1930s—he takes that something with him; however, Soupspoon retains it and feels compelled to share it with an audience. The idea of Johnson appearing and disappearing at will, while enjoying more mobility than the average Black man in the Jim Crow South, harks back to Wardlow and McCormick's list of the various names Johnson used as he moved from community to community. In order for Soupspoon to share his memories of Johnson, he must speak his story into a tape recorder, tapping into the African American oral tradition, with the ultimate goal being his memories' inclusion in a written text.

The fact that Soupspoon can articulate his memories of Johnson is important because those memories inform the coming-of-age stories that he shares about his own life in the blues. In this case, it is useful that Soupspoon sees Johnson as a shadowy figure. If Johnson is an apparition that is here one moment and gone the next, Soupspoon can conjure him up, access the memories, and document them through a tape recorder and eventually the written word:

> The memory of Robert Johnson was so strong in him that he sometimes felt that he could actually talk to the guitar man. He'd walk around Kiki's studio apartment, while she was at work, imagining RL was at his side talking about women he'd known and how many records he could play from memory. It all came in one big rush; too much for him to make sense of. He tried to write it down but the words were flat and toneless. He turned on the cassette recorder that Kiki brought home from Radio Shack and tried to talk out his stories. But when he played the tape back he was reminded of a hapless baby-sitter trying to tell a fairy tale that he couldn't remember. Finally he asked Kiki to help. "Just listen to me," he said. "I'm a storyteller. Storyteller need somebody wanna hear what he got to tell."

Here Soupspoon expresses an important truth about the way that storytelling works. An oral storyteller needs a listener to help shape the story—without eager listeners, who ultimately became participants in the story's circulation, the Stagolee legend would not exist. Similarly, Big Mama Thornton's stories about Elvis Presley and Janis Joplin in that van in chapter 2 were made all the richer by her listeners' responses to her calls. In his role as biographer, Soupspoon is taking on the responsibility of telling the larger story of the blues. When he tracks down his friend and bass player Alfred Metsgar, he hopes to include more forgotten voices in his blues biography: "I'm yo' old friend, Alfie. Soupspoon. We used t'play together. I wanted t'tell the story about that night [their guitarist friend Quickdraw's possible murder] if I could get you to remember. I wanted t'tell some stories 'bout the blues 'fore they all gone. You. Me." Alternatively, when Soupspoon tells his story about Johnson, he focuses on Johnson's engagement with the devil and gestures toward the crossroads tale. Soupspoon starts by talking about how one night Johnson played "Love in Vain" and then, predictably, "Me and the Devil." He introduces a young female character named Booby Redman who was overwhelmed by Johnson's music, and ultimately drawn to Soupspoon because his music was gentler: "I guess RL's music was too much for Booby, because she come across the street, really it was just a graded dirt road, to hear my soft sweet blues. Satan wasn't after me. That's why I'm still here in the flesh." Soupspoon's description of Johnson's music reinforces the idea that Johnson was possessed by the devil: "We played and played. The nickels fell like hail. Everybody was movin' to RL's evil moods."[43]

When the county sheriff arrives to break the street concert up, firing shots in the air, with Black folks running in terror in different directions, Soupspoon and Johnson are caught by the big, mean, white sheriff, Heck Wrightson. The sheriff takes Soupspoon and Johnson to a makeshift jail in the back of the local white barbershop. While Soupspoon tries to communicate with Johnson, Johnson acts strangely, breaking unexpectedly into song: "That's when Bob started in. 'Ohhh, momma yeah. Yeah, yeaaaaahhhh,' he sang out. 'Ohhh, momma, I,' he cried. Then he th'ew his head back and crooned a long high note." Johnson's crooning captures Heck's attention, and he demands to know what is wrong with Johnson: "'RL got spells,' I told him. I figured it was true."[44] Soupspoon does not actually know if Johnson has "spells," but he assumes that a possessed man might. The idea that Johnson would experience periods of disorientation—even more so than the usual dream he exists within—that manifests itself in song could fit in with the spirit of the crossroads tale. After all, if the devil grants a musician mastery over their instrument in exchange for their soul, and there's always a catch, as the devil is the ultimate trickster, perhaps the devil might want to collect on his investment earlier than agreed on. And maybe Johnson's musical expression is made to become a tortuous experience while he is still alive, whether due to his "spells" or his cursed guitar in *Reservation Blues*.[45]

Soupspoon is unfazed when Heck proceeds to beat Johnson up; yet after each blow Johnson gets back up and keeps singing:

> Heck hit Bob so hard that the poor boy rolled across what little floor they was. But he jumped right up into a crouch and scrabbled back to his corner and started singin' again. And Heck hit him again. But this time RL had his behind anchored. You could see how hard the slap was but RL just shuddered, shuddered and moaned. The Sherriff was a little worried when he seen that his slaps didn't bother RL. So he turned to me and said, "What's wrong with him?" "Spells," I said. I hunched my shoulders up to my ears. "Had'em since he was a babe," I lied. That time Heck used his fist on RL. That boy's

head rolled back and so did his eyes. He slid down on his side but he was still singin', "Ohhhh, momma yeah. Yeah." And a sweet smile crossed his beat-up face. Heck backed on away from him then. He looked down on that po' bluesmaster with a kind of awe. He whispered, "Spells." "Bad ones," I tells him.

These "spells" might also offer a clue as to why Johnson is silent—silenced really—throughout the novel. He has few lines of dialogue in the narrative, and when he does speak he is confused, as in this exchange after Soupspoon finds him after the two men are separated when they are released from jail: "'Bob!' I says. 'Bob, it's me, Soup, Soupy!' RL huddle down in the yellah dirt and sobbed. I helped him up and got'im t'walk wit' me. I told 'im that we could get some whiskey if we went back to Mary's general store. Back then the general store was also a juke joint, what they call a nightclub nowadays. RL says, 'Why you got my guitar, man?' 'Just carryin' it till you want it back, RL. Ole Heck almost busted it.' RL looked at me so wary I didn't think he knew who I was." Later Soupspoon even suggests that Johnson may have forgotten about jail and their run-in with Heck: "RL took his guitar and we headed for Mary's. He didn't even say nuthin' 'bout bein' in jail. I don't even think it was real fo' him. It was more like we had passed through a dream and now he was back to where we was."[46] Johnson wanders through the narrative as if he is dreaming, and Soupspoon engages Johnson in his memories as if he, too, is dreaming. This is also why the memories are so close to the foreground of his mind; he interacts with Johnson as if he is in the room with him as he speaks—as if by magic across time and geographical distance. The only way it would be possible for Johnson to be in the room with Soupspoon would be if Johnson were a ghost, or if Soupspoon was in a dream state.

Johnson's ethereal state is explained when Soupspoon asks him how he learned to play the blues: "'Made a trade fo'it, Soup.' That's what he said! Give up his right eye to the blues. Made a blood sacrifice with a witch woman down Clarksdale. Soiled his hands in the blood of an animal, then goes out to the crossroads. He said that and then he jammed his hand under Linda's skirt." This is a variation on the usual crossroads tale in which Johnson does his business directly with Satan, circumventing the witch, but it is every bit as compelling. It is also important to note that Johnson speaks for himself in that moment. He is able to share a key autobiographical detail in his own words, but Soupspoon tells the rest of the crossroads story for him. Soupspoon also tells the tale about how Johnson, the character, died—invoking the mythical Satan encounter allegedly experienced by the real-life Johnson: "They said Satan come got him in a little place outside Greenwood, Mississippi. Satan or a jealous man."[47] Johnson is unable to speak for himself throughout the novel because he is not fully present in his body. In Soupspoon's imagination Johnson exists in a liminal space between the physical plane and some form of after- or underworld, so others are able to speak for him.

As Soupspoon attempts to tell the full story of the Robert Johnson he remembers, he visits his ex-wife, Mavis, who had a sexual liaison with Johnson before becoming involved with Soupspoon. Mavis met Johnson on the night of a deadly juke joint fire that killed four people. This was also the last time that Soupspoon saw Johnson. After saving Mavis's life by helping to put out the fire that had begun to consume the hem of her dress, Johnson took her home, made love to her, and then told her about his life. Mavis in turn is another person who speaks for Johnson—sharing his autobiography: "He told me all 'bout his girl down around Robinsonville. Just fifteen but she still died with their baby. He cried like Chirren do, all lost and sad. I could see by the way he felt her death how he could play such strong music. He told me how everybody hated him. First his stepdaddy who beat him and then later all the folks who made fun'a him not workin' in the fields. Even the musicians didn't want him to play nuthin' but mouth harp. They bad-talked him until he trained hisself to play right."[48] This is a moment in the text that is based on Johnson's real-life biography. When Johnson was roughly eighteen years old, in 1929, he married a teenager named Virginia Travis, who in 1930, at sixteen years old, died in childbirth, along with her baby.[49] As Mavis tells Johnson's story, Soupspoon reflects on his own failed relationship with Mavis and wonders if their relationship ever had a real chance, since he met her after she had been involved with Johnson: "There was a loud thought in Soupspoon's mind. He never knew that Mavis had met RL at Panther Burn; at the fire that marked the last time he was ever to see his friend. He felt a double loss. It seemed to him that RL had raised up out of his grave to steal his wife away. Mavis had never been his because she had never, even from the start, opened her whole heart to him."

Soupspoon's own romantic ideas about Johnson cause him to feel inferior to him, and place Johnson in the dual role of friend and rival.

At the end of the novel, as Soupspoon waits for death in his hospital bed, he sees RL: "When the young man [Kiki's boyfriend Randy] lit his cigarette Soupspoon could see RL's evil, handsome face in the flame. Even after he blew out the match his face stayed alight. He smiled but his cold eyes told Atwater that he was finally going to die. RL didn't say anything, but that didn't surprise Soupspoon. He knew that ghosts couldn't talk like men anymore. All they do is to haunt you with what they once looked like."[50] Throughout the narrative Johnson is represented as a ghost even though he is supposedly alive, and at the end of the story the close third-person narrator finally refers to Johnson as such. The narrator even focuses on Johnson's silence, suggesting that he does not speak because he is a ghost. This is particularly striking given the fact that Johnson barely talks while alive throughout the novel. He was, in reality, a ghost all along, a mere figment of Soupspoon's dreams. Soupspoon invented this ghostlike character named Johnson to perhaps replicate the unknowability of the real-life Johnson. Soupspoon has been engaging a myth with a temporary body the entire time. Johnson's tenuous attachment to the physical world allows others to speak for him and provides the opportunity for Soupspoon to become the storyteller he longed to become, and to participate in the narrative blues tradition.

In Sherman Alexie's *Reservation Blues,* the Robert Johnson character is a minor one who, as in *RL's Dream,* catalyzes the main character's participation in the blues tradition through storytelling and mythmaking. While the protagonist, Thomas Builds-the-Fire, is already known as an unrelenting storyteller, it is Johnson's wayward guitar—imbued with special powers due to black magic—that motivates him to start a Spokane Indian rock band called Coyote Springs. When Johnson wanders onto the Spokane Indian reservation, the community immediately takes notice: "The entire reservation knew about the black man five minutes after he showed up at the crossroads. All the Spokanes thought up reasons to leave work or home so they could drive down to look the stranger over." The first person Johnson encounters is Thomas Builds-the-Fire: "The black man waved at every Indian that drove by, but nobody had the courage to stop, until Thomas Builds-the-Fire pulled up in his old blue van."[51] Thomas is a familiar Alexie character (along with Victor Joseph) whom he first introduced in his short story "This Is What It Means to Say Phoenix, Arizona," from *The Lone Ranger and Tonto Fistfight in Heaven,* and who later appears in the film *Smoke Signals.* It makes sense that Thomas would take an active interest in meeting Johnson and learning about his background, given Thomas's obsessive need to tell stories. The real-life Johnson's crossroads tale is told over and over in books, films, and other media—reflecting the repetition Schroeder describes as part of Native American storytelling and the blues.[52] Thomas also participates in this sort of repetition, as he is prone to telling the *same* story over and over again: "Thomas repeated stories constantly. All the other Indians on the reservation heard those stories so often that the words crept into dreams."[53] This is, of course, reminiscent of the African American folkloric tradition, in which stories are passed along, with modifications—sometimes minor, often significant—from person to person, and from generation to generation. The Stagolee and "Freddie" tales from the opening chapter are obvious examples of the repetitive nature of this sort of folk storytelling. What Thomas describes is similar, though it is particularly compelling to imagine his stories appearing in people's dreams. This suggests that the repetitive nature of Thomas's narrativity creates spaces for his tales to live well beyond the original, or even subsequent, retellings in waking life. Instead, the stories permeate the listeners to such a degree that they appear in their dreams. This is obviously fitting, given Thomas's fascination with Johnson, and the nature of Johnson's mythos—that of a dreamlike figure—and it suggests that Johnson and Thomas are mirrors of one another. Johnson is associated with a fictional story that has been attributed to him with no proof but nonetheless remains of great interest and is told and retold by generations of blues fans. Thomas, through his engagement with Johnson, finds validation for his unrelenting desire to tell his own stories on a seemingly endless loop.

In *Reservation Blues,* the crossroads tale drives the plot. When Thomas meets Johnson, Johnson has a guitar with him, but he is careful to keep his hand at his side rather than shaking hands with Thomas. Johnson also refuses to say the guitar's name aloud due to fear of conjuring "The Gentleman"—another name for Satan. As the omniscient narrator states, "The Gentleman held the majority of stock in Robert Johnson's soul and had chased Robert Johnson for decades. Since 1938, the year he faked his death by poisoning and made his escape, Johnson had been running from the Gentleman, who narrowly missed him at every stop." The Gentleman originally approached Johnson by offering him his deepest desire for a steep price: "'What do you want, Mr. Johnson?' asked the Gentleman. A handsome white man, the Gentleman wore a perfectly pressed black wool suit in the hot Mississippi heat. He leaned against the crossroads sign, picking at his teeth with a long fingernail." Johnson exchanges his freedom for guitar prowess, and he now hopes to undo the pact. Johnson has traveled to the reservation to find Big Mom, a Spokane Indian elder who counsels young musicians, viewing them as the embodiment of the slaughtered Native American horses—or the metaphorical Indian peoples—that white men killed several generations earlier: "With each successive generation, the horses arrived in different forms and with different songs, called themselves Janis Joplin, Jimi Hendrix, Marvin Gaye, and so many other names. Those horses rose from everywhere and turned to Big Mom for rescue, but they all fell back into the earth again." Big Mom, like Johnson, is a mythologized figure who is the subject of many tales: "There were a million stories about Big Mom. But no matter how many stories were told, some Indians still refused to believe in her." Johnson wishes to see Big Mom because he "Made a bad deal years ago. Caught a sickness I can't get rid of." The narrator conflates Johnson's "sickness" with Thomas's insatiable need to tell stories: "Thomas knew about sickness. He'd caught some disease in the womb that forced him to tell stories. The weight of those stories bowed his legs and bent his spine a bit. Robert Johnson looked bowed, bent, and more fragile with each word." While Johnson is unable to speak for himself in *RL's Dream,* in *Reservation Blues* he has a voice that grows stronger as the story unfolds. At the end of this exchange, Thomas agrees to bring Johnson to the base of the mountain where Big Mom lives, and he tells Johnson that he has to now walk on his own. Johnson leaves his guitar behind on the floor of Thomas's car, and Thomas takes it, thus beginning his new life as a bass player and songwriter in a rock band.[54]

Thomas's obsessive nature is demonstrated in his dependence on the instrument: "Thomas had carried Johnson's guitar around with him ever since then. He so strongly identified with that guitar that he wrapped it in a beautiful quilt and gave it a place of honor in his living room. When he went out for his daily walks, Thomas cradled the guitar like a baby, oblivious to the laughter all around him." While at first it is difficult to understand Thomas's relationship with Johnson's guitar, it is soon clear that the guitar has magical, human attributes, including the ability to talk and play itself. When Victor—Thomas's future lead guitar player—breaks the guitar, it even fixes itself.[55]

Johnson disappears after climbing the mountain to see Big Mom, and he reappears in the middle of the novel. During his absence, Thomas forms Coyote Springs, with Victor, the recipient of Johnson's possessed instrument. During the band's rehearsals in Irene's Grocery Store, the guitar is hot to the touch, hot enough to burn its owner: "Victor wore gloves when he played Robert Johnson's guitar but still suffered little burns and scratches. At first, Thomas had worried that his amplified bass and Junior's drums would overwhelm the acoustic lead guitar, but Victor could have kicked the guitar around the floor and it would have sounded good enough. Even without an amplifier or microphones, Robert Johnson's guitar filled the room." Part of Johnson's allure centers on how immediate his vocals and guitar sound on his recordings, so a magical Robert Johnson guitar would need to fill a room despite having to compete with amplified instruments. And lest the reader forget how the guitar came to be, on the way to an early Coyote Springs gig, the band ends up at a crossroads: "The blue van, tattered and bruised, cruised down an anonymous highway on the Flathead Indian Reservation and searched for the dirt road that led to the Tipi Pole Tavern. . . . The blue van suddenly stopped at a Crossroads."[56]

When Johnson returns to the story, he has regained his physical health and he is well rested, yet he worries about his guitar. He is sure that it will come back to him, even though he has, in the past, done everything in his power to lose it: "He buried that guitar, he threw it in rivers, dropped it off tall buildings. But is always came back to him." Importantly, it is not Johnson himself who is haunted in this novel—he arrives at the reservation tired and frail, but he is not possessed. It is the guitar that holds all of the power, and Johnson is both afraid that it will return to him and guilty that it has possibly latched on to the members of Coyote Springs. As the narrator states, "The guitar would never let go of those Indians now. It held onto Victor even harder than it ever held Johnson."[57]

Johnson's response to his fears is to sing a blues song, one that the entire reservation can hear:

> I's up this mornin'
> Ah, blues walkin' like a man
> Worried blues
> Give me your right hand.

This performance taps into a collective blues experience, with Johnson's blues speaking for African American *and* Native American struggle: "Then the music stopped. The reservation exhaled. Those blues created memories for the Spokanes, but they refused to claim them. Those blues lit up a new road, but the Spokanes pulled out their old maps. Those blues churned up generations of anger and pain: car wrecks, suicides, murders. Those blues were ancient, aboriginal, indigenous." While many Spokanes denied their stake in the blues, Thomas, tapping into his connection to the music vis-à-vis his role as storyteller, feels the connection between African American and Native American blues:

> In his bed, Thomas Builds-the-Fire had recognized Robert Johnson's voice as those blues drifted down from Big Mom's mountain. But Thomas also heard something hidden behind the words. He heard Robert Johnson's grandmother singing backup. . . . Johnson's grandmother was not alone in that cabin. Other black men, women, and children sang with her. The smell of sweat, blood, and cotton filled the room. . . . Thomas listened closely, but the other Spokanes slowly stretched their arms and legs, walked outside, and would not speak about any of it. They buried all of their pain and anger deep inside, and it festered, then blossomed, and the bloom grew quickly.[58]

Thomas hears this song, and understands how it applies to Spokanes, because he uses his own type of song—in story form—as a way to share autobiographical and biographical details about himself and others. When Johnson sings a song that expresses his own individual experience, while also allowing others to tap into that experience in a collective way, Thomas can relate because he does that with his stories and with his band. Big Mom also taps into a collective experience.

During the novel, Big Mom counsels the young members of Coyote Springs and a lost and bewildered Robert Johnson. After hearing the legends about Big Mom's profound impact on American popular music, the band with two additional members, sisters Chess and Checkers, go up the mountain to be mentored by Big Mom before their audition with the ominously named Cavalry Records in New York City: "Indians all over the country would play a scratched record of Elvis, Diana Ross, Chuck Berry, and strain to hear the name *Big Mom* hidden in the mix. 'Didn't you hear it? Elvis whispers *Thank You, Big Mom* just as the last note of the song fades.' . . . Still, Big Mom had her heart broken by many of her students who couldn't cope with the incredible gifts she had given them. Jimi Hendrix, Janis Joplin, Elvis. They all drank so much and self-destructed so successfully that Big Mom made them honorary members of the Spokane tribe."[59] While the members of Coyote Springs visit Big Mom, Thomas confides in Chess that while he is scared of Coyote Springs experiencing success or failure, he is particularly afraid of the band becoming self-destructive rock stars. As the narrator states,

> Thomas closed his eyes and told this story:
>
> Coyote Springs opens a show for Aerosmith at Madison Square Garden. We get up on stage and start to play. At first, the crowd chants for Aerosmith, heckles us, but gradually we win them over. By the time our set is over, the crowd is chanting our name. *Coyote Springs. Coyote Springs. Coyote Springs.* They chant over and over. They keep chanting our name when Aerosmith comes out. They boo Aerosmith until we come back out. For the rest of our lives, all we can hear are our names, chanted over and over, until we are deaf to everything else.

Thomas is afraid of the band becoming so successful that they lose touch with reality. After rehearsing with Coyote Springs for a week, Big Mom says goodbye to the band. She does not promise them fame, but she tells them that whether they become famous or not, few of her former students have ended up happy.[60]

Coyote Springs' audition for Cavalry Records is a spectacular failure when Victor is unable to play Johnson's guitar because it becomes dangerous to do so. According to the narrator, "The guitar bucked in his hands, twisted away from his body. He felt a razor slice across his palms." After Coyote Springs returns to the reservation, Betty and Veronica, two white former Coyote Springs groupies, sign with Cavalry Records. After the recording session with Coyote Springs fails to work out, Phil Sheridan and George Wright, the Cavalry Records label executives, decide to market the two white girls as Native Americans. Sheridan and Wright reinvent Betty and Veronica through creating a fabricated biography. As Sheridan states,

> I mean, they had some grandmothers or something that were Indian. Really. We can still sell that Indian idea. We don't need any goddamn just-off-the reservation Indians. We can use these women. They've been on the reservations. They even played a few gigs with Coyote Springs. Don't you see? These women have got the Indian experience down. . . . Can't you see the possibilities? We dress them up a little. Get them into the tanning booth. Darken them up a bit, Maybe a little plastic surgery on those cheekbones. Get them a little higher, you know? Dye their hair black. Then we'd have Indians. People want to hear Indians.[61]

In order for Betty and Veronica to become Native American, they simply have to change their appearance, and trade on their connection—however tenuous—to Coyote Springs. The women agree to be sold this way and are therefore participants in a culturally and politically problematic version of autobiographical self-invention.

At the end of the novel, Johnson decides to stay on the reservation: "I think these Indians might need me. Maybe need my music. Besides, it's beautiful here." Johnson's statement reinforces the notion that the blues resonates in both African American and Native American communities. He is also no longer haunted by the Gentleman's guitar. Thomas, Chess, and Checkers leave the reservation to move to nearby Spokane—a mere hour away. However, as Thomas says, "Anywhere off the reservation . . . is a long ways from the reservation."[62] Their move demonstrates their resiliency and their desire to live in honor of Big Mom's dead Indian horses. It is ultimately Johnson's crossroads tale that serves as a catalyst for Thomas's autobiographical storytelling, as well as Johnson's own reinvention as a free man whose spiritual debt is paid to the Gentleman. It is a fictional tall tale, rooted in African American folklore, that brings Johnson to the Spokane Indian reservation. And it is the remnant from that tale—the possessed guitar—that leads Thomas on his own ultimately successful spiritual quest, ending with his leaving the reservation and beginning his life anew.

■

We now turn to Geoffrey Becker's "Black Elvis," a work that dismantles romantic ideas about racialized blues authenticity. In "Black Elvis," identity is a more fluid construct. This story takes a postmodern approach to engaging the question of blues authenticity and subverts traditional ideas about blues signification. In this fictive world, race—and identity in general—is slippery, with characters putting it on and taking it off, like clothing. This sartorial Blackness is foreshadowed in the second sentence of the story, as Black Elvis impersonator Black Elvis chooses his outfit: "He laid out his clothes, the dark suit, the white dress shirt, the two-tone oxfords."[63] When white radio listeners in Memphis first heard the real-life Elvis on record in 1954, they thought he was Black. (Elvis himself was thus the first Black Elvis.) In his first radio interview, the disc jockey, Dewey Phillips, deliberately quizzed Elvis about the high school he attended to settle the race question in their minds.[64] So the second sentence of the story reflects the questions surrounding the real-life Elvis's racial background when he first emerged as a recording artist in 1954: Is he Black—the dark suit? Is he white—the white dress shirt? Or is he more like the two-tone oxfords—neither Black nor fully white? The oxford brogues are also important because they evoke the young, brash Elvis Presley. Black Elvis is impersonating the sharp-dressed rockabilly cat rather than the overweight, complacent, establishment star he had become by the end of his career. Elvis's musical work—and initial popularity—owes a great debt to Black gospel, blues, and R & B. Thus, when Black Elvis chooses to imitate early rock and roll Elvis Presley, he puts on early Elvis's version of whiteness, a version infused with notions of authentic Blackness. The term "Black Elvis" is, in reality, redundant. A better title for this story might be "*Blacker* Elvis."

Black(er) Elvis waits to be called by Butch, the manager who runs the blues jam, in his usual spot at the bar in Slab's barbecue joint. He has been doing the jam for four years, and the crowds love him. Butch instead introduces a new face:

> "We got a real treat here tonight," he said. "Let's all give it up for Mr. Robert Johnson. I'm serious now, that's his real name. Give him a nice hand." From somewhere in the back, a person in an old-fashioned-looking suit and fedora worked his way up through the crowded restaurant, holding a black guitar case up high in front of him. Trailing out from the back of the hat was a straight black

ponytail. When he reached the stage he opened the case and took out an antique guitar. He turned around and settled into a chair, pulling the boom mike down and into place for him to sing, while Butch arranged another mike for the instrument. Black Elvis just stared. The man was Chinese.

Black Elvis, transfixed, stares intently at the Chinese Robert Johnson as he performs. Johnson, the character, makes sure that all of the so-called authentic blues signifiers are at play. He wears a pinstriped suit and fedora like the real-life Robert Johnson wore in that iconic photo in which he sat cross-legged with a guitar on his lap. The antique guitar is even more compelling. The old guitar signifies authenticity, as it is a given that vintage instruments are a connection to a simpler, less technologically advanced time. Technology is somehow less authentic, so a newer guitar would not have the same effect. The close third-person narrator states, "Black Elvis drank some more beer and listened carefully as Robert Johnson began to play the Delta blues. He was good, this boy. Probably spent years listening to the original recordings, working them out note for note. Either that or he had a book. Some of those books had it like that, exact translations. But that wasn't important. What was important was on the *inside*. You had to *feel* the music. That just didn't seem likely with a Chinese man, even one that came from Memphis." The narrator is convinced that a Chinese man, despite being from Memphis, could never play Delta blues, as only Black people can play the blues authentically. The Chinese Robert Johnson could do a good imitation, or perhaps even pass for a song with the aid of a book with "exact translations," but he could never be an authentic bluesman. The narrator states, "He did 'Terraplane Blues.' He did 'Sweet Home Chicago' and 'Stones in My Pathway.' He played 'Love in Vain.'"[65] This roll call of some of the most popular (and frequently covered) songs by the real-life Johnson indicates that Johnson, the character, is aware of what it takes to both attract and keep his audience coming back for more.

As Johnson continues to play, Black Elvis becomes increasingly anxious. What if he is wrong? What if Johnson *is* authentic? Will he be left behind? Or is Johnson just better than him? According to the narrator, "Black Elvis felt something dark and opiate creeping through his blood, turning harder and colder as it did so. On the one hand, it should have been him up there, making the crowd love him. But the more he watched, the more he was convinced that he simply could not go on after Robert Johnson. With his pawn shop guitar and clumsy playing, he'd just look like a fool." Black Elvis owns a cheap used guitar "stowed in a chipboard case held together by a bungee cord," while Robert Johnson's guitar is an expensive antique.[66] Both guitars are old, but from Black Elvis's perspective only one of them signifies commodified blues expression. Paradoxically, in Black Elvis's mind, Johnson's new "antique" guitar is more representative of the necessary commercial polish than his beat-up guitar. Of course, the joke here is that Black Elvis believes that he should possess an expensive guitar that signifies blues authenticity, and Black musical authenticity more generally, rather than his inexpensive, pawn shop guitar that the real-life Robert Johnson might have actually been able to afford in his time.

Throughout the story, Black Elvis expresses concern about his place in the musical pecking order at Slabs, as well as in his music career in general. Some of his anxieties are temporal in nature. After Johnson finishes his set, the narrator states, "He stood and bowed, antique guitar tucked under one arm. Black Elvis felt he was watching the future, and it was one that did not include him."[67] It is striking that Black Elvis sees Johnson, the character, as the future, when in an historical context, real-life Robert Johnson died just a few years after real-life Elvis was born. The fictional interactions between these two iconic figures, whose images continue to circulate widely in a variety of American cultural spaces, are rich with historical relevance. While I do not agree with Patricia Schroeder's suggestion that Johnson "may yet become the Elvis Presley of the New Millennium," given Johnson's relative obscurity among those who do not follow music closely, I do agree that their circulating images do similar kinds of cultural work.[68] Their names have become free-floating signifiers. The words "Elvis Presley" can signify an important contributor to American musical history or a storehouse for all that is wrong with American commodification and consumption of popular music. "Robert Johnson" too can be the soulful, outside-of-modernity, folk blues exemplar or the haunted, self-destructive, tragic blues outlaw, and everything in between.

Later in the story, Black Elvis has a frank discussion with Johnson in which he asks him if he is from "Memphis, China," prompting Johnson to tell him he is Korean American. When Black Elvis asks him what kind of guitar he plays, he states, "Martin. 1924 00–28 Herringbone. I wish I could tell you I found it in an attic or something, but it's not that good a story. I paid a lot for it. But it's got a nice sound, and it fits with the whole Robert Johnson act, you know?" This moment could not be any more overt in its enunciation of the tropes of Black American blues authenticity. Johnson is not only in on the joke, but is, in fact, helping to extend the punch line. He recognizes that possessing the antique guitar is positive, but he would have a much better "story" if he just happened to find the guitar rather than actively pursuing it. Johnson tells Black Elvis that he loves his look: "I love your hair, incidentally. I mean, if I looked like you, Jesus. I'd be working all the time. You just have that natural blues man look. You could be John Lee Hooker's cousin or something." Blues authenticity is clearly marked on the body. A Black man would, of course, have "that natural blues man look," while a Korean American could not. So in this story, the character Robert Johnson constructs the persona of a Black bluesman with a vintage guitar, the right clothes, and the perfect name. Even though he does not actually have the correct guitar for blues, and can't claim to have come by it in an "authentic" way, he readily acknowledges that lying about the origins of his guitar might help his career. This demonstrates Johnson's awareness of the power of a constructed autobiography to invent or reinvent one's personality. He may not be in the correct body, but he can still participate in blues self-fashioning. Black Elvis then tells Robert Johnson,

> "I don't care much for blues music, said Black Elvis. He sniffed. "Never have."
>
> "Really?"
>
> "I like that rock and roll."

While Black Elvis's overt disdain for blues music, despite his Black body, helps to undercut racially essentialist ideas about music production and consumption, it is also unsettling. In most critical accounts, rock and roll evolved from the blues. In fact, Muddy Waters even wrote a song with Brownie McGhee called "The Blues Had a Baby and They Named It Rock and Roll." So these two fictional figures are participating in an important historical conversation. The real-life Elvis would not have existed if it were not for the real-life Johnson and the other Black blues legends who paved the way. Yet *Black* Elvis chooses (white) rock and roll over the blues. The narrator even locates Black Elvis's musical selections in the early part of the real-life Elvis's career when he routinely covered blues (and country) songs, with the cover song serving as a metaphor for blackface: "For the most part he was a Sun Sessions man. 'That's All Right, Mama' for an opener. 'Hound Dog.' 'All Shook Up' 'Milkcow Blues Boogie.'"[69]

"That's All Right" was a blues tune written and performed by Arthur "Big Boy" Crudup, and "Milkcow Blues Boogie" was based on "Milk Cow Blues" by Kokomo Arnold. And as is fitting for this postmodern story, "Hound Dog," as performed by Black Elvis, was composed by two Jewish Americans from the East Coast, Jerry Leiber and Mike Stoller, specifically for Big Mama Thornton. Of course, the song was a hit for her in 1953, but it became an even bigger hit for the real-life Elvis in 1956. As a result, many music fans are unaware of Thornton's version. Curious as it is to hear a character named Black Elvis disparage the blues, perhaps his perspective suggests a reclamation of rock and roll, the child of the blues—and maybe even rock, the grandchild that passes for white—as Black music.

Despite Black Elvis's lack of interest in the music Johnson plays, he is impressed with Johnson's marketing ability. When he asks Johnson for help with his career—"Should I be doing something else? You play good, you sing good, you know about marketing. Just tell me and I'll listen"—he is showing why he sees the future in Johnson.[70] The fictional Johnson's ability to turn himself into a commodity rather than letting others do that for him redresses, at least in this short story, the real-life Johnson's historical commodification. Of course, the real-life Elvis is also a commodity, but his whiteness allowed him to reap the significant financial rewards in his lifetime that the real-life Johnson never saw. In this fictional world, Johnson and Elvis trade places, as the Black impersonator of the white artist is still unable to reap significant financial rewards from his artistic output.

"Black Elvis" subverts notions of racialized blues authenticity through autobiographical self-creation. The Robert Johnson character in "Black Elvis" is able to reinvent himself as an "antique" blues musician despite having the wrong guitar and the wrong body. And Black Elvis, who has "that natural bluesman look" and plays music derived from the blues, wants no part of them.[71] Both characters face questions about the commodification of their work, and their resistance to prescribed racial roles runs along a parallel track. As the characters take control of their racialized images, they gain the confidence to carve a place for themselves commercially. Both of these characters express themselves musically on their own terms, resisting the proscribed, racialized tropes of blues authenticity specifically, and Black musical authenticity more generally.

This postmodern blues story stands in stark contrast to the romanticism and racial essentialism of "Stones in My Passway, Hellhound on My Trail," *RL's Dream,* and *Reservation Blues.* In these more modernist texts, Johnson is a figure of genius whose tortured demeanor is consistent with his mythologized biographical representation. Compelling here are the ways in which the Johnson character, though mostly silenced, provides an opening for other characters to participate in autobiographical and biographical blues expression. Even when the fictionalized Robert Johnson is not overtly undermining the concept of blues authenticity, his role as a blank canvas on which others can project ideas allows these characters to tell their own stories and the larger story of the blues. And as I have argued throughout *Fictional Blues* so far, this storytelling is an essential component of the blues tradition.

4 From John Anthony Gillis to Jack White

A Study in Blues Self-Invention

Jack White is a singer, songwriter, and guitarist whose former band, blues-rock duo the White Stripes, enjoyed immense critical and commercial success during the aughts and into the first few years of the second decade of the twenty-first century. He is also a member of two other critically acclaimed rock bands: the Raconteurs, formed in 2004 in Detroit, Michigan, and the Dead Weather, who performed for the first time in Nashville, Tennessee, in 2009.[1] In 2012, White released his debut solo record, *Blunderbuss*. His second and third solo works, *Lazaretto* and *Boarding House Reach*, were released in June 2014 and March 2018, respectively. White is a producer and a record label executive. In 2009, he broke ground on the brick-and-mortar location for his Nashville-based Third Man Records, and in 2015, he opened Third Man Records Cass Corridor in Detroit, Michigan. Third Man Pressing, a vinyl record pressing plant, launched in Detroit in February 2017.

White has always been straightforward about his conflicted feelings around being a white man playing blues-based music. He has expressed this sentiment in various interviews over the years, including a moment in the 2009 documentary *It Might Get Loud* when he frankly admits to trying to "get away with" being a white man who sometimes plays in a traditional Delta blues style.[2] In a March 2010 interview in the *Observer,* White describes one of his strategies as aesthetic misdirection: "With the White Stripes we were trying to trick people into not realising we were playing the blues. We did not want to come off like white kids trying to play black music from 100 years ago so a great way to distract them was by dressing in red, white and black."[3] White, who came of age in Detroit during the 1990s, used costuming and graphic design to construct an image for the White Stripes that invoked childhood innocence, and created a fictionalized autobiographical backstory for himself and drummer Meg White, with the goal, in part, to preemptively insulate the band from charges of cultural appropriation. Given cascading debates about racialized blues authenticity, John Gillis, in his guise as blues revivalist "Jack White," an artistic persona developed at the end of the twentieth century, has an awareness of the politics of blues legitimacy in a way that the previous generation of musicians did not. In the 1960s, Cream, the Rolling Stones, Led Zeppelin, and other young British blues rockers were in the self-consciously odd position of introducing American blues music to a generation of young white American audiences. Given that most white American teenagers had little exposure to blues music and that Black American youth, attracted to rhythm and blues and then soul, had deemed it old-fashioned, the British were not, at first, accused of cultural appropriation and inauthenticity—though these attacks would later come in droves.[4] White, in contrast, had to anticipate such charges from the very beginning. In fact, early articles about the White Stripes attempted to situate the band within the authenticity paradigm. In a 2002 article for Pitchfork.com, William Bowers suggests that their second record, *De Stijl,* avoids the "blues-aping caricatures, or the diluted Caucasian appropriations that clog rock history."[5] Across the Atlantic, in a 2003 article in the *Evening Standard,* Steve Jelbert describes an experience that mirrors that of Eric Clapton and the other young 1960s British blues revivalists:[6] "The White Stripes' loving appropriation of the blues is hardly novel, but to a young audience they present something unfamiliar, while older listeners can appreciate their skill at reviving an ancient art."[7] Jelbert deems the White Stripes' blues appropriation harmless since it simultaneously soars over the heads of their young and predominantly white fan base while pleasing their older fans. Yet as the White Stripes' fame grew, some people, such as Tim Duffy—founder of the Music Maker Relief Foundation, an organization that offers Southern American roots musicians financial support—expressed dismay in a 2006 issue of the *Orlando Sentinel* at the unequal distribution of financial rewards for those who play American roots music based on differences in artists' ages, races, and class backgrounds: "It's hard for the true traditional artists to have any platform because they have no expertise competing against white college-educated kids. How can you compete against a guy like Jack White of the White Stripes?"[8] This pointed critique is one of the reasons why White developed an alternative blues persona early in his career.

While White's construction of a highly stylized image for the White Stripes was certainly motivated by his desire to avoid the scrutiny of critics who might accuse him of cultural theft, it is also important to note that White has never been shy about his interest in image and persona and the necessity for a musician to tell a story that relies on both art and artifice. In 2007, White told the *New York Times*, "Everything from your haircut to your clothes to the type of instrument you play to the melody of a song to the rhythm—they're all tricks to get people to pay attention to the story."[9] And in a 2002 interview with *Guitar World*, White asserts, "Anything involved in presenting yourself onstage is all a big trick. You're doing your best to trick those people into experiencing something good, something they haven't thought about before or haven't thought about in a long time. I'm doing my best to be that vaudeville trickster, to help that happen. But the image stuff all stemmed from the music—just the childishness and how it relates to anger and innocence and these colors and what they mean to us, and us being children together. It all comes from that childishness, really."[10]

White, a self-proclaimed "trickster," extends his engagement with myth into the realm of his autobiography. While the mythical trickster figure can be found in many different cultures, White's trickster moves suggest the kinds of "indeterminacy" and "ambiguity" that the African diasporic trickster figures Esu and the Signifying Monkey represent, situating him within the blues storytelling tradition.[11] His deliberate fabrication of key autobiographical details about the nature of his relationship with Meg White is one obvious example. White's interviews are sites for many of his fabrications, while his autobiographical obfuscations also exist in his musical performances on record, in concert, and in music videos. White's autobiographical misdirection has helped him to invent—and reinvent—himself in different phases of his career. When Jack White defines the White Stripes' playful and childlike visual aesthetic, he is inventing personalities for himself and bandmate Meg White, thus performing an autobiographical act—or, considering the subterfuge involved, it might be more accurate to call it an *anti*-autobiographical act—that allows him to participate in traditional blues self-fashioning. All of this supports my larger argument: that White self-consciously, and quite adeptly, through his autobiographical blues self-invention, inserts himself into the tradition of blues self-mythologization.

This chapter will explore White's ever-evolving identity: from John Anthony Gillis, a young, self-conscious, white blues disciple determined to stand apart from his contemporaries and the white bluesmen who preceded him, to "Jack White," a solo artist, producer, and businessman who takes an unapologetically postmodern approach to his work as a musician and as a music industry executive. In the first part of the chapter, I examine the visual presentation White constructed for himself and Meg White during the White Stripes era. In the second part, using music scholar Andrew Legg's gospel taxonomy, I analyze sonic aspects of White's blues self-creation through his vocal performance in "Ball and Biscuit" from the 2003 White Stripes album *Elephant*. And in part three, I look at postmodern pastiche in White's solo work, specifically in his 2011 collaboration with Insane Clown Posse on W. A. Mozart's scatological 1782 vocal canon "Leck mich im Arsch" and in his video for *Blunderbuss*'s "Freedom at 21."

THE WHITE STRIPES' GREAT ART PROJECT

Jack White's concerns about blues authenticity motivated his use of visual aesthetics as an antidote to his racial and temporal misplacement. White, through a deliberate clash of visual and musical signifiers, turned his White Stripes persona into a postmodern Pop art performance. This extended *anti*-autobiographical performance demonstrates the slippery nature of Black blues signifiers and allows White to signify on entrenched ideas by some blues scholars, critics, and fans of how an authentic blues figure should look.

When asked about his blues influences, White most consistently mentions three closely-related Delta legends—Charley Patton, Son House, and Robert Johnson—and one Atlanta-based contemporary, Blind Willie McTell. In *It Might Get Loud,* which features three generations of iconic guitar players—Jimmy Page, the Edge of U2, and White—White declares House's "Grinnin' in Your Face" his favorite song. In 2013, White's Nashville-based Third Man Records label, in collaboration with Document Records, reissued recordings by Charley Patton, Blind Willie McTell, and the Mississippi Sheiks exclusively on vinyl. At the end of 2013, a partnership between Third Man Records and American Primitive blues guitarist John Fahey's Revenant Records yielded *The Rise and Fall of Paramount Records: Volume One, 1917–1927,* the first installment of a projected reissue of every race recording released by the titular early twentieth-century race label in a sprawling archival box made to resemble a portable Victrola. The collection features early recordings by classic Black American artists such as Blind Lemon Jefferson, Louis Armstrong, Ethel Waters, and Ma Rainey in both vinyl and digital formats. *The Rise and Fall of Paramount Records: Volume Two, 1928–1932* was made available at the end of 2014. Given White's fetish for historical revival and accuracy, and in order to place White's goals for his blues music expression in its proper context, it is important to explore the artists who have directly or indirectly influenced him.

Despite what White's predominantly white contemporary rock audiences might assume, his imagistic gymnastics—his playfully unorthodox approach to his self-presentation—do not wholly set him apart from the Delta blues players. Some of these musicians share White's love of on- and offstage showmanship and a propensity toward autobiographical trickery. Blues pioneers such as W. C. Handy, Charley Patton, and Tommy Johnson laid the groundwork for White to construct an invented biography for the White Stripes. Famously, throughout the band's existence and beyond, White maintained that he and Meg White were siblings, despite the fact that the press uncovered both their marriage and divorce certificates at the beginning of the aughts. As White admits, "Nothing that is said in an interview or onstage into a microphone—just like nothing in the Bible—should be taken literally."[12] Like blues harmonica player Aleck Miller, who renamed himself Sonny Boy

Williamson even though there was already a famous blues harmonica player from Tennessee with the same name, and blues musicians such as Muddy Waters, Son House, and Lead Belly who allowed themselves to be presented by record industry professionals as more rural and "exotic" than they actually were, White effectively places himself within the tradition of the self-mythologizing bluesman through his use of autobiographical fabrication.[13] The representation of Jack and Meg's relationship as a natural sibling bond, rather than a grown-up, postdivorce business partnership, helped White to create an image for the White Stripes that subverts conventional notions of blues authenticity. This approach helps White sidestep charges of cultural appropriation, while the masking of his musical intentions through visual distraction propels his anti-autobiographical performance forward.[14]

Charley Patton and Tommy Johnson were both consummate Delta performers who took pride in their ability to entertain crowds in juke joints, barrel houses, and outdoor country dances. Most likely born "in April 1891 in the area between Bolton and Edwards, Mississippi," Patton was an extremely important Delta blues originator.[15] Not only would Patton have a profound influence on the work of Son House, Tommy Johnson, Booker White, Howlin' Wolf, and Muddy Waters, but he was also a progenitor of what now are seen as commonplace, even clichéd, rock and roll stage antics. As Ted Gioia writes, "Patton played the guitar behind his back, or between his legs, sometimes flipping it over, or snapping the strings, or tapping on it like a big drum. All the strutting and flaunting we associate with rock stars since Jimi Hendrix were already part of Patton's repertoire in the 1920s."[16] Patton was a passionate entertainer, but his flamboyant style carried over into his personal life in the form of numerous run-ins with law enforcement, mostly having to do with public drunkenness, multiple marriages, fighting, and general hell-raising.

Patton's stage shenanigans, his bold personality on- and offstage, and the conflicting accounts of his biography—he apparently recorded songs for Paramount Records under three different monikers: Charley Patton; the super heroesque Masked Marvel—as part of a Paramount Records free giveaway to a customer able to guess his identity; and Elder J. J. Hadley—make him White's spiritual ancestor. As Gioia notes, "Casual acquaintances often surmised that Patton came from the North. His brashness and assertiveness seemed so out of character for a black man from Mississippi."[17] Apparently, Patton was full of confidence or, depending on one's view, braggadocio, particularly about his sexual exploits. Son House once complained about Patton, "You could hardly get a word in edgeways yourself, not when Charley [was] around. His woman yesterday, the day before yesterday, all what he done to the woman."[18] That confidence represented a sense of freedom that most other Blacks, facing stultifying oppression on many fronts, could admire. Patton's sexual confidence also served as his autobiographical expression, given his lack of access to print media. Instead of writing a book, Patton orally narrated his story.

Tommy Johnson was another Delta blues singer who was heavily influenced by Charley Patton. LeDell Johnson told David Evans about his brother Tommy's purported visit to the crossroads with his guitar in order to become a better player.[19] And Robert Palmer describes Johnson as having "affected a trickster's personality. He took to carrying a large rabbit's foot around with him and displaying it often, and his performances were spectacularly acrobatic."[20] White, too, shape-shifts into a wild man onstage. Though he does not twirl his guitar or play it between his legs or behind his back, during live performances his body is in perpetual motion. He lunges forward and back, kicks out his legs, bows like a spasmodic folding chair, and bobs his head, occasionally quite violently, to the music. At times he attacks the guitar so viciously that it ends up covered in blood. This sanguine sacrifice serves as a signification of his commitment to the music, all the while cementing his own legend. White's larger-than-life onstage persona also plays out in music videos and on-camera interviews, effectively serving as postmodern pastiche, an unruly mix of traditional blues mythology and, as we will see, 1960s British visual aesthetics.

As one of the few blues pioneers to write an autobiography, W. C. Handy left traces in print of the self-conscious mythologizing tendency that would later inspire White. Widely known as the "Father of the Blues," Handy was a Black American bandleader, composer, and music publisher whose 1914 tune "Saint Louis Blues" has been recorded by numerous jazz and blues artists. There have been short and feature films about the song, and even a National Hockey League team, the St. Louis Blues, bears its name. Handy's assumption of the title "Father of the Blues" came with a certain amount of controversy, since many of his compositions are more jazz or pop than twelve-bar blues. He also famously claimed in his 1941 book *Father of the Blues: An Autobiography* to have "discovered" the blues accidentally at a train station in Tutwiler, Mississippi, in or around 1903: "A lean, loose-jointed Negro had commenced plunking a guitar beside me while I slept. His clothes were rags; his feet peeped out of his shoes. His face had on it some of the sadness of the ages. As he played, he pressed a knife on the strings of the guitar in a manner popularized by Hawaiian guitarists who used steel bars. The effect was unforgettable. His song, too, struck me instantly. Goin' where the Southern cross' the Dog. The singer repeated the line three times, accompanying himself on the guitar with the weirdest music I had ever heard."[21] This written-down story is the inverse of the unwritten legends that surround Johnson and Patton, narrated from the perspective of the trained urban musician rather than the itinerant country entertainer—Handy hardly needed to sell his soul for musical knowledge: he had had lessons on the pipe organ at church. The lyrical form that Handy describes certainly sounds like the blues, and in his autobiography he makes no attempt to hide the fact that he merely committed to paper a music style already in existence that proved to be popular with white and Black audiences. Handy, a successful bandleader, was a talented businessman before anything else, and he understood that this largely unknown regional music could cross over to a national audience, particularly with the right amount of romantic myth attached.

The veracity of many details in Handy's books has been called into question by people who knew him before his great success, as well as by a handful of journalists and scholars along the way. As Francis Davis asserts, "All the best stories are apocryphal, especially any told by Handy, who wasn't just one of the new century's most important bandleaders, composers, and musical publishers, but also, in common with men like Henry Ford, a bootstrap entrepreneur savvy enough to know that the creation of personal myth came with the territory."[22] In fact, a controversy about the location where Handy composed "St. Louis Blues" flared up in 1947 when Robert C. Ruark, a *Scripps-Howard* staff writer, suggested that Handy even lied about where he wrote the song in his autobiography. In *Father of the Blues* Handy paints a dramatic, even cinematic picture: "I could feel the blues coming on, and I didn't want to be distracted, so I packed my grip and made my getaway. I rented a room in the Beale Street section and went to work. Outside the lights flickered." The legend went that Handy rubbed elbows with the rough characters on Beale Street, Memphis' famous red-light district, allowing him to write authentic blues music. After staying up all night to complete the song, he continues, "The same day on Pee Wee's cigar stand, I orchestrated the number and jotted down scores for the men of my band."[23] But, according to Ruark, in an interview published with Handy in 1947 with the headline "Legend Takes Beating on Conditions under Which Handy Wrote His Blues," Handy tells him, "I didn't write St. Louis Blues in Peewee's Café on Beale Street. I wrote it in 1914 on the second floor of the Solvent Savings Bank in Memphis, where I had set up the Pace & Handy Music Co."[24] Ruark professed to be disappointed that Handy had not hung "around the low dives in Memphis, notably a place called Peewee's Café, consorting with gamblers and sweet men and easy ladies."[25] When Ruark laments at the end of his article that "Handy's melodies reek of the easy streets, but Handy is a hardheaded businessman who toots his cornet for fun," he misses the point. It is possible to be a businessman and an artist simultaneously. It is also possible to be a musician who takes his or her art seriously, while also holding loosely to the objective truth of an autobiography.

Contemporary autobiographies by Eric Clapton, Bob Dylan, and Keith Richards—"authentic" musicians all—demonstrate the ways in which the autobiographical genre can serve as a vehicle for artistic blues self-creation, allowing that the subjective details delivered in these works may or may not be independently verifiable as "truth."[26] Each of these musicians was heavily influenced by blues music and, in the case of Richards and Clapton, they aspired to be what they perceived as so-called authentic bluesmen. Unlike White, who relied on distraction and artistic tricks to free himself from the waiting charge of white blues appropriator, these earlier revivalists engaged the Black bluesman tropes directly, participating in historical practices of racial mimicry.

Chronicles: Volume One by Bob Dylan (2004), *Life* by Keith Richards, with James Fox (2010), and *Clapton: The Autobiography* by Eric Clapton (2007) begin as bildungsromane about the early formation of white blues players. Each book details the moment when the young blues acolyte in question discovers Robert Johnson. Dylan describes the "stabbing sounds" emanating from Johnson's guitar and the numbness he felt after taking it all in.[27] Clapton experiences a sense of revulsion during his first exposure to Johnson's music: "At first the music almost repelled me, it was so intense."[28] Richards suggests that during his first encounter with Johnson he "was astounded at what [he] heard."[29] Jack White describes a similar response to Johnson's music and the impact it had on his musical development in an interview with Kurt Loder on MTV.com. Unlike Clapton, Dylan, and Richards, who worry about this later, he is immediately consumed by fear of being labeled "inauthentic": "Somehow Robert Johnson really snapped something in my brain. I really felt like I had to find a way that I could play this music that felt so real and so cathartic for me, and figure out how I could attack that and share it with other people without getting this 'white-boy blues' thing labeled on me." In these accounts, the writers use words like "numb," "repelled," "confused," and "snapped" to describe the visceral effect the blues sounds have on the listener, suggesting that the music provokes physical disorientation.[30] This disorientation correlates with tropes about how *real* Black music is dangerous to whites.

In *Near Black: White-to-Black Passing in American Culture,* Baz Dreisinger casts white-to-Black passing as a function of white Americans' close contact with Black Americans. For Dreisinger, many of the white subjects in her study were able to take on a shroud of Blackness due to living or working near or among Black people. Dreisinger argues, "Because 'blackness,' so to speak, is imagined as transmittable, proximity to blackness is invested with the power to turn whites black." And the idea that Blackness might be transmitted through art, specifically jazz music, caused a significant amount of anxiety among many whites during the 1920s and 1940s: "When critics and medical experts argued that the sound of jazz would bring out the barbarian in white listeners, they were essentially declaring that jazz could transform white to black."[31] These tropes also correlate to the moment in Black blues mythology when the protagonist meets the devil. It is as if he or she is "repelled" or experiences "numbness" as a reaction to shaking the devil's ice-cold hand.[32]

Richards is explicit in his book about his youthful desire to be not only a bluesman but a Black bluesman, with Chicago blues as the catalyst: "We [the Rolling Stones] soaked up the music, but it didn't change the color of our skin." Even though Richards admits to wanting to change his whiteness at the start of his career, he acknowledges that he learned over time that it is unnecessary to be Black to play the blues.[33] In contrast, Clapton appears to be particularly concerned about his authenticity as a blues musician, and he is stuck in racially essentialist notions about what constitutes blues authenticity. In his autobiography, Clapton reveals acute anxieties about his whiteness in the context of playing blues music, and his actions serve as a cautionary tale for what can happen to a white blues artist who endeavors to function within the narrow confines of blues authenticity rather than subverting it. His self-consciousness is clear as he admits, "The fact is, of course, that through my playing people were being exposed to a kind of music that was new to them, and I was getting all the credit for it, as if I had invented the blues." He also shares his experience when Hendrix performed with Cream in London in 1966: "It scared me, because he was clearly going to be a huge star, and just as we were finding our own speed, here was the real thing."[34] To Clapton, Hendrix was real because he was Black. Clapton, assuming, perhaps unawares, the position that Norman Mailer had notoriously called the White Negro, is fixated on Black visual appearance as an indicator of musical authenticity.[35] As Ulrich Adelt suggests, "Although Clapton began to identify with what he considered a white sound during his Cream stint, his search for a white identity coincided with his pseudo-Afro hairstyle, an imitation of either Jimi Hendrix or Bob Dylan, whose Jew-fro did not need artificial enhancement, whereas Clapton had to resort to perms."[36] Clapton did what he could to override his whiteness, but his interventions were unsustainable. Clapton tried to change his physical image, particularly his straight hair, to appear phenotypically Black, or at the very least to look like the cool white musicians in the Jimi Hendrix Experience. White, on the other hand, embraced his own pale skin and long, floppy, phenotypically Caucasian mane, leaving only aesthetics and invocations of childhood innocence to deflect attention away from his manifest whiteness.

JOHN ANTHONY GILLIS BECOMES JACK WHITE

Of course, "White" wasn't his real name. Jack White, né John Anthony Gillis on July 9, 1975, grew up the youngest of ten children—as he reports, the seventh son—in a Catholic family in the lower-middle-class neighborhood of Mexicantown in Southwest Detroit, far away from the American South, the putative birthplace of American blues music. Thus, according to White, he "went to an all-Mexican grade school and an all-black high school [Cass Tech]," and his peers at school and in his local community were more likely to listen to hip-hop, techno, or house music than countrified Americana such as the blues.[37]

At fifteen, Gillis apprenticed to a local upholsterer and family friend named Brian Muldoon. Muldoon introduced White to garage and punk bands such as the MC5 and the Cramps, and the duo formed a band called Two Part Resin—and later the Upholsterers—with Muldoon on drums and White on guitar. In 2000 they released a seven-inch single called "Makers of High Grade Suites." When Gillis's apprenticeship with Muldoon ended, he formed his own upholstery business, Third Man Upholstery, for which he created a yellow, black, and white visual aesthetic in which everything from the van he drove to his business cards bore those colors. By this time, Gillis was familiar with electric blues artists Howlin' Wolf and Willie Dixon and blues-rock band Led Zeppelin; however, as we saw previously, blues music did not resonate deeply with him until he heard acoustic country styles from the Mississippi Delta.[38]

When Gillis was still a teenager, a friend introduced him to the music of Son House: "He played me 'Death Letter', and then this a cappella song, 'Grinnin' In Your Face'. I heard the song I'd been waiting to hear my whole life. It said, 'Don't care what people think. Your mother will talk about you, your sister and your brothers too. No matter how you try to live, they're gonna talk about you still.' We had a big family, I didn't have that many friends, and I was paranoid. I thought everybody was talking about me all the time."[39] It was Gillis's introduction to Southern roots artists such as Son House and Robert Johnson, rather than the kind of electrified blues one could have found on any weekend even in turn-of-the-twenty-first-century Detroit, that White says inspired him to play blues music: "If people really love music, they're going to start being drawn toward honesty, and if they're drawn to that, it's a direct line right back to Charley Patton and Son House. I'm very skeptical of musicians who say they love music and don't love the blues."[40] However, not only was he tentative about playing amplified country blues music from his twenty-first-century, white, urban subject position, but he was loathe to be lumped in with aging 1960s-era white blues rockers Clapton, Richards, Page, and Jeff Beck, or worse, find himself tethered to a more conventional contemporary white blues revivalist such as Joe Bonamassa. Influenced by English and Irish blues artists such as Clapton, Beck, and Rory Gallagher, instead of the Black American Delta blues musicians, Bonamassa is viewed by some music critics as a technically proficient guitar player whose performance style lacks heart.[41]

Gillis's wariness of the "white-boy blues thing" played a significant role in his approach to his own band, the White Stripes.[42] After teaching his then wife, Meg White, a simplistic drumming style, White saw an opportunity to form an under-the-radar blues duo.[43] He hypothesized that evoking the cultural innocence of childhood might circumvent charges of cultural appropriation: "I would feel really fake sitting down, adopting a black accent, and singing about trains or something. My easy way out of that is to just go into childhood, because that honesty seems to reflect the same nature that the blues was reflecting. That's my way of getting involved in that tradition."[44] When White talks about the blues, he frequently uses variations of the words "truth" and "honesty." As self-consciously constructed as the White Stripes were, White places a high value on, if not a purist's view of blues authenticity, then perhaps a punk rock truthfulness that lends authenticity—according to which brashness, immaturity, and raw emotion are privileged commodities. This brand of truthfulness is not necessarily always correlated with a commitment to objective facts but rather is tied to a particular set of performative approaches—high-energy live shows and a bold, tell-it-like-it-is interview style, for instance—that reads as the opposite of artificial. White's focus on childlike honesty also reinforces the idea of the country blues as a simple, and perhaps more innocent, music. In this context, the blues emerges during the "childhood" of American popular music. White here shows a tendency to racially essentialize the country blues and its practitioners. That blues musician that Handy "discovered" in Tutwiler, Mississippi, immediately comes to mind. Handy's description of the "primitive" young man—"A lean, loose-jointed Negro had commenced plunking a guitar beside me while I slept. His clothes were rags; his feet peeped out of his shoes. His face had on it some of the sadness of the ages"—harks back to the racist image of the childlike darkie or Uncle Tom figure from the antebellum South that appeared on sheet music covers of the time.[45] Handy and White both invoke this image: the man on the platform is not a child, but his ability to "happily" play music, in spite of his oppressive circumstances, suggests a level of unsophistication befitting a child, supporting the artificial construction put forth in blackface minstrelsy. While few scholars would disagree with the notion that formal blues structure is simple, more than a few would offer the caveat that the musical form is deceptively simple, with originators, like

Patton, laying the groundwork for completely new musical forms such as rock and roll.[46]

White's alignment with the Delta blues players in particular placed him in a unique quandary. The country blues, which emerged early in the twentieth century but was not recorded until the 1920s and 1930s, originated largely among field hands in the agrarian Jim Crow South amid extremely harsh socioeconomic circumstances. Even the natural environment could be dangerous, unpredictable, and destructive, as evidenced when both country blues artist Charley Patton and classic blues artist Bessie Smith notably memorialized the deadly Great Mississippi Flood of 1927 in "High Water Everywhere" and "Homeless Blues," respectively. In contrast, amplified blues is the sound of the African American Great Migration: not only a transition from Southern country to Northern city life, but the sound of African Americans definitively entering modernity.[47] Coming from Detroit, a key destination for that Black Northern migration, White had to figure out how to not only cross race-based boundaries to achieve blues authenticity but also overcome regional and class boundaries.

Rather than attempting to emulate the visual style of Black Delta blues figures, White constructed an image that appears antithetical. He takes this approach to offset what Les Back, in his discussion of the "coloring" of the sound made by the predominantly white Muscle Shoals house band, refers to as "the visual regimes of racism." Given that most people thought the Muscle Shoals band was Black, the musicians themselves and the Black artists they worked with did not go out of their way to disabuse unsuspecting audiences of that notion. Back reasons, "In [recorded] sound there was the potential for expression in which the strictures of racial categories were partially transcended. This was not a matter of 'passing as black,' but rather of becoming more than white and, in so doing, creating music that could not be reduced to racial categories." Back glosses over an element of white privilege here: after all, it was no doubt easier for the Muscle Shoals musicians to become "more than white" than it would have ever been for Black musicians, even in the studio, to become "more than black"—perhaps only ace Wrecking Crew drummer Earl Palmer, laying down the groove for the Monkees, got close. Even so, the fact that the session players were largely hidden did make it possible for audiences to listen for so-called authentic Blackness with their ears rather than their eyes. Muscle Shoals drummer Roger

Hawkins admits to being self-conscious when playing in a more public setting. Hawkins reasons, "I'm not comfortable unless I have my own little corner to play in and my own set of headphones. On stage I feel like an insurance salesman playing all those hot grooves."[48]

Jack White could never have been "more than white," given his place in a post-MTV musical landscape where sound and visual image go hand in hand. He sidesteps the passive visual indicators of the "unmarked" racial interloper by avoiding casual, everyday clothing that on his Caucasian body would be categorized as white and male. He instead makes the proactive gesture of moving as far away as he can from either a white working-class or a Black American Delta blues persona. With 1960s Pop art rockers the Who, the 1920s Dutch De Stijl art movement, and the western Pop art movement as foundational models, as well as his own artistic background in upholstery and furniture restoration as a precedent, White rigidly controlled the fabric of his band's identity, cultivating a highly stylized red, white, and black visual aesthetic.[49] This color palette was used not only for the White Stripes' stage clothing but also for their instruments, stage gear, backdrops, lighting, and marketing materials. White explains, "The White Stripes' colors were always red, white and black. It came from peppermint candy. I also think they are the most powerful color combination of all time, from a Coca-Cola can to a Nazi banner. Those colors strike chords with people. In Japan, they are honorable colors. When you see a bride in a white gown, you immediately see innocence in that. Red is anger and passion. It is also sexual. And black is the absence of all that."[50] White's inclusion of the Coca-Cola can and the Nazi banner—the former the premier symbol of Western capitalism and consumer democracy, and the latter equally symbolic of Western totalitarianism—as two historical examples of the use of the red, white, and black color palette is notable, as both feature the kind of highly abstract, mass-produced sign language that Pop art would later mine for formal cues. White was very clear about the political and psychological power of this color combination *itself* as a sign, so it follows that by choosing it he challenged his audience to recognize the essentially political, manufactured nature of even the most "traditional" blues signifiers.

The Pop art elements of White Stripes–era performances are striking because they provide a framework wherein White negotiates questions of racial authenticity. Pop art began as separate movements in the United States and Britain. Pop art in the United States was spearheaded by two important exhibitions—*Art 1963: A New Vocabulary* in Philadelphia and *The New Realists* in New York—and included Pop artists Andy Warhol and Roy Lichtenstein. In Britain, the movement began with artist Richard Hamilton, an instructor at the Royal College of Art; art critic Lawrence Alloway; and artist and teacher Eduardo Paolozzi serving as important conduits. All three were members of the Independent Group, a collective of young London visual artists, art critics, and architects who challenged entrenched ideas about modern art. Emerging in Britain in the late 1950s and in America in the early 1960s, Pop art, according to Simon Frith and Howard Horne, took "seriously as artists the people involved in designing cars and furniture, producing packages and pop stars." It advocated that "fine artists too should apply the aesthetic lessons learned from a study of mass culture, using in their own work the organization of colour and shape found on the streets and the billboards, incorporating mass-produced images into their own individual statements."[51] By the end of the 1950s, Pop art theory had made its way into British art schools. The British art school system profoundly affected a generation of British rock musicians who came of age during the 1960s.

Even a partial list of soon-to-be-famous British musicians who attended art school during the heyday of Pop art in the late 1950s and 1960s is a Who's Who of rock royalty: Syd Barrett (Pink Floyd); Ray Davies (the Kinks); Pete Townshend (the Who); Charlie Watts, Ron Wood, and Keith Richards (the Rolling Stones); Jimmy Page (Led Zeppelin); Jeff Beck (the Yardbirds); John Mayall (the Bluesbreakers); Eric Clapton (Cream); and John Lennon (the Beatles). Not only did a significant number of British rock stars, many of them blues rockers, attend art school, but some—the Who, the Rolling Stones—took the Pop art ethos to heart as they sought control of their own commercial images.

By the late 1950s and 1960s, fashion became, for the first time, an important pathway for the successful manipulation of rock and roll visual presentation. According to Frith and Horne, "The history of rock, in Britain at least, is a history of image as well as sound, a history of cults and cultures defined by clothes as well as songs. Whether in pursuit of authenticity or artifice, romantic truth or postmodern paradox and pastiche, musicians use the language of fashion, and this may be the point at which art schools have their most important musical impact."[52] The teddy boys and the mods were important British working-class youth subcultures that emerged during this timeframe and affected fashion trends that resonated with future rockers. Both demonstrated an affinity for Black American music, while crafting a bold visual style through fashion. In the 1950s, the teddy boys, whose name derived from the updated take on the aristocratic Edwardian Savile Row suits they wore, became infatuated with rock and roll, a form of crossover music that had sprung in part from rhythm and blues, a musical form played predominantly by Black musicians. The mods emerged in the 1960s; they appreciated Black American music, including soul and R & B. Style was also important to this group, though there was a stark contrast in dress. Dick Hebdige notes, "Unlike the defiantly obtrusive teddy boys, the mods were more subtle and subdued in appearance: they wore apparently conservative suits in respectable colours, they were fastidiously neat and tidy. Hair was generally short and clean."[53] The mods were more respectable than the teddy boys, though they still fell into disfavor with the older generations, particularly parents and the media. The Who, a self-professed mod band with Pop art sensibilities, became an important model for Jack White and the White Stripes.

The Who titrated their embrace of Black music and culture with a heavy dose of art school theory. The very name "mod" pointed toward a theoretical acceptance of modernism in visual and performance culture. Frith and Horne state, "Townshend himself . . . saw his own musical activities in terms of performance art, which meant seeing the Who's stage act itself as the moment of artistic creation and exploring the constraints on this. . . . Townshend was a remarkably self-conscious pop performer, unusually able to articulate what his shows were about." Townshend's course of study at art school exposed him to Pop art theory, and he often referred to the Who as a Pop art band, blurring the lines between high and low culture, art and commerce: "The importance of Townshend's use of Pop art rhetoric (and what distinguished him from the r & b bohemians) was that it referred not to music-making as such—to the issue of self-expression—but to commercial music-making, to issues of packaging, selling and publicizing, to the problems of popularity and stardom."[54] This is the similarity between Townshend and White; both white artists are fascinated with music played predominantly by Black people, and neither musician is conflicted about being an artist and a product at the same time as long as they are firmly in control of their own images and cultural productions.

The Who and the White Stripes, however, faced generationally different concerns regarding racialized musical authenticity. The Who took a commercial approach to what can be seen as commercial music: Motown/soul. Berry Gordy and Motown were themselves somewhat mod, taking a contemporary pop—secular—approach to gospel music, so the Who's "Maximum R & B" did not face the same problems of canon and authenticity that Jack White did with the White Stripes' mythologized version of the blues. In this context, framing Motown's "Sound of Young America" as European-style Pop art was no different from Andy Warhol's infamous work with Brillo boxes and Campbell's Soup cans. As Pop visual artists incorporated mass-produced images into their work, the Who were emboldened to incorporate those types of images into their own efforts—or even commodify themselves. The White Stripes were engaging an iteration of blues music that was neither contemporary nor commercially mainstream in a twenty-first-century urban context. White's attempt to evade the role of the white appropriator by copying 1960s Pop art performance, while playing blues music that predates Pop art, was thus much more of a gamble.

White also displays a specific self-consciousness about his visual presentation. The White Stripes' second record, *De Stijl,* is named after the post–World War I Dutch art and design movement that prized formal simplicity, relying only on the use of primary colors, along with white and black. White has noted the De Stijl movement's influence on the White Stripes' approach to their performance and their music: "We walked into a drugstore and saw this bag of peppermint candy and I said 'That should be painted on your bass drum because you've been drumming like a little kid.' . . . I was really into furniture design for that [his time as an upholsterer] and I liked Gerrit Rietveld—he did a red-blue chair for De Stijl. And it really had meaning to me and to the band and the music and the aesthetic of our live performance."[55] The White Stripes' visual aesthetic exists on a continuum. It begins with De Stijl, and evolves into Pop.

THE ROLE OF CLOTHING IN BRITISH ROCK AND AMERICAN BLUES

When the curtain rises on the White Stripes' performance of their hit "Seven Nation Army" at the 2004 Grammy Awards telecast in Los Angeles, the audience hears the now familiar bass-register riff from White's down-tuned, octave-pedal-reinforced 1950s Kay hollowbody archtop—

White is well known for his love of off-brand vintage instruments. In a theater-in-the-round at the Staples Center, Jack White wears a plain black T-shirt, trousers with one red leg and one black, and red shoes. Meg White is dressed in a black sleeveless top and white pants. Strobing black and white circular targets bounce off the black scrim behind them. Meg's kit, notably the heads on her snare and bass drums, features red and white peppermint swirls; the amplifiers, too, are red. "Seven Nation Army" is an up-tempo, contemporary rock song with little in the way of blues or even blues-rock flourishes, so the bottleneck on White's left pinky finger, at first, seems incongruous.[56]

From the beginning of the Grammy performance, the band's color palette is on full display through their instruments and light show, but the Pop art cartoonishness of the Stripes' appearance is captured most starkly by their clothing. On this occasion, the Stripes mainly wear black and white, with Jack's pant leg offering a hint of red, but in other performances the color red might predominate. The style of clothing also changes depending on the venue—stage performance, interview, promotional materials, or album cover. For instance, instead of a T-shirt and trousers, Jack might wear an outfit designed by H Bar C during a photo shoot.[57] When Frith and Horne discuss clothing as an important component of British rock music, with musicians speaking the "language of fashion," the argument can certainly extend to American bluesman Robert Johnson's iconic pinstriped suit and fedora and White's emulation of that style both during his tenure in the White Stripes and in his solo career.[58] The White Stripes' art school conceptualization, by way of De Stijl and Pop art, is expressed through bold primary colors, along with black and white, and a playful yet stylish sensibility.[59]

After two verses of "Seven Nation Army," something quite unexpected happens. The White Stripes launch into a frenetic version of Son House's "Death Letter Blues," initiating a spectacular clash of musical and visual signifiers. House's tune is traditional, rural, Mississippi Delta: *acoustic.* The simple fact that Jack White is plugged in while playing the song presents a stark contrast between premodernity and technology. White plays his vintage Kay guitar, a favorite, along with his red JB Hutto Montgomery Airline guitar, and given that artists such as Jimmy Reed and Howlin' Wolf played the same guitar, it is a blues music signifier. House, though, never played electric. White is playing House's acoustic blues with a sound that is associated with amplified Chicago blues artists. The bottleneck slide fits more comfortably in a song that originated in a Delta blues framework, as it is a signifier of both Delta and urban blues: Blind Willie McTell, Son House, Muddy Waters, and Elmore James all used a bottleneck at one time or another. Over time, the slide became a rock signifier, with guitarists such as Jimmy Page and Jeff Beck serving as important channels, so the fact that White plays with it during the "Seven Nation Army" guitar breaks makes sense in retrospect. White's use of the Kay and the slide, signifiers of old or vintage equipment, as well as the blues, suggest that White is playing in a legitimate blues style. These items are signs of blues authenticity.

But every other signifier at play systematically dismantles any claim to blues legitimacy. The corporate Grammy crowd and the theater-in-the-round staging in the middle of the Staples Center—a twenty-thousand-seat arena that houses NBA and NHL sports teams and hosts world-famous pop, rock, country, R & B, and hip-hop acts—are certainly at odds with this early twentieth-century rural song that in its time period was commercially unsuccessful.[60] On stage, the peppermint swirl on Meg's drums signifies candy, which evokes both childhood innocence and consumer goods. The swirl also raises the specter of advertising, of the colorful toys incessantly marketed to children of all ages. Although White himself equates the honesty of children with the truth he sees emanating from the blues, childlike imagery or crass commercialization was never a standard element of the blues tradition.[61] It was not commonplace, for instance, for Delta or urban blues musicians to sing about children or childhood or to wear clothing that evoked the same.[62]

But it is through the color and lighting that the White Stripes' Grammy performance highlights their postmodern, Pop art style. The swirling black and white targets, alternating between circular and square-shaped, turn red, as does the entire backdrop, as soon as the opening riff of "Death Letter Blues" begins. The red is blinding, and the now colorful targets are reminiscent of Jasper Johns's 1955 neo-Dada painting *Target with Four Faces*. The work features four faces from the nose down above a green and yellow target set against a red background.[63] David McCarthy suggests that Johns's piece paved the way for Pop because he "painted these shapes in a gestural, though nonetheless representational style, that simultaneously emphasized the painted and objective, or created and factual, qualities of the resulting work." This juxtaposition between what is *real* and what is constructed is the under-

Figure 3. The White Stripes at the 46th Annual Grammy Awards Show, 2004. L. Cohen/WireImage/Getty Images.

current of much of White's creative output during the White Stripes era. Peter Blake, an important Pop artist, created another target in 1961 as homage to Johns's impact on Pop art called *The First Real Target?* That work has a black, white, blue, red, and yellow target set against a brown background, with the title of the painting at the top.[64]

Just as "Seven Nation Army" contains musical signifiers of modern rock, including White's use of 1990s-era effects pedals such as the DigiTech Whammy, the guitar solo at the end of "Death Letter Blues" speeds up so fast that it almost sounds like hardcore rock rather than Delta blues. White's willingness to mix and match the visual and musical signifiers in this Grammy performance apparently offended some blues purists. According to White,

> When we played our first shows, a lot of people were really mad at the colours we wore. To me, how we presented ourselves was to show people how stupid it is for them to think that, to play authentic blues, I'd have to dress like I'm from fucking Mississippi. Eric Clapton, for example, said he didn't like The White Stripes. He thought

we were having a laugh about Son House, playing "Death Letter" on the Grammys. People in that Stratocaster white blues scene didn't understand that we could dress in red and white and black, play in the simplistic way we did, and still be the blues.

White's use of the red, white, and black color scheme while playing a Delta blues cover on a national—and international—stage was deliberately designed to demonstrate just how arbitrary the racialized signifiers of so-called authentic blues are. White believes in blues authenticity, but he prefers to achieve it through autobiographical misdirection—using red, white, and black symbolism to mask his debt to red clay and Black bluesman iconography—and a punk rock ethos. For White, the blues is, above all, about honest self-expression as espoused in punk rock subcultures, and as long as he and Meg are delivering their version of the truth—in this case, passionately playing the music they love—to an audience, they are "the blues."[65] What they wear, and specifically how region affects their fashion, or how their stage is set up, has no bearing on their ability to play blues music.

In the White Stripes' official video for "Hardest Button to Button," Jack White wears the same outfit he had on for the Grammy show, though he is pretending to play his red Airline guitar instead of the Kay. Meg, however, is dressed differently. She is barefoot, wearing a red tank top and black pants. The video utilizes stop-motion animation and shows Meg and Jack playing music in the streets of New York City and in the PATH train station. In this uniquely self-referential video, the stop-motion editing visually simulates the song's musical sounds, as Jack and Meg move forward a step on each beat, with, at the end of the song, Jack and Meg appearing and disappearing in time to the music. The video's director, Michel Gondry, recalls, "When I heard the song, it was so incredible, I knew I had to do the video. It's the shape of the song that gave me the idea. The pattern, how it goes 'doot-doot-doot, doot, doot, doot, doot, doot.' This makes me think of 1, 2, 3, 4 . . . 4, 8, 12, 16 . . . 2, 4, 8, 16, 32."[66] The colorful and playful nature of the visuals draws attention to the constructedness of the video, underscoring the Pop art dichotomy of the concrete and the imaginary. Due to the stop-motion effect, Jack and Meg are rendered blues-rock fantasy figures.[67]

Even more striking than the video is animated television program *The Simpsons'* homage to the "Hardest Button to Button" video in the "Jazzy and the Pussycats" episode, which aired September 17, 2006. This installment signifies wittily on the source material, underscoring Jack White's and the White Stripes' self-conscious visual presentation in service to showing their audience the precarious nature of blues authenticity. Bart Simpson becomes obsessed with practicing the drums. One day while drumming in the street, as "Hardest Button to Button" plays in the background, Simpson literally runs into the White Stripes. Mimicking the stop-motion animation from the original video, and because Meg and Jack are also drumming in the street, the trio crash into each other at an intersection. Meg and Jack are wearing the same outfits from the video, while Bart is wearing an orange T-shirt with blue shorts and blue shoes. His drum kit is blue. It is notable that the show's director gave Bart a color scheme as well. At the start of the clip, Bart drums from home to the school bus—the driver comments, "Ooh trippy"—to school and beyond, advancing on the beat like the original video. The concept of arty cartoonishness evolves from Hamilton's, Lichtenstein's, and Warhol's use of cartoons as Pop art to the White Stripes' cartoonish live show to Gondry's decision to use stop-motion—a cartoon animation technique—in his video to that same technique being mimicked in an animated television series in which the White Stripes themselves become cartoon characters.[68]

Within the context of Pop art, the White Stripes' trajectory from cartoonish live action figures to animated characters on an iconic television series is the logical next step. Given that an important element of Pop art is the artist's embrace of mass culture, the White Stripes' cartoonish self-representation for a mass audience falls neatly within Pop art principles. And it is the White Stripes' Pop art performance that helps them forge a blues identity, despite their complicated racial and historical challenges. White discovered that his band could overcome a potential political obstacle with an art project. The White Stripes used Pop art to playfully appropriate and depoliticize extremely powerful techniques of persuasion and control in order to "resolve" the complicated racial history of the blues. After all, behind the discourse of blues authenticity stands genuine racial, political, and socioeconomic oppressions.

When White asserts that red, white, and black are "the most powerful color combination of all time, from a Coca-Cola can to a Nazi banner," should audiences be disconcerted by his casual invocation of a fascist regime that similarly set out to glamorize the politics of racial authenticity with a powerful visual aesthetic that encompassed fashion, propaganda, and mass media?[69] In her 1975 article "Fascinating Fascism," Susan Sontag laments Nazi Party filmmaker Leni Riefenstahl's then recent social and political rehabilitation. She believes that audiences are willing to accept whitewashed accounts of Riefenstahl's past due, in part, to the Pop art movement. With the erosion of the division between high and low culture, audiences are able to view "Nazi art with knowing and sniggering detachment, as a form of Pop art." Sontag continues, "The ironies of pop sophistication make for a way of looking at Riefenstahl's work in which not only its formal beauty but its political fervor are viewed as a form of aesthetic excess."[70] Pop art's apolitical orientation allows for audiences to engage with images that in other contexts may be unpalatable. As a result, a Coca-Cola can or a Nazi banner can be aesthetically pleasing to an audience if a Pop artist inserts the image into a larger work of art or an audience member reads the image through a Pop art lens.

Did the White Stripes' use of Pop art visuals distract their audience from pertinent concerns about race and the blues, or did they simply enact a liberating free play of musical and visual signifiers? I contend that when Clapton suggested that the White Stripes were "having a laugh" at Son House, he misunderstood their intentions.[71] They were not laughing at Son House; they were responding to the joke of signification around race and blues authenticity.

White once asserted, "I always said that if you can't handle how the White Stripes looked, then we can't be in this room together sharing this same music. Don't bother with us, go find a different band."[72] Jack White invented himself as a postmodern hybrid of the early to mid-twentieth-century blues figure as seen through the lens of a 1960s British visual aesthetic, creating a new type of white blues band. The White Stripes' visual presentation did not disrupt their fans' positive reception of the music, as the band's raw, stripped-down musical style supported popular notions of the simple but passionate nature of the blues. White's efforts allowed him to sort out the audience members who did not get the joke, and that tactic served the band well during their fourteen-year run.

THE WHITE STRIPES' "BALL AND BISCUIT" AND THE FICTIONAL OUTLAW BLUESMAN

During the White Stripes era, Jack White enunciated a sustained autobiographical performance through a highly self-conscious visual presentation and intentional fabrication of his biography through the music press—but how is White's autobiographical self-invention expressed *sonically?* In this section, I explore White's vocal sounds and lyrical performance of the mythical blues bad man in "Ball and Biscuit" from the White Stripes record *Elephant.*[73] In a short article White wrote about Charley Patton for the *Observer* in November 2003, he stakes out an unequivocal position: "The blues are closer to honesty than the sort of music that's been going on for the past 20 or 30 years. Patton, Robert Johnson, Bukka White were doing honest, truthful music 80 years ago—it's the most beautiful music ever made. It's the twentieth century art form that will never be surpassed."[74] When White speaks of the blues it is clear that he holds very specific ideas about what is at the root of both *the blues* generally—as a tradition, as a feeling—and blues as a form of musical performance.

In the January 2010 issue of *Rolling Stone,* White claims that Jay-Z's music is resonant for him because it is suggestive of the blues: "I think that what he's saying in his lyrics is honest. His ideas about metaphor are really reflective about what struggle is."[75] At first glance it may seem as if Son House or Blind Willie McTell has little to do with hip-hop, but for White it is the element of struggle, both in the life of the artist as well as in their music-making process, that is most compelling. For White, the blues *is* struggle, and he does all he can during his own performances to ensure that he both experiences and evokes hardship. As White explains in the documentary film *The White Stripes: Under Great White Northern Lights,*

> I like to do things to make it *really* hard on myself. Like, for example, if I drop a pick, to get another pick I've gotta go all the way to the back of the stage to get another one. I don't have picks all taped to my microphone stand. I put the organ just far away enough that I have to leap to get to it to play different parts of a song. It's not handy to jump from one thing to the next. I always try to push it a little bit farther away, so I have to work harder and get somewhere.[76]

This view of the blues as a form born of personal difficulties goes hand in hand with the privileging of the rural, primitive, mysterious, and dangerous bluesman archetype. Elijah Wald ticks off the clichés associated with the "popular [white] image of an old-time blues singer" in his book *Escaping the Delta:* "He is male and black, of course. He plays guitar. He is a loner and a rambler, without money or a pleasant home. He is a figure from another world, not like the people next door, or anyone in your family, or anyone you know well. And his music is haunting, searing, and cuts you to the bone." Patton is one such "figure from another world," as suggested in White's words: "Listening to Patton's music may be difficult for some nowadays. It requires a certain bit of attention to, or ignorance of, minute scratches, and whistles to really feel the emotion of his music. But when it clicks, you are entranced, and are drawn into a new mysterious world, where Patton is the reporter of the troubled times."[77] White is correct, of course, to mention the difficult historical context from which these early blues artists emerged. What can be problematic is when a given historical context, or the specific origin stories of some early blues artists, becomes a fixed, timeless, essential identity that is applied to all. Or at least to the so-called *authentic* blues artists. While White carefully resists the conventional, earnestly appropriative path of the white bluesman for himself, in his article about Patton he advances familiar tropes about authentic bluesmen's otherworldly qualities.

Historian Grace Hale rejects the idea, implicit in accounts as far back as Handy's 1941 autobiography, of the blues as a primitive music made by a primitive people. She sees the blues as an artfully constructed form of music that allowed an oppressed people agency through the power of self-creation:

> With their sounds and words, blues musicians created a rebel persona, a romanticized black figure who said no to hard work and yes to personal pleasure. The blues rebel announced that transformation was possible, that individual black lives could not be contained and controlled by whites. It is more than ironic, then, that later white fans understood the music as the somehow pure, "outside of history" voice of rural black southern "folk." . . . Rather than an artistic and commercial creation, the blues rebel became a "real" black identity, proof that African Americans—especially southern rural

people "uncontaminated" by modernity—lived and felt more deeply than modern whites repressed and alienated by modern life.[78]

When White asks, "Can the modern listener used to albums recorded on computers let down his or her guard enough to hear Patton's story?" he is using a general fear of technological alienation to reinforce the concept of the unspoiled, authentic Black blues performance.[79] And in "Ball and Biscuit," White, through his vocal performance and his lyrics, does his best sonic impersonation of an authentic, hypersexual, and potentially violent Black bluesman—further perpetuating the myth of the bad man. While White's vocal performance is undeniably an exercise in racial mimicry, his track also layers, through his music and lyrics, elements of his own autobiography on top of the preconstructed blues narrative, extending the archetype while signaling White's acceptance of the fiction involved in even the most "authentic" autobiographical tropes of the bluesman.

Exploring White's blues self-fashioning, here I focus on his vocals while listening through the horn of what is commonly referred to as a Delta blues style of singing. In his seminal work *Deep Blues,* Robert Palmer writes, "The Mississippi Delta blues musicians sang with unmatched intensity in a gritty, melodically circumscribed, highly ornamented style that was closer to field hollers than it was to other blues."[80] Wald adds, "There is no mistaking the traces of traditional moans and hollers in popular blues songs, and still more so in the performance styles of many, if not most of the singers."[81] These "moans" and "hollers" are such a mainstay in modern American popular music that they are largely taken for granted; however, an early twenty-first-century Northerner like Jack White must self-consciously adopt the styles for songs such as "Ball and Biscuit." In Andrew Legg's detailed taxonomy of gospel vocal styles he draws close connections between the sounds of gospel and other popular music forms. As he notes, "Researchers are beginning to now credit African American gospel music as being one of the key underpinning influences in the development of the juggernaut that has become contemporary popular music throughout the twentieth and twenty-first centuries."[82] Legg sees gospel vocals as closely tied to blues singing styles, and a common link from early moans and hollers to the sounds of the blues, R & B, rock and roll, and other popular vocal forms.

White's vocals in "Ball and Biscuit" have a distinct gritty, almost dirty tone. Legg refers to this as "gravel tone": "The tonal characteristics of the African American gospel 'voice' are as rich and as varied as the number of singers. The 'gravel' in the voice—alternatively referred to as 'rasp' 'grit' or 'hoarseness'—used by many singers is a commonly applied general vocal characteristic that also functions as a means of creating an impassioned emphasis and added intensity to a word or phrase."[83] This gravelly sound is a characteristic of White's singing voice in a general sense, but it is more pronounced when he sings quieter blues numbers rather than screamed-out rock tunes. For White, the gravel serves as a mark of passion, feeling, and struggle. As we have seen, White positions struggle as an index of blues authenticity, so whether he is attempting to represent or to participate directly in struggle through vocal or guitar performance, or even by nonergonomic stage setups, the feeling of struggle is his self-conscious, expressive goal. One of White's favorite Delta blues artists, Son House, sings with a gravel tone in songs like "Grinnin' in Your Face" and "John the Revelator." It is not difficult to hear the similarities in vocal inflection between White and House, but it is most pronounced when White adds what musicologists identify as a "blues inflection" to selected words throughout "Ball and Biscuit."

According to Legg, "Gospel singers will often superimpose a 'blues inflection' or minor pentatonic improvised embellishment on a gospel melody that is of a predominantly major tonality, resulting in a marked shift in both sound, intent and affect that recalls the 'down home' sound of the blues."[84] When Legg says "down home," he refers to stereotypical notions of blues legitimacy: the "down home" blues sound is possible only if produced by Black, rural, socioeconomically-oppressed people. At 00:26 White sings the first two lines: "It's quite possible that I'm your third man, **girl /** But it's a fact that I'm the seventh **son.**" In addition to the gravel already present in White's voice, he adds a blues inflection to the bolded last word of each line: "girl" and "son," at 00:29 and 00:33, respectively. It is this blues inflection that comes closest to a reproduction of that elusive sound of struggle that so many would-be blues performers strive for, and, within the narrow confines of blues authenticity, fail to capture. White puts emphasis on those words that help add emotion and a sense of pain to the song. His voice serves as an aural representation of grief or sadness as it reveals a small catch, like the crack that comes at the onset of tears. It rather faithfully mimics the "gritty, melodically circumscribed, highly ornamented style" Palmer praises.[85] White places emphasis on the exact same words as he repeats the same lines three more times during the song. White makes a conscious choice about which lyrics to emphasize, and throughout the song he uses the blues infection for the words "girl" and "son" without exception. Why does White choose those words to emphasize and imbue with emotional resonance? It is probable that he sees himself as a narrator and character, and the people he sings about as other characters in a story. He speaks directly to a female character whom he calls "girl," and speaks about himself alternately as a "man" and a "son." By emphasizing "girl" and "son," he communicates who the two most important people in the story are to the audience. These two words, "girl" and "son," common in blues songs, hark most directly back to childhood, although, of course, the blues are not normally correlated with children. Later in the song, White uses the blues inflection as his narrator suggests that his would-be paramour find out more about his reputation—his special gifts. In these lines, otherwise mundane words such as "know" and "it" can refer to either the narrator's sexual prowess or perhaps his supernatural powers. It is important for those words to stand out, as they point toward the narrator's unique masculine gifts: he is either a regular human who happens to be an outstanding lover—the best this girl will have had to date, or perhaps ever—or he is a magical being who will cast a love spell over her.[86]

Another vocal inflection White uses in most of his songs, live and on record, is the soft grunt. Legg asserts,

> The use of the "grunt" . . . is in evidence in two early field recordings of "Jumpin' Judy" from the 1930s (Afro-American Spirituals, Work Song, and Ballads). In the liner notes, [Wayne D.] Shirley writes; "The rhythmic grunts on this record indicate the work blows of the pick or axe". The Arkansas version illustrates a constant drum-like pulse underlying the work song, whilst the Mississippi version of the same tune includes a wider-spaced, more punctuating percussive "grunt" to which Shirley refers. In its gospel context, the grunt occurs less frequently and is usually a loud, short expulsion of air on a non-specified pitch which punctuates sentences and phrases, underlining the pulse or beat within the phrase.

When White grunts "yeah," he uses it as punctuation, but his grunts tend to both accentuate a sentence and introduce a new, musical one. Most of the time, White's grunts occur just before or in the middle of an extended guitar solo, as at 01:46, where his "yeah" comes before his first guitar break. Rather than being reminiscent of the "work blows of the pick or axe," his grunts are seductive and alluring.[87] He uses his voice to almost hypnotize his intended. If she is not intrigued by his words, perhaps she will be won over by his voice or his guitar.[88]

These grunts also sometimes blur into longer raps or a line of talk-singing. Legg refers to this as "song-speech." According to Legg, "Song-speech is similar to operatic recitative where the gospel singer delivers a lyric that is either half sung/half spoken or vacillates between a melodic and a spoken phrase."[89] White exhibits song-speech throughout most of the song. His style is a hybrid, with talking for most of a line and the feel of singing coming through the blues inflection at the end of the line. Even so, his overall vocal performance is still reminiscent of singing when compared to his extension of grunts that turn into entirely spoken lines. When White says "Yeah" at 00:39, he uses the spoken words that follow as an aural form of swagger, in line with the "rebel persona" Hale discusses.[90] Like a peacock, he struts in front of the woman he is trying to impress and coerce into bed. He bookends his guitar solo with such spoken lines, giving the guitar a chance to speak for him and his erotic power when words fail him. Here, he is the mythical violent bluesman who is willing to do whatever it takes to assert his masculinity, to be known as an outlaw or a bad man, including conjuring up the old racial stereotype of the hypersexed, Black male rapist. If the girl does not catch his drift, that is, will not sleep with him, he just may have to force her, harm her, or even kill her. Here the threat of violence is interchangeable with sexual coercion, as White's voice contains all of the suggestive sexual energy and menace he can muster.[91]

Lyrically, there are numerous lines that suggest sexual innuendo, coercion, and possible violence, but for all of the obvious and amusingly crude insinuations, there are some more subtle double entendres. The first example is the title of the song. The "ball and biscuit" is the nickname of a vintage condenser microphone, the 1935 Standard Telephones and Cables 4021. White's fascination with period instruments and recording processes is well documented, so the title aligns with White's musical aesthetic. If he uses a ball-and-biscuit microphone and records, if not on wax discs, at least on analog tape, he might be able to replicate the sound of those great Black bluesmen. Fittingly, the title evokes a sort of sexual liaison plus a snack, as numerous blues songs, across generations, contain such references. It is through the self-conscious construction of the title of a blues song with such a double meaning that illustrates White's willingness to add to an existing fictional bluesman narrative. Writing a song called "Ball and Biscuit," which is, on the surface, about a vintage microphone with a funny shape but is really about sex, death, and braggadocio, allows White access to the pantheon of blues players whose wild, studio-constructed personas did not necessarily have much to do with their regular lives.

White writes his own entry in the ledger of bluesman mythology when he adds an autobiographical reference in a line he repeats in the song: "It's a fact that I'm the seventh son." This line, like many of White's lyrics, is a biblical reference, which fits with elements of White's stated autobiography: White grew up the youngest of ten children in a Catholic family, and both of his parents worked for the Catholic Church. These are undisputed facts, but White does have a reputation for fictionalizing pieces of his biography in the vein of rock stars before him such as Jim Morrison and Bob Dylan. Despite audiences and the press being fully cognizant of White's marriage to, and divorce from, Meg White, White continued to refer to her as his "big sister" even after the White Stripes disbanded. As a result, many fans and members of the media assume that embellishments of other elements of White's autobiography might be discovered.

White gave a series of interviews in conjunction with the release of *Elephant* that suggest his statements about his upbringing are accurate. When profiled on *60 Minutes* in 2004, he told Mike Wallace that he almost chose a different career path: "I'd got accepted to the seminary in Wisconsin, and I was gonna become a priest, but the last second I thought, 'I'll just go to public school.'" When Wallace asked him what made him change his mind, he replied, "I had just gotten a new amplifier in my bedroom, and I didn't think I was allowed to take it with me."[92] And in an interview in a 2004 issue of Britain's the *Observer*, when talking about what he was like as an adolescent, White stated, "I wouldn't let myself enjoy anything. And remnants of that are still there. I don't do drugs, I don't get drunk, I don't vote. Girls I don't do. With this whole band, it's obvious how much we're forcing ourselves and limiting ourselves all the time."[93] If White was truthful in both interviews, in service to good, dramatic storytelling, he might have seen the necessity of creating a suitably rebellious bluesman character in "Ball and Biscuit." If White almost went to a seminary at fourteen and did not have sex, do drugs, or get drunk as a twenty-nine-year-old rock star, then in "Ball and Biscuit" the performer in him has no choice but to construct an alter ego just like the early twentieth-century bluesmen did.

White's autobiographical fictions extend to the realm of figures. He is known to be obsessed with the number three, an eccentricity that continues to pique the curiosity of fans and critics alike. The first line of "Ball and Biscuit," "It's quite possible that I'm your third man, girl," is just one in a long, but hardly exhaustive, list of autobiographical references to the number three: he uses "Jack White III" in his production credits, his record label is called "Third Man Records," his production company for his concert documentaries is called "Third Man Films," his publishing company is called "Third Man Books," and his vinyl pressing plant is called "Third Man Pressing." Both the White Stripes and the upholstery company he owned in Detroit—"Third Man Upholstery"—used a three-color scheme. He has mentioned in interviews that the film, *The Third Man,* is one of his favorites. White also changed his name for the duration of his 2005 U.K. tour to "Three Quid." When White brings his tripartite obsession lyrically into "Ball and Biscuit," it marries a persona he created as part of his verifiable autobiography to the blues tradition of autobiographical self-invention. When White renames himself Three Quid, he participates in the type of self-creation that Herbert Leibowitz, Timothy Dow Adams, and Paul John Eakin discuss in their texts as the necessary and inherent fictions within the autobiographical genre. White also takes part in the tradition of blues self-fashioning by artists such as W. C. Handy, Robert Johnson, and Tommy Johnson.

While White is the seventh son born into his nuclear family, in African American folklore and blues mythology it is the *seventh son of a seventh son* that is supposed to be endowed with special powers by God or by Satan. But this moment of self-mythologization, so convenient for Muddy Waters—in his lyrics for "I'm Your Hoochie Coochie Man," after the narrator claims that he was delivered into the world on July 7 at 7:00 by seven doctors, he states

He was born for good luck
And that you'll see
I got seven hundred dollars
Don't you mess with me . . .

—is useful for White's fictional rock star persona as well as his fictional blues persona.[94] After all, as the true seventh son of a seventh son, he would have out-of-this-world powers that would awe his would-be woman in the bedroom and outside of it.

BLUES IN THE PAST, HIP HOP IN THE FUTURE—MORE THAN JUST POSTMODERN PASTICHE

In this final part of the chapter, I examine the ways in which Jack White's solo work in various forms—an unexpected musical collaboration and a provocative hip-hop-style music video—serves as postmodern pastiche and allows for his artistic and autobiographical reinvention. White is seen by many as a man out of step with the current music scene, privileging musical production and dissemination techniques that eschew digital technology. However, according to Josh Eells in his 2012 *New York Times* article "Jack Outside the Box: Jack White Is the Coolest, Weirdest, Savviest Rock Star of Our Time," "White famously doesn't own a cellphone, but he isn't the Luddite he's often made out to be. He has an iPod; he knows how to Skype. His friend Conan O'Brien says he'll occasionally e-mail to say he laughed at a tweet."[95] He prefers vintage instruments and analog recording practices. Yet, as a post–White Stripes solo artist and producer, he has collaborated with mainstream recording artists Jay-Z, Beyoncé, Alicia Keys, and Insane Clown Posse; he used Pro Tools to edit his 2018 album *Boarding House Reach;* and the video for "Freedom at 21" from *Blunderbuss* utilizes standard hip-hop and grindhouse video tropes with a dash of 1980s hair metal aesthetics thrown in. It is important to note that even though "Freedom at 21" is a rock song, for White, the blues is the foundation for all of his music, regardless of style: "With The White Stripes, I wanted to have a new blues . . . 'Seven Nation Army' has become a soccer chant to some people, but to me it's a blues song, a struggle of one person against the world. The sound, the rhythm, is not what someone would label blues, and I think that happens with a lot of songs on this album [*Blunderbuss*] as well. I consider all of it to be the blues, but I'm trying to present it in a way that shakes it up for me and the listener."[96]

It is precisely White's manipulation of image and autobiographical fabrication that keeps the audience and media off balance and allows him to form a hybrid musical and personal identity as an iconoclast who is equal parts pop sellout and indie hipster. Rather than viewing him as inauthentic, I believe it is more useful to see White's autobiographical self-fashioning as a self-conscious pastiche that has allowed for an unruly yet productive artistic expression. His postmodern approach to his creative and business affairs gave White the freedom to engage blues music as an art project while he was in the White Stripes, and this tack enables White to thrive as a label head, producer, and solo artist who defies musical categorization and subverts his reputation as a humorless *artiste*. This particular description has become so entrenched, mainly due to his long-standing, vocal opposition to fans' use of cell phones and social media during his live shows, that in 2006 the music blog *Stereogum* published an entry with the headline: "Jack White Does Have a Sense of Humor," in which the author relays a story of White's friendly and relaxed interaction with fans during a Raconteurs video shoot.[97] In 2012, while on the road in support of his first solo record, *Blunderbuss*, White played for less than one hour at a concert at New York City's Radio City Music Hall because of poor sound and a lack of audience enthusiasm, and he attempted to ban social media usage altogether during other shows on the tour.[98] White's decision to use a visual medium—video—to signify on this aspect of his reputation is not a surprising choice, given that visuals, moving and still, can vividly tell an individual's life story.

In "Posing: Autobiography and the Subject of Photography," Paul Jay examines photographer Cindy Sherman's self-portraits as works of autobiography. As part of a 1987 retrospective at the Whitney Museum of Art in New York City, Sherman offered a three-part series in which the first set of photographs evoke familiar pop culture images. Jay asserts, "Each pose confronts the viewer with banal forms of subjectivity utterly familiar from a mass culture in which not only dress and gesture but personality itself is constructed out of a social nexus of commodified images and ideal types." In one photo from the first set, *Untitled #90*, Sherman poses in shadow with light illuminating her face and one of her legs. A cigarette dangles from her mouth, and her head is slightly cocked back in a haughty rock star pose. In the second part of her series, her self-portraits turn those mass-marketed, socially desirable images on their head. For example, in *Untitled #137*, Sherman faces forward, in muted light, wearing a V-neck shirt under a rumpled robe. Her hair is unkempt and she appears pale and dazed. Jay posits, "In the first series the underlying sense that her subjects are dominated by subtle and not-so-subtle forms of social and cultural discipline—which erases any trace of individual subjectivity—surfaces in the second series in an explicit way as Sherman poses herself as a woman profoundly disturbed, disoriented, and defeated." In the final series of images, body parts are photographed in a chaotic manner, as in *Untitled #167*, in which a nose, an ear, and a hand, are strewn across a patch of dirt.[99] Jay sees the evolution of the self in these three sets of photographs as, if not an unfolding conventional autobiography, a set of images that can "be construed as recording her 'life,' even her experience and her likeness," with the larger narrative arc speaking to the inevitability and consequences of objectification. Jay explains, "The self starts out in these photographs as a wholly commodified object, descends into images that bespeak the eventual horror such a situation can lead to, and finally explodes the individual amidst a pile of rubble."[100] In Jay's reading of Sherman's photographs, commodification enacts violence on bodies and creates a seemingly permanent rupture—but what can be made of a subject who willingly commodifies his own image? What autobiographical story would such a figure tell?

White's subversive solo projects, in which he is firmly in control of his brand, allow for his autobiographical self-creation. As Jay posits, "Visual memory, the 'reading' of images from the past—be they fixed in a photograph or fluid in the mind's eye—can often be integral to the construction of that identity in autobiographical works."[101] For Jay, a photograph does not have to be literal; it can instead be an image that the mind conjures. And autobiography does not have to be a conventional, book-based enterprise. I will take this argument further and suggest that a photograph does not necessarily have to be in the distant past to create a memory; the memories can be created in real time with each camera click.

In 2011, Jack White collaborated with Insane Clown Posse on Mozart's bawdy "Leck mich im Arsch," which literally translates to "Lick Me in the Arse."[102] Additionally, his video clip for "Freedom at 21," created by the renowned hip-hop director Hype Williams, who has helmed music videos for Tupac, Biggie Smalls, L. L. Cool J, Jay-Z, and Kanye West, was released in 2012. I read both of these works as a series of photographs that together offer White an opportunity for self-representation and, ultimately, self-invention and even reinvention. Furthermore, it is

White's inventiveness with postmodern pastiche that demonstrates the fluidity of his hybrid artistic expression. He is an artist and a businessman who retains the legal rights to the master recordings for his work with the White Stripes, Raconteurs, Dead Weather, and his solo efforts. As Eells explains, "White walked back to a room called the Vault, which is maintained at a constant 64 degrees. He pressed his thumb to a biometric scanner. The lock clicked, and he swung the door open to reveal floor-to-ceiling shelves containing the master recordings of nearly every song he's ever been involved with. Unusually for a musician, White has maintained control of his own masters, granting him extraordinary artistic freedom as well as truckloads of money."[103] He owns his music and his self-presentation. He is both the product *and* the producer.

In the trailer for "Leck mich im Arsch," White, dressed in a black T-shirt, peacoat, and bowler hat, is straight-faced while a member of his crew, similarly dressed in a black suit and matching hat, playing the role of a reporter, asks him about Third Man Records' upcoming projects. White feigns ignorance as Joseph Utsler, a.k.a. Shaggy 2 Dope, and Joseph Bruce a.k.a. Violent J, of Insane Clown Posse (ICP), sneak up on him and his interviewer. ICP walks all the way up to the camera, until they are in extreme close up. It is important to note here that ICP is a frequent target of almost universal critical scorn. In *Blender*'s September 2003 list of the "50 Worst Artists in Music History," the writers gleefully declared ICP number one, with this brutal description of the group: "Two trailer-trash types who wear face paint, pretend to be a street gang and drench cult devotees in cheap soda called Faygo, Violent J and Shaggy 2 Dope are more notorious for their beef with Eminem (who pistol-whipped an ICP homey [*sic*] in 2001) than their ham-fisted rap-rock music. They claim that a 'dark carnival' visited them one night, prophesied impending apocalypse and made them its messengers. Between this circus gospel, they find plenty of time to rap about 40-ouncers and venereal disease."[104] White's grim face, as Shaggy 2 Dope and Violent J, wearing full clown makeup, loom in the frame, signifies on his reputation as a serious artist who only collaborates with fellow critical darlings, revealing his playful side. In fact, this clip allows the audience to watch White transform, in real time, from an indie artist, producer, and label head who, in certain circles, enjoys a godlike status, to a transgressor who is willing to bless an unholy collaboration between Mozart and Insane Clown Posse regardless of how many fans and critics he may alienate.[105]

The editing in the trailer, with its cuts on the beat as the duo move ever closer to the camera, is reminiscent of a series of still camera clicks with the resultant snapshots acting as autobiographical puzzle pieces, each pose propelling White's evolving identity and personality forward in real time. This is reminiscent of the idea advanced by Paul John Eakin and others that autobiography is a necessarily fictive structure in which one self-creates as they construct their narrative.[106] An autobiographical narrative is not comprised of the static experiences of a life. It is a vehicle for the emergence of that life, with its subject finding him- or herself as a result of the storytelling process. White's movement from unsullied critical darling who works with artists such as Loretta Lynn and the Rolling Stones to potential sellout who gives a platform to suspect performers such as Insane Clown Posse is reflected in this brief video clip.[107]

White's black coat and hat and ICP's clown makeup also support the fictional element of autobiography. In an interview with Camille Dodero in the *Village Voice,* Violent J talks about his experience working with White: "The one thing that was really interesting? When it came time to film the pictures? We put our make-up on. He put his hat on. You know what I'm saying? He put on his black hat and his black coat and we put on our makeup. We both had our thing. . . . We went back to the studio, and we put our normal clothes back on, and we took our make-up off. He had [his] shtick and we had ours. He has to have his black hat everywhere." By the end of the video teaser, we know White has unapologetically produced a hybrid of high and low culture through his pairing with ICP, while offering a meta experience of the same, with Mozart's "Leck mich im Arsch" itself being an example. The transgressive potential of such hybridity was not lost on Violent J: "People are tripping out because the respected meets the non-respected in every way. That's what the whole news about this is."[108]

In "Freedom at 21," after the grindhouse-style title screen with the names of the song and video director, we see two of White's public selves. One self is more or less the persona he has held to since the formation of the Dead Weather in 2009. He is wearing a black leather jacket with a boa on one of the lapels, black print trousers, and mirrored sunglasses. The other White is an outlaw, perhaps the outlaw in the White Stripes' "Ball and Biscuit" come to life. This White wears a black pinstriped suit and a fedora, like an out-of-context Robert Johnson, living in an altogether different temporal, regional, racial, and gendered moment. The protagonist of "Ball and Biscuit," a stand-in for a Delta or Chicago bluesman, would most likely not be in an interracial sexual situation, speeding in a lime green 1970 Hemi Cuda, and getting arrested by a *female* police officer. It is also ironic that, in an era of mass incarceration, a video for a song called "Freedom at 21" would take place, in part, in a jailhouse. Throughout the video, both Whites are glam and wearing heavy eyeliner, perhaps as homage to 1980s hair metal videos, complete with a video vixen on the hood of the automobile. Both Whites wear pancake makeup, but the lawbreaker's powder is heavier. The outlaw's look makes him seem more alien, even more of a fictional autobiographical self—perhaps the part that can relate to Charley Patton and other early bluesmen.[109]

In this segment of the video, White poses as he sings, without his guitar, in front of a wall. His movements are playful; he even sticks out his tongue. The stuttering imagery on the beat is similar to the cutting on the beat in the trailer for "Leck mich im Arsch." This effect serves as a series of still photographs, capturing White's expression as his identity and autobiography evolve. It is unlikely White would have made this video fifteen years ago. In fact, he was public in his disappointment in the 2003 Sophia Coppola–directed video for the White Stripes' cover of Burt Bacharach's "I Just Don't Know What to Do with Myself." The video featured a pole-dancing Kate Moss, which White deemed too sexy.[110]

"Freedom at 21," a rock song, with its hip-hop and grindhouse features—including the video vixens, a fast car, outlaw behavior, and even White singing in front of a wall, 1990s hip-hop style—once again demonstrates his musical hybridity. And his mixing and matching of high and low culture in "Leck mich im Arsch" and multigenre signification in "Freedom at 21" demonstrates White's determination to grapple with the well-worn racial stereotypes and cultural appropriations inherent in white interpretations of the blues, and other forms of music originated by Black Americans. White's use of stereotypes reshapes arguments about American music, and showcases the fundamental influence of Black musicianship and style on all of American culture.

White is truly a postmodern figure, as he does not engage in conventional approaches to authenticity. While in the White Stripes, he avoided that path, recognizing the unresolvability of the problem of blues authenticity. Post–White Stripes, in his artistic work, and in his business dealings, White's identity has remained fluid. He is as comfortable producing and performing with Alicia Keys, Jay-Z, or Beyoncé as he is working with Loretta Lynn or Wanda Jackson. He can play the role of the antitechnology-blues-rock icon or he can blithely produce an obscene Mozart canon for Insane Clown Posse, one of the most reviled musical acts of this generation. For White, it does not really matter, as he heartily embraces the fictions behind the construction of a self and the freedom they bring.

In the video for "Freedom at 21," White revels in his self-commodification, and he does not show any obvious signs of regret over his participation in the various hip-hop, hair metal, and grindhouse tropes, including the highly sexualized and objectifying female images. In his collaboration with Insane Clown Posse, White gleefully "explodes the individual [his own hipster icon image] amidst a pile of rubble." All of these actions constitute a process of autobiographical self-invention and reinvention for White. Jay further clarifies how an autobiography can unfold, even unintentionally, during the act of artistic expression: "[Sherman's] portraits examine the cultural conditions in which identity is fashioned, and as selected and shown by Sherman they are given the shape of a narrative about that investigation. Seen from this perspective, her self-portraits take the shape of something like an autobiographical metanarrative about the course of one artist's investigation of subjectivity, scrutinizing the very concepts of identity and subjectivity in a way that turns that act into a memoir of itself."[111] In White's case, his autobiographical, and sometimes anti-autobiographical, acts are enacted in a conscious manner. Yet the general idea of an artist telling an autobiographical story about him or herself, simply through the act of selecting his or her art materials or making a decision about how to dress or how to present him or herself in a music video or in a *Rolling Stone* interview, is also valid. Jack White enunciates his evolving autobiographical identity through all of these processes, with a full understanding of, and apparent comfort with, his fluid position as both an objectified commodity and the subject in control of his own commodification.

5 The Blues Apprenticeship

Racialized Conventions of the Acolyte

During the 1920s, Charley Patton mentored Chester Burnett, who would later be known as Howlin' Wolf. In the decade that followed, Son House mentored young, aspiring Delta bluesmen, including Robert Johnson and Muddy Waters. And more than a generation later, in the 1960s, Texas bluesman Mance Lipscomb offered advice to a young blues guitar player named Taj Mahal.

A new generation of young African American artists work within a variety of American musical traditions and styles, many of which normally fall outside of the American commercial mainstream, who have or are currently engaged in musical apprenticeships. Classically trained vocalist, multi-instrumentalist, and singer-songwriter Rhiannon Giddens is a solo artist, and a founding member of the Americana group Carolina Chocolate Drops, whose work falls within the categories of Black old-time string music, blues, classic country, and Scottish mouth music; singer and multi-instrumentalist Valerie June performs in a variety of

American roots musical styles, including blues, gospel, soul, country, and bluegrass; and Gary Clark Jr. began his career as the next big thing in blues music—in fact, in a 2013 *Rolling Stone* article, blues icon Buddy Guy states, "He's as good as it gets. Gary reminds me of T-Bone Walker more than anybody I've ever seen. We're all trying to do this to keep this music alive, because the blues is not being played"—but he resisted that label and in recent years has branched out into R & B, soul, gospel, and hip-hop.[1] These artists have had white (and in one case, Black) mentors who helped them along their musical paths and aided them in achieving various degrees of notoriety and critical and commercial success. For Clark, it was blues guitarist Jimmie Vaughan; for Giddens, it was Black string band legend Joe Thompson and musician and producer T Bone Burnett; for June, it was Dan Auerbach of blues rock band the Black Keys; and for Howard, it was blues-rock musician and producer Jack White.

White has been on both sides of the apprenticeship paradigm. When he was fifteen years old, and living in Detroit, Michigan, he apprenticed to a local furniture upholster. It was during that time that White learned about the work of the Dutch De Stijl artist Gerrit Rietveld, whose simple primary colors inspired the White Stripes' color palette. Post–White Stripes, he has had brief apprenticeships in which he has served as a master for Brittany Howard, vocalist and guitarist for the band Alabama Shakes, who performs in various musical styles, including blues rock, Americana, and soul, and Ruby Amanfu, who is a singer-songwriter who provided vocals for White's solo record *Blunderbuss* and toured with his female backing band, the Peacocks. The Alabama Shakes also opened for White during the 2012 *Blunderbuss* tour. Both Amanfu and Howard recorded seven-inch singles for his Third Man Records Blue Series. Third Man Records serves as a vehicle for the development of emerging artists who record seven-inch singles produced by White. These collaborations are abbreviated apprenticeships, as they sometimes help launch the artists into a new level of public awareness and commercial success.

This chapter interrogates the role of the interracial apprenticeship in the development of a narrative blues persona. Where does autobiographical and biographical storytelling fit within these paradigms, and how do the participants use narrative to invent and reinvent themselves? In this chapter, I will consider the racial dynamics in organic, long-term, face-to-face apprenticeships, such as the ones between Clark and Vaughan, as well as short-term, institutionalized apprenticeships that are connected to state arts commissions and humanities foundations, such as the Mississippi Arts Commission Folk Art Apprenticeship program and the Sherman Holmes Blues Apprenticeship sponsored by the Virginia Foundation for the Humanities. I will also explore unconventional blues apprenticeships that exist across time and space, as exemplified by what I see as writer Ralph Ellison's influence on Clark's and Giddens's approaches to their artistic works.

This chapter also considers the role blues authenticity plays in the master-apprentice dynamic, necessitating a focus on the sociocultural backgrounds of the participants. It is understood that the blues master is so because he or she is an authentic exemplar of the blues, but to what degree is this designation bound up in restrictive approaches to blues authenticity? What impact do race, gender, class, and geographical background have on the normative blues apprenticeship pairings, and in what ways do the artists in this chapter subvert those expectations?

A standard feature of many state arts commissions and organizations is the folk apprenticeship program. These initiatives are meant to ensure the continuation of arts or crafts that might otherwise become extinct in coming generations unless they are passed on through formal, short-term apprenticeships. These relationships are generally predicated on the idea that both the master and the apprentice have experience working within the artistic discipline or craft, with the master bringing significantly more experience and expertise to the partnership. Perhaps not surprisingly, the organizations that offer blues apprenticeships are almost exclusively located in the southern region of the United States. Some examples of institutions that offer blues apprenticeships include the West Virginia Humanities Council West Virginia Folklife Apprenticeship Program, the Mississippi Arts Commission Folk Art Apprenticeship, the Virginia Humanities Virginia Folklife Apprenticeship Program, the Tennessee Arts Commission's Traditional Arts Apprenticeship Program, the South Carolina Arts Commission Traditional Arts Apprenticeship, and the Texas Folklife Apprenticeship Program.[2] Most of these apprenticeships strongly suggest that the master and apprentice have a shared cultural background. The West Virginia Folklife Apprenticeship Program, for instance, states in its application materials, "It is preferred, though not required, that masters and apprentices belong to the same cultural community."[3] The Mississippi Arts Commission Folk Art

Apprenticeship says that "preference will be given to master artists and apprentices who are members of the same community or cultural group"; the Virginia Humanities Virginia Folklife Apprenticeship Program mentions, "it is also preferred, though not required, that masters and apprentices belong to the same cultural community"; and the Louisiana Folklife Apprenticeship Program is most direct when it states that "preference is given to apprentices coming from the same culture as the master. This is not a program to teach traditions cross-culturally."[4] There are some formal apprenticeship programs, however, that do not dissuade interracial partnerships. For instance, even though the Texas Folklife's Apprenticeships in the Folk Arts program defines the traditional arts as "art forms practiced by a group of people who often share cultural values and/or heritage," they notably do not state a preference for intracultural apprenticeships.[5] Even the Virginia Folklife Program, one of the programs that sought to dissuade interracial apprenticeships, invited legendary Black Piedmont blues guitar player John Cephas and his white apprentice Marc Pessar to participate in 2006. Noting the racial and cultural differences between the two, Cephas asserts, "Whenever there is a listening ear, that's where I want to play. I don't have no preference. . . . These blues—this Piedmont style—touched Marc the way it has touched so many. It came from the black community, but has come to affect every ethnic group in the world."[6] Cephas's statement gestures at the politics of blues authenticity and cultural appropriation, with its many enduring questions: Does blues music belong to Black people? Do nonblack people have a legitimate right to play it? Do Black people play the music most authentically? Can nonblacks also play the blues authentically? And, perhaps most importantly, who benefits most from the blues financially? When you consider these questions in the context of the blues apprenticeship, where the (normatively Black) blues master shares his musical techniques and knowledge of blues history with someone who is not Black, and in most cases is white, these couplings can be fraught.

In many of the formal blues apprenticeship relationships, whether they are between people who share the same cultural background, or are comprised of people from different races, ethnicities, or cultures, the storytelling is a crucial component. As the West Virginia Folklife Apprenticeship Program states in their application materials, "These apprenticeships aim to facilitate the transmission of techniques and artistry of the forms, as well as their histories and traditions." While the art and craft of the blues might be passed down through limited verbal communication, with a mostly aural approach, the only way to disseminate its "histories and traditions" in a manner that reflects its connection to, and continuation of, folk storytelling is through the oral tradition.[7]

During the 2017–18 cycle of the West Virginia Folklife Apprenticeship Program, blues singer-songwriter Doris Fields, a.k.a. "Lady D," worked as a mentor to Xavier Oglesby, a blues and gospel performer. According to a July 2018 article in the *Charleston Gazette-Mail*, the pair, both African American, had a previous musical relationship that dated back to the 1990s, when they performed together in a play that lasted for years. In their new roles as master and apprentice, rather than focusing on playing music together, during their sessions they mostly spent their time talking. As Oglesby states, "You can take a form of music and like what you hear, but if you don't know the history behind the music, you don't appreciate it as much. . . . We as black people, we created this music. It teaches you to really appreciate what our history is in this country and the contributions that we have made. I value the blues. When she told me this history, it taught me to value that music more."[8] The idea that one needs to understand the historical and cultural context of the blues in order to fully appreciate its value is distinct but not all together divorced from the notion that one might be better suited to play the blues if one has had a certain set of experiences, or has been born into a particular body. These ideas situate the blues as more than just a style or form of music. The blues instead is an extension of the African American folk storytelling tradition in which it is the strength of the various tales—as measured through the emotional resonance and entertainment value shared in blues lyrics, stage banter during live performances, constructed blues personas, and promotional interviews in print or on film/television—that matters the most.

In the rest of this section, I will focus my attention on Debbie Bond, a white blues singer and guitarist, and former executive director of the Alabama Blues Project, a nonprofit organization that promotes the Alabama blues through educational and arts programming, who has participated in multiple interracial apprenticeships. Some of her musical partnerships are informal, as in the case of her pairings with legendary Alabama-based blues singer and guitarist Johnny Shines, and Mississippi/Alabama blues guitarist and singer Willie King. Bond also participated in an Alabama/Georgia State Council on the Arts Apprenticeship with blues guitarist, singer, and songwriter Eddie Kirkland, who was born in Kingston, Jamaica, and raised in Alabama.[9] For each of these relationships, I will consider the ways in which the politics behind the interracial blues apprenticeship can be even more complicated when more than one gender is represented. In this section, I will also focus on the storytelling aspects of the apprenticeship—those crucial moments where the master shares his knowledge about the blues, or teaches by telling stories about his own life.

Debbie Bond was born in California, but she moved with her family to Brighton, England, when she was eight years old. At twenty-four, she moved back to the United States, settling in Tuscaloosa, Alabama, where she became involved in the local blues scene. It was around this time that Bond met Shines. As she states in a fall 2018 interview with me, "My plan was to visit friends and work for a summer here in Tuscaloosa, Alabama. I heard Johnny Shines lived nearby in Holt. I had heard about Johnny and about his significance—that he had hung out with and really apprenticed himself to the notorious Robert Johnson." As one of the few living blues musicians who had known and played music with Johnson, Shines was sought out for information about the blues icon by scholars, critics, and fans during the 1960s blues revival and until his death. However, as Bond adds, "Johnny said that Robert wasn't too anxious to share his knowledge, although they were friends and traveled well together, that in fact Robert would make it hard for him to see his licks!"

Shines would prove to be a more generous master. After Bond shared a recording of her band—the Kokomo Blues Band—with him, he invited her to play music. In fact, the Kokomo Blues Band played many shows with Shines, eventually becoming his main local backing band. Bond did not play guitar in that band but instead sang background vocals and a few songs in a duet with Shines. Beyond what Bond undoubtedly learned playing music with Shines, it appears that she gained a deep sense of what it means to be a blues artist and how to approach one's craft through Shines's words. She shares that Shines gave her important advice as a young artist: "Debbie, if you are going to sing the blues—you're gonna get ugly sometimes." And to her question about why he had multiple jobs—including as a house painter and steelworker—and was a student until well into his seventies of various vocational trades, he responds, "Debbie, you always have to have something to fall back on." These lines might seem obvious, or even mundane, but I would argue that they demonstrate the ways in which a blues apprenticeship encompasses so much more than shared musical performance, or the teaching of musical technique or theory. Words, whether expressed through storytelling or communicated wisdom, are hallmarks of the blues apprenticeship. Autobiographical storytelling, particularly the act of sharing personal details about one's childhood or family life, can play a particularly strong role in these relationships. As Bond notes, "Besides my mentors sharing their stories through their songs, we were very close friends. When you travel the roads together, there is much shit-shooting and gabbing in the van. You stay together in the same hotels and hang at each others' houses. These people were my friends and mentors. Yes, I talked about my life with them too." Once again, these ideas are rooted in African American folk traditions. As we have seen through multiple examples throughout *Fictional Blues*, stories are sometimes passed from stranger to stranger, but more frequently these tales are shared between friends, or told by a parent to a child. These close friendship and familial bonds are an important component of the blues tradition because it is through these networks that people learn how to tell stories, as well as the cultural role and impact of these tales. As Bond elaborates, "He would tell me stories of his days on the road, hopping trains, his days on Beale Street in Memphis and Maxwell Street and the clubs in Chicago—how he knew musicians like Memphis Minnie, Howlin' Wolf, Muddy Waters, Big Mama Thornton. He described the joints, the music unions in Chicago, how he made money doing everything from house painting to photography in the blues places to make ends meet."[10] What is most striking here is the conversation Shines has about the other blues performers he has encountered throughout his long career. His telling stories about Big Mama Thornton or Howlin' Wolf demonstrates the importance of camaraderie between blues artists. This idea is reminiscent of Thornton sitting in the back of the van telling stories, with Muddy Waters to her right and Big Joe Turner over her left shoulder, in chapter 2. For Big Mama in that moment, her stories were certainly important, but even more so, it was vital for her to receive feedback from her blues peers in the form of positive call and response when she talked about her successes with "Hound Dog" and "Ball and Chain." While here Shines is not sharing stories with a peer, he is training his mentee to continue this tradition with her own peers, and with other artists whom she will mentor in the future.

Bond's relationship with Eddie Kirkland grew out of their working together at various "blues-in-the-schools programs." After the success of these programs, the Alabama Arts Council approached Bond about doing an official apprenticeship with Kirkland. As Bond explains,

> We received a grant to work together over a period of six months, meeting whenever we could as our schedules permitted—when Eddie was passing through Alabama or when we managed to also have a show together. I was always struck by Eddie's dogged determination—his cars and gear always duct-taped together. Another great musician who did not get the recognition he deserved. He was so creative musically—always thinking outside the box, finding different ways to play things. He told me to play guitar every day—even if for just ten minutes—good advice.

While this interaction was relatively short lived, Kirkland also communicated his wisdom to Bond, which she remembered in an interview more than two decades later. But, more importantly, this apprenticeship—one that was structured to have an artificial start and end date—was wonderfully unstructured. And this makes sense, as they already had a relationship prior to the formal partnership. But it also shows that these apprenticeships are predicated as much on the master's demonstration of the blues lifestyle as it is on storytelling. In her apprenticeships with Shines and Kirkland alike, Bond notes both of her masters' strength and unwavering work ethics in the face of significant financial hardships and a depressing lack of structural support for blues artists who carry important knowledge that should be passed on so it does not die out. For Shines, that lack of support led to his need to work "multiple jobs" into his seventies in order to survive, while for Kirkland, he had to find ways to get a good sound out of gear that was "duct taped together."[11] These are the lessons that convey important aspects of the blues musician's lifestyle, and they can also be shared with Bond's peers and future mentees.

Bond met Willie King a few days after Johnny Shines's death. They played together at a fundraiser for Shines's funeral expenses, and then he participated in multiple blues-in-the-schools programs through the Alabama Blues Project. Eventually, they began playing together regularly in juke joints: "Willie said the juke joint was the most important place to learn to play the blues. He said that if you could make the people happy in a juke joint you could play the blues anywhere." This is another example of an apprenticeship forming naturally between master and apprentice. In this case, it also appears that this pairing offered the most comprehensive apprenticeship relationship for Bond:

> This was the most in-depth mentorship I experienced—working with Willie. I was his fulltime guitar player and I was very nervous about it—I did a lot of wood-shedding! I wanted very badly to honor his sound and give him what I thought he wanted. Willie was nothing but deeply encouraging. He also encouraged me with my own music—and no matter where we were—he let me do one of my own songs on every set—whatever small or large stage we were on—and always insisted I did solos. The last thing he said to me was "Keep on pushing!"

In earlier apprenticeships, Bond expresses a reluctance to play the guitar in front of these esteemed blues guitar players, but King not only actively encourages her to play the guitar in his band but also showcases her talents by insisting she take solos:

> Willie showed me how important tone is—which is partly equipment—but more important the magic he had in his touch of his fingers on the fret board. It was scary the magic he had in his fingers. He also, like Eddie, played through old beat-up equipment—a non-American-made cheap Strat that he named the Red Rooster. But he knew how to make the strings sing and his guitar talk. I also learned a lot from Willie about stage presence. He was so relaxed and natural on stage—he didn't have a separate persona but was himself. . . . He also was very big on telling his story, the meaning of the music and the song. The blues tells a story; "look for the meaning in the music," he would say. He was also—what a great improviser. He taught me the magic of really being in the moment—making up words in the moment—getting the soul and spirit of the blues.

This affirms the blues as a storytelling art in which improvisation is central. Like the African American folk tradition in which storytellers build on existing stories to create new ones, the blues musician makes up verses based on the familiar experiences of themselves and others.

Whether these tales are based on fact or fiction makes no difference when expressing "the soul and spirit of the blues."[12]

Bond was frequently the only woman in the various bands when she performed with Shines, Kirkland, and King, but she felt comfortable in these spaces, though her gender did make her vulnerable to the male gaze and unwanted sexual advances:

> I grew up with two brothers, so maybe that helped being a woman in a man's world. I was always comfortable hanging and being one of the guys—and liked it. I was always treated with respect by all these bluesmen and they encouraged me. I think Eddie was the only one who was a big flirt—but nothing I couldn't handle, though I was single at the time. Jerry McCain tried it on one time—again when I was single—and I was able to affectionately laugh it off. I think they all appreciated my being a woman and wanting to play the blues and treated me with respect.

While Bond felt comfortable with the gender dynamics in her various apprenticeships, the intersecting racial and gender dynamics prove to be more fraught. Bond and Kirkland faced a series of potentially violent experiences while traveling together on the road, specifically because they were a Black man and white woman: "I know Eddie and I experienced some weird stuff traveling together, bordering on threatening behavior by white redneck men. For example, during our apprenticeship I was checking Eddie into a motel near my house. We were outside the motel talking by his car. A redneck screeched up aggressively in his pickup truck near where we were standing and looked at us menacingly. Eddie pulled out his gun and stood there casually but clearly with it in his hand resting on the hood of his car so the guy could see his gun. The dude pulled out and left."[13] What happens here is made possible by Bond's and Kirkland's different races and genders. The disapproving white man in the pickup truck is a reflection of racist anxieties about interracial relationships between Black and white people, specifically Black men and white women. It is unlikely that this man would have had an opinion if Bond had been a white man, and he certainly would not have noticed Kirkland talking to a Black woman. The interracial and mixed-gender apprenticeship can bring its own unique set of dangers because, as happened here, someone from the outside may misinterpret the relationship with potentially violent consequences.

As has been noted throughout *Fictional Blues*, blues authenticity hinges on the idea that Black people are the natural owners of the blues, and therefore are its most authentic and effective disseminators. The fact that Bond is not only white but also a woman raises questions about her blues legitimacy. When considering race in Bond's apprenticeship with Willie King, the question of blues authenticity, and who has the right to play the blues, quite unsurprisingly emerges. As Bond admits,

> I felt self-conscious about myself in terms of issues of authenticity and just being good enough on guitar or vocals. One way I have made peace with this is that I don't sing songs about things I haven't lived. You won't hear me singing songs about living as a sharecropper or living under Jim Crow. I take Big Bo's [an Alabama harmonica player, singer, and songwriter] advice and remember I can only be myself. That helped me to write my own songs. I have also felt self-conscious about my voice. But like Bo said, I can only be myself and trust that passion and love that makes me want to sing. Meanwhile, I have worked on my singing voice—knowing it's an instrument just like guitar. I know I have to keep growing as an artist with my unique instrument.

While Bond has found ways to play blues music without appropriating it, and erasing the contributions and experiences of others, she has still occasionally found herself caught in the thicket of racialized blues authenticity. As she shared with me,

> I have experienced some negative behavior from white blues aficionados who wanted Willie King's band to be all black. That wasn't Willie's thing. He liked having a diverse band, in terms of race and gender. He felt that's what his blues was all about. Willie was thrilled to be included in the Martin Scorsese documentary on the blues. However, he resented that Rick and I were edited out of the film because they wanted Willie to fit into their narrative of the African roots of the blues. They came to shoot at Bettie's Place but edited us out. You can hear Rick's voice, in his British accent

saying "Check, check!" Willie talked to us about this and also how he had experienced pressure occasionally from some black musicians or promoters that thought his band should be all black. But, ironically, I think he got this more from white folks who wanted him to fit their image of what his band should be like—a backwoods, all black, rootsy juke joint blues band.[14]

As I discussed in the previous chapter, and will explore in the next section, there are expectations in the contemporary blues scene—comprised almost entirely of white fans—that authentic blues must be played by Black people. The fact that what is considered to be authentic blues is being filtered through the expectations and projections of predominantly white audiences is not lost on contemporary Black and white blues performers alike.

Besides her work with the Alabama Blues Project, Bond has found other ways to give back to the music that has enriched her life. She has repaid her debt to Johnny Shines, Eddie Kirkland, and Willie King through mentoring young blue performers:

> One of the students that came out of the Alabama Blues Project, Rachel Edwards—we have continued to work together off and on, write together and record together. She has gone on to do some very original, awesome work—doing her own music that is highly blues and soul influenced but very contemporary and original. I consider her one of my blues babies—and like a good blues-mentoring mama, I've had to let her go and watch her fly with her own awesome original wings. She sang on my last CD and I'm hoping she does so on my next one![15]

While the previous section looked at formal and informal conventional blues apprenticeships, where a master and an apprentice have a relationship that occurs face to face, this section examines relationships that are both conventional and unconventional, with apprenticeships sometimes occurring across space and time, and sometimes even without the master's awareness.

Ralph Ellison confronted the notion of apprenticeship in an unconventional way. His example was novel, as his masters were men he never met. They were other writers—some of whom were long dead before he was born. For Ellison, white Western writers and thinkers were as important to his development as an artist and intellectual as were African American folk traditions. As Robert G. O'Meally notes, "Sophocles, Homer, Dostoevsky, Bergson, Freud, Jung, Raglan, Burke, Eliot, Joyce, Wright, and Malraux; spirituals, blues, and minstrels' jokes; personal experiences rendered symbolically—all figure in *Invisible Man*."[16] Many of Ellison's ideas—some at least two generations in the past—could easily find a home today in our postsoul moment.[17] Notions of anti-essentialist and fluid—or as Ellison might suggest, *improvisational*—approaches to Black creative expression, as well as the acknowledgment and celebration of multiple Black identities, are of great value in the twenty-first century.

In his classic essay "The Little Man at Chehaw Station," Ellison asserts that "the man behind Chehaw's stove also serves as a metaphor for those individuals we sometimes meet whose refinement of sensibility is inadequately explained by family background, formal education or social status . . . it would appear that culturally and environmentally such individuals are products of errant but sympathetic vibrations set up by the tension between America's social mobility, its universal education, and its relative freedom of cultural information."[18] Ellison suggests that it is the relatively unfettered movement of culture, music in particular, across educational and socioeconomic boundaries that facilitates this uniquely American brand of self-creation. And given the ways in which jazz, and particularly blues, serve as a foundation for other more contemporary musics—rock and hip-hop immediately come to mind—it is important to examine the ways in which current musicians create self-fashioned identities as artists and people. This becomes a political concern, as the racialized musical authenticity/inauthenticity binary persists in the largely white blues and Americana music scenes. As such, Ellison's capacious approach to his artistic and intellectual work provides a useful model for contemporary Black musicians working within those genres.

Rhiannon Giddens and Gary Clark Jr. are two such artists who, like Ellison's approach to writing, deploy artistic individuality as they blur the dividing lines between musical styles while resisting narrow ideas by some critics, fans, and fellow musicians about what constitutes so-called legitimate Black creative expression. As David Grazian, Adam Gussow, and Roger Gatchet assert, racial and class-based essentialism continue to undergird notions of blues authenticity in a contemporary context.[19] And

Jennifer Stoever's work on the "sonic color line" is useful in interrogating why some twenty-first-century audiences, critics, and musicians persist in believing that race can be detected through musical sounds.[20]

These complicated interracial interactions, which I read as musical apprenticeships, are frequently sites of tension where the African American artists are subjected to raced and gendered essentialist responses to their works by their mentors or those outside of the relationship. These interactions can also prove liberating, however, and serve as models for other Black musicians for how to contest reductive representations of Black cultural expression.

In this section, I will explore the concept of the conventional and unconventional musical apprenticeship as demonstrated in the work of Ellison, Clark, and Giddens. I will focus on Ellison's discussion of the power of the musical apprenticeship to undermine well-worn representations of Black people, and I will interrogate how Ellison's exploration of the unconventional jazz apprenticeship resonates in the twenty-first century vis-à-vis Clark and Giddens. I will also demonstrate that despite Ellison's careful guarding of his writing time, and his unwillingness to nurture large numbers of younger Black writers while he was still alive, his influence reverberates in the works of these two Black singer-songwriters/musicians a generation after his passing.[21] Ultimately, I argue that Clark and Giddens take Ellisonian approaches to undermining static ideas of authentic Black artistic expression through the use of cross-racial musical apprenticeship models, experimentation with diverse musical genres and transgressive collaborative projects, and a spirit of productive ambivalence.

Allan Moore's definition of authenticity is again useful here.[22] His "*authenticity of execution*, . . . or 'third person authenticity' . . . arises when a performer succeeds in conveying the impression of accurately representing the ideas of another, embedded within a tradition of performance."[23] This concept of the "authenticity of execution" can also be used to critique artists such as Clark who fit the criteria for "first person authenticity" but transgress those boundaries. Clark, like Ellison and Giddens, self-fashions his creative identity as a way to manage his ambivalence about being policed into a proscribed artistic category predicated on his racial background. Ellison's reluctance, after *Invisible Man* and *Shadow and Act*, to participate in artistic projects organized by young, political Black writers and activists during the 1970s; Giddens's anger at being questioned about her legitimacy as a performer of Scottish mouth music; and Clark's distaste at being forced to focus his musical talent on the blues are all examples of the Black American creator who holds fast to an improvised American artistic identity.

During the 1960s, in the midst of the American country blues revival, Ellison contested prevailing ideas about racial essentialism and musical authenticity. He famously engaged in literary debates with LeRoi Jones, speaking back to Jones's work. In *Blues People,* Jones is very particular about not only what constitutes authentic blues expression but also what is considered to be an honest expression of *Blackness.* Jones correlates the dilution of Black art to the emergence of a Black American middle class at the beginning of the twentieth century that wanted to move away from so-called authentic Blackness. According to Jones, "They did not even want to be 'accepted' as *themselves,* they wanted any self which the mainstream dictated, and the mainstream *always* dictated. And this black middle class, in turn, tried always to dictate that self, or this image of a whiter Negro, to the poorer, blacker Negroes." Jones is clear in his text that authentic Black people, and, by extension, authentic Black artists—those who Moore would suggest represented "first person authenticity"—can be found exclusively among the working class.[24] Jones extends his critique to classic blueswomen such as Bessie Smith and Ma Rainey, who from his perspective lost their claims to authenticity when their music became too commercially successful, thereby attracting a white mainstream audience.[25]

Ellison's essay "Blues People" in 1964's *Shadow and Act* directly engages Jones's text. Ellison questions Jones's conflation of social class with both Black cultural legitimacy and Black reception of art made by other Blacks.[26] Ellison also takes issue with the idea that the mainstream merely influences African Americans instead of acknowledging Black people's impact on the mainstream. As Ellison argues, "Negro musicians have never, as a group, felt alienated from any music sounded within their hearing, and it is my theory that it would be impossible to pinpoint the time when they were not shaping what Jones calls the mainstream of American music." This reinforces Ellison's philosophy that Black and white Americans have had a lasting and profound impact on each other's cultures. In much of Ellison's nonfiction he passionately argues for the existence of Black artistic expression, particularly in the areas of music and literature, disseminated in an interracial context, allowing for cross-cultural influence between Blacks and whites. Ellison writes about this cross-racial engagement in a way that echoes the classic apprenticeship in which a master craftsman teaches a young acolyte his or her trade. He frequently acknowledges the literary mentoring he received from white poets and writers such as James Joyce, T. S. Eliot, and Mark Twain. In "Change the Joke and Slip the Yoke" Ellison asserts,

> I use folklore in my work not because I am Negro, but because writers like Eliot and Joyce made me conscious of the literary value of my folk inheritance. . . . I knew the trickster Ulysses just as early as I knew the wily rabbit of Negro American lore. . . . And a little later I could imagine myself as Huck Finn (I so nicknamed my brother) but not, though I racially identified with him, as Nigger Jim. . . . My point is that the Negro American writer is also an heir of the human experience which is literature, and this might well be more important to him than his living folk tradition.[27]

As an "heir" to literature, the Black American writer, even at a distance, is apprenticed to those great poets and novelists who came before, regardless of race or nationality.[28] Thanks to recording and dissemination technologies, from sheet music and the vaudeville circuit to digital streaming, musical apprenticeships can be similarly unconventional. In his essay "Homage to Duke Ellington on His Birthday," published in 1969 in Washington, DC's *Sunday Star,* Ellison suggests that an established Black musician can be a mentor for an aspiring one, even if they do not meet face to face. In fact, Ellison regards Ellington as a mentor: "Then Ellington and his great orchestra came to town—came with their uniforms, their sophistication, their skills; their golden horns, their flights of controlled and disciplined fantasy. . . . They were news from the great wide world, an example and a goal, and I wish that all those who write so knowledgably about Negro boys having no masculine figures with whom to identify would consider the long national and international career of Ellington and his band, and the thousands of one-night stands played in the black communities of this nation."[29] When Ellison refers to "all those who write so knowledgably of Negro boys having no masculine figures with whom to identify," he is referring to Daniel Patrick Moynihan's 1965 article "The Negro Family: The Case for National Action," otherwise known as the "Moynihan Report." In the text, Moynihan determines that the growing number of households headed by Black women poses a serious threat to the Black family and contributes to the social, economic, and political problems facing the Black community. Moynihan states, "In essence, the Negro community has been forced into a matriarchal structure which, because it is so out of line with the rest of the American society, seriously retards the progress of the group as a whole, and imposes a crushing burden on the Negro male and, in consequence, on a great many Negro women as well."[30] This is Ellison's reminder that a musician, even from the stage, can act as a stand-in for a missing parent or be, as Ellison suggests, "an example and a goal."[31] In this case, his or her mere presence can prove inspirational and show the mentee what is possible. Ellison's invocation of the musical apprenticeship is transgressive, as it allows for a diversity of experiences in Black family life and demonstrates the different ways that young Black children can receive positive mentorship. Strikingly, Ellison, too, engaged in literary apprenticeships with some of the younger Black writers at a distance, the inverse of his relationships with white Western novelists.

In her chapter "The Timbre of Sincerity: Mahalia Jackson's Gospel Sound and Ralph Ellison's *Invisible Man*," Emily Lordi discusses Ellison's treatment of Mahalia Jackson's performances at the 1958 Newport Jazz Festival and Newport's Mount Zion AME Church that Sunday in his essay "As the Spirit Moves Mahalia." Ellison examines Jackson's "timbre of sincerity," suggesting that her vocal sound evinces her profound religious devotion.[32] Given that Ellison describes Jackson's vocal style as one that accesses varied musical forms (gospel, blues, folk, flamenco, and jazz), Lordi recasts Ellison's concept of "the timbre of sincerity" as "an integrative expressive practice that conveys ambiguities with clarity." She takes this idea further by introducing her concept of ambivalence. For Lordi, ambivalence is a positive enterprise that "convey[s] conflicting ideas or emotions," yet "does not privilege one meaning over the other but instead foregrounds simultaneity and indeterminacy."[33] In this section, I will build on the idea of ambivalence as I discuss two artists who not only work across various musical styles and forms but also experience that "simultaneity and indeterminacy," as they desire to play certain forms of Black American roots music, while not wanting to be tethered to those same forms as a result of racial essentialism and the cult of musical authenticity.[34] My use of the concept of ambivalence will also interrogate the ways in which interracial apprenticeships may open the

Black artist to a larger commercial realm while simultaneously shrinking his or her possibilities for eclectic musical expression due to exposure to critics and audiences who may not recognize the varied approaches to Black artistic expression.

For Clark, his musical apprenticeships have been particularly significant in his artistic development, while presenting a racially complicated experience. Clark was born on February 15, 1984, in Austin, Texas. At the age of twelve he taught himself to play the guitar. At fifteen, he started playing gigs in downtown Austin with his friend Eve Monsees. As teenagers, the duo performed in shows at clubs along Sixth Street, finally catching the eyes and ears of Clifford Antone, owner of famed Austin blues club Antone's. Antone invited Gary and Eve to open for blues guitarist Jimmie Vaughan—Stevie Ray Vaughan's older brother and a member of the Fabulous Thunderbirds—at an anniversary show. At seventeen, Clark was fully entrenched in the Austin blues scene, with Vaughan serving as his mentor.[35] In some ways, Clark's decade-plus apprenticeship with Jimmie Vaughan was every bit as unconventional as Ellison's with his distant literary mentors. While Clark enjoyed a traditional, face-to-face relationship with Vaughan, their apprenticeship took the cross-racial element featured in Ellison's mentorships much further. Not only is Vaughan white, but the contemporary Austin blues scene is also predominantly Caucasian. And to offer some perspective on how white the blues scene is in Austin, Texas, in a 2012 interview with Neil McCormick in the *Daily Telegraph*, Clark told a story about a Black school friend who asked him why he played the guitar. According to Clark, "He said, 'Black people don't play the blues.' It kind of blew my mind."[36] Even so, Austin has long been a site for the interracial blues apprenticeship. As Josep Pedro asserts, Antone's was "a mecca for experienced African-American bluesmen and emerging white blues musicians. As such, Antone's became Austin's 'Home of the Blues,' an underground connective hub for face-to-face musical learning, intergenerational and interracial dialogues that contributed to identity hybridizations." Older local Black blues players such as W. C. Clark and Henry "Blues Boy" Hubbard, as well as blues legends such as Muddy Waters, B. B. King, Albert Collins, and Freddie King have acted as mentors to younger white players in the Austin scene, including Stevie Ray and Jimmie Vaughan.[37] Given the continued foregrounding of racialized blues authenticity, it is significant that a young African American blues musician would have been shepherded through the process of becoming a professional musician by white mentors. Gary Clark Jr. turned down a full scholarship at the University of Texas at Austin to tour with Vaughan and promote his first LP, *Worry No More.*[38] Clark had already achieved a good deal of notoriety in his hometown. When Clark was just seventeen, the mayor of Austin declared May 3, 2001, "Gary Clark Jr. Day."[39] However, it was Clark's performance at the 2010 Crossroads Guitar Festival that proved to be his coming-out party.[40]

It was Clapton's guitarist, Austin native Doyle Bramhall II, who recommended Clark to Clapton, and it is Bramhall's voice at the beginning of Clark's performance from the *Crossroads Eric Clapton Guitar Festival 2010* DVD. He states, "I'm so happy that Gary Clark Jr. was invited to be on this festival. I think he's a player that doesn't exist anymore. He has a voice that's just phenomenal. He can sing soul music. He can sing Delta. He can sing Chicago blues. And he's *really* authentic." Bramhall speaks of Clark in romantic terms. He describes him as "a player that doesn't exist anymore." In other words, Clark is the embodiment of a cultural myth. He is the early twentieth-century blues figure come back to life. Bramhall gives Clark the ultimate accolade, "authentic," a term that may be meant positively, but can become a trap for an artist who is then tasked with creating within its narrow confines.[41] As David Grazian states in *Blue Chicago: The Search for Authenticity in Urban Blues Clubs*, a sociological, ethnographic study on contemporary Chicago blues performers at the end of the 1990s, "While audiences appreciate the performative aspects of the musician's stage act, they nevertheless demand to hear performances based, in part, on preconceived expectations regarding the authenticity of the stereotypical black blues player." This need for a specific brand of blues authenticity correlates with Moore's "third person authenticity," as the audiences in these contemporary blues clubs want the performers to evoke an earlier time and place.[42] So even though the Chicago musicians, like Clark, would appear to be imbued with Moore's first-person authenticity based on their race, they are tasked with performing in an expected "authentic" blues style whether they are invested or not. As Adam Gussow, an associate professor of English and Southern studies at the University of Mississippi and a blues harmonica player who was part of the New York City–based blues duo Satan and

Adam states in 2007's *Journeyman's Road*, "White blues hunger is epitomized by the creepy phrase 'keeping the blues alive,' the mantra of more than a few well-intentioned, white-run blues organizations. What many white folks want to keep alive, to be blunt, is what might be called the Pristine Black Folk Subject, the postmodern reincarnation of the Old-Time Negro. Aging Old-Time Negroes are great—the real bluesy deal from Chulahoma, Mississippi!—but Young Old-Time Negroes are even better." While within the pages of *Living Blues*, or certain contemporary blues spaces, Black blues performers are perceived as authentic, leading to their valorization by white fans, critics, and musicians, the authenticity paradigm frequently creates a power imbalance that is in service to the "white blues hunger" Gussow notes.[43] As E. Patrick Johnson offers, "When white Americans essentialize blackness, for example, they often do so in ways that maintain 'whiteness' as the master trope of purity, supremacy, and entitlement, as a ubiquitous, fixed, unifying signifier that seems invisible."[44] In this case, the "hunger" both derives from and leads to the sense of "entitlement" that Grazian discovered in the Chicago blues clubs.[45]

In recent years, Clark has expressed a desire to disentangle himself from critical and audience expectations. In 2012, his major-label debut, *Blak and Blu*, disappointed some critics and fans who thought it too slick and who were unhappy with Clark's embrace of postblues genres such as hip-hop and neo-soul—Jon Pareles of *Rolling Stone* opines that "on this album, it's still his blues that cut deepest."[46] In a 2013 *London Evening Standard* article Clark states, "There's definitely a blues police who will come and write you up for not staying in the structure. It just seems like a natural thing to branch out and find your own place, knowing at the same time that what you do is held down by those blues roots."[47] If Clark's cross-racial apprenticeship was not Ellisonian enough, the quotation that follows reveals Clark's frustration with reductive audiences and critics who have little imagination for diverse Black experiences and methods for Black musical expression. Clark's quotation is reminiscent of a passage from Ellison's "Blues People" essay. In a 2013 *Rolling Stone* article by Patrick Doyle that is appropriately titled "Gary Clark Jr.: The Chosen One," Clark states,

> If it were up to everybody else, I would do Hendrix covers all the time. I saw this comment from somebody online the other day, say-

> ing, "We need you to play more Chicago or Louisiana blues—we want the raw shit." Well, I'm not from Chicago or from Louisiana. I'm not from that time period. There was segregation. That music was the popular music at the time. People were doing what they did in that moment in time to express themselves. It's a different time. So why am I going to pretend? I'm not some poor kid who grew up in the middle of nothing.[48]

Given that Clark was born in the post–civil rights movement/post-soul era, his response is expected. In this case, his reclamation of his factual autobiography allows him to speak for himself and stay true to his artistic vision. Rather than allowing himself to be persuaded to take on a persona that does not interest him—the out-of-time and -place Chicago Bluesman—he proudly shares details about his middle-class upbringing. His thoughts also, strikingly, correlate with Ellison's own ideas about the multiple Black experiences some fifty years earlier:

> One would get the impression that there was a rigid correlation between color, education, income and the Negro's preference in music. But what are we to say of a white-skinned Negro with brown freckles who owns sixteen oil wells sunk in a piece of Texas land once farmed by his ex-slave parents who were a blue-eyed, white-skinned, red-headed (kinky) Negro woman from Virginia and a blue-gummed, black-skinned, curly-haired Negro male from Mississippi, and who not only sang bass in a Holy Roller church, played the market and voted Republican but collected blues recordings and was a walking depository of blues tradition?[49]

Clark's reaction to audiences and critics who attempt to limit his musical expression to the blues has been to keep taking musical chances, as he proclaimed to the *New York Times* in 2012: "Someone said something to me the other day: 'People like to keep you where they found you.' . . . I'm totally comfortable shaking that up."[50] Clark performed at the 2014 NBA All-Star Game with popular soul singer-songwriter Janelle Monáe; released *Blak and Blu: The Mixtape*, featuring Mississippi MC Big K.R.I.T., R & B singer Bilal, and Brooklyn-based hip-hop artist Talib Kweli in 2014; and sang "Higher Ground" with Beyoncé at the Stevie Wonder Grammy special in February 2015. This last performance, in particular, was in line with what Clark calls "shaking" things up. After all, authentic blues performers do not often appear on television with high-profile, massively successful pop divas.[51]

As Clark continues to resist the efforts of blues purists to determine his musical course, he demonstrates his ambivalence by producing work both independently and with collaborators that cross musical boundaries. As he states in a 2015 interview for the Associated Press, "If it's an artist I'm willing to work with, I'm going to do it. I'm not going to put any boundaries on my music. I like to sit and play the piano, I picked up violin, I love to play horns. This bluesy thing is my foundation. But you never know. I might pop up playing the accordion somewhere. . . . One thing I don't want to do as an artist is to not be free artistically."[52] In September 2015, Clark released his second major label record, *The Story of Sonny Boy Slim.* According to Jewly Hight in an article for npr.org, the "album title came from both the guitar-prodigy character he played in the 2007 film *Honeydripper* and a family nickname."[53] Given that the title invokes pieces of Clark's personal and fictional identities, and Clark produced the record himself, this release provides an opportunity for Clark to continue creating music that resonates with the stories *he* wants to tell. As such, the record includes songs that fall within the genres of R & B, funk, gospel, and even a concessionary blues rock hybrid called "Grinder" that A.V. Club writer Corbin Reiff suggests is the "closest Clark comes to fulfilling the visions others likely have for him—those who see him as their savior of blues-rock."[54] And after providing a guitar solo—one that is unmistakably of the rock variety—for the song "What Did I Do?/God as My Witness" for rock band the Foo Fighters' 2014 record *Sonic Highways,* he opened for the Foo Fighters during September and October of their 2015 North American tour.

In a YouTube video about the making of "What Did I Do?/God as My Witness," Clark, dressed all in black save his brown fedora, sits on a couch next to drummer Taylor Hawkins. Producer Butch Vig explains that the band has four tracks available as they record, so Clark has room to experiment: "I don't want you to have to think you got to work out a part. I think you just play and we can always take the best bits and put it into a master comp. It's cool." Clark's quick smile, before the video cuts away to his blistering offering, serves as a foreshadowing of sorts. He has worked as a hired gun for other popular contemporary artists, so he certainly knows what is expected. But more than that, he is on the precipice of taking control of his musical output by serving as his own producer for *The Story of Sonny Boy Slim*. That smile suggests that he is certainly capable of giving the Foo Fighters what they want—a piece of Clark's blues rock brand—while he knows that he can do more. What he does do is create a rock solo on the spot that impresses everyone in the room: Hawkins is visibly giddy as Clark's solo builds—his face contorting at the sound of each note; and Dave Grohl, who has been listening in the other room, exclaims, "All I hear is your guitar. . . . I don't even hear the track. . . . That's rad!"[55]

While Clark's musical contribution is undeniably successful, it also serves as a representation of his ambivalence about his branding as the next big bluesman. In an article for *Faster Louder*, Clark explains how the solo came about: "Well they had the track done for the most part musically so they were just like 'Man, play a solo here. Just do what you do. Just be badass.' [laughs] So no pressure there . . . I just went in and ripped it. I brought like a 125 hollowbody guitar, which is completely wrong for a session but I thought it would be cool and different. It was a total fail but Pat Smear hooked me up with an SG and let me rip. I think it came out really well plus he let me keep the guitar, which is not a bad deal."[56] It is noteworthy that Clark brought a Gibson ES 125 hollowbody to the session, a vintage guitar manufactured during the 1940s and 1950s and mainly associated with jazz, country, and blues artists. Rockers do not generally use the 125 hollowbody; however, the Gibson SG is the guitar of choice for many iconic rock stars, including Angus Young of AC/DC, Pete Townshend of the Who, and Tony Iommi of Black Sabbath.[57] Here Clark shows his ambivalence: He wants to move past the blues, yet he brings a guitar that is associated with American roots music to a session with a hard rock band that includes former members of iconic grunge band Nirvana (Dave Grohl) and seminal LA punk band the Germs (Pat Smear). He wants to play the blues, and he does not want to play the blues. Clark retains part of his blues brand by showing up with his hollowbody but then undermines any expectations the band might have had about what the bluesier solo might sound like by using Pat Smear's guitar. As Lordi states, "The timbre of sincerity goes one step further in describing double meanings that do not alternate but instead coexist." Lordi uses "America the Beautiful" by Ray Charles and "My Favorite Things" by John Coltrane as examples of artists who exhibit sincerity by "signifying on or critiquing their source material while also earnestly engaging it—both 'meaning it' and not meaning it."[58] In the case of Clark, however, he means it when he plays the rock solo, but he also meant it when he brought the blues guitar. He wants to play the blues; he just does not want to be trapped by it.

Rhiannon Giddens, like Clark, is closely identified with American roots music. Although Giddens is a trained opera singer, and she grew up with significant exposure to other forms of European classical music, after college she fell in love with the Black American string music tradition. Similarly, as a young musician Ellison gravitated toward Western classical music, as well as African American forms such as jazz and blues.[59] Given that audience members generally do not know that Black Americans played in string bands during the nineteenth and early twentieth centuries, on tour Giddens and each of her band mates in the Carolina Chocolate Drops assume the role of educators. As the band introduces audiences to the history of Black participation in rural string band music, they simultaneously carve a space for themselves. As the banjo, for many, invokes (white) country music, slavery, and the minstrel tradition, Giddens and the rest of the Carolina Chocolate Drops seek to recuperate the banjo as an instrument with African origins and an important role in African American musical history. As Giddens states, "A lot of the music we play has been bowdlerised, ignored or demonised. As a people, we have taken that era and swept it under the rug. And there's so much great music in it, and so many fantastic performance styles."[60] On the surface it appears that Clark and Giddens have vastly different concerns—Clark's dilemma centers on his need to create distance between himself and a style of music that has long been associated with Black people, while Giddens labors to reclaim her music as Black—yet they share in common a desire to experiment with different musical styles, and resist racially essentialist reactions to their work.

Giddens was born on February 21, 1977, in Greensboro, North Carolina, to a white father and Black and Native American mother. She grew up in a musical family, with her parents and extended family being dedicated fans of various styles of music. Her father played in rock bands, while her mother enjoyed classical music. Her maternal grandparents were admirers of jazz and the blues, and one of her paternal uncles played in a bluegrass band. At seventeen, Giddens successfully auditioned for a prestigious summer choral camp at the Governor's School of North Carolina in Raleigh. Based on the exuberant reactions of the choral teachers during her audition, she realized that she might have a future as a singer. After studying opera at the renowned Oberlin Conservatory of Music in Ohio, Giddens returned to North Carolina, where she joined a Celtic band and worked as a contra dance caller.[61]

In 2005 she attended the Black Banjo Gathering at Appalachian State University in Boone, North Carolina. It was there that she met the two men who would become her bandmates: fiddler Justin Robinson and harmonica, guitar, and jug player Dom Flemons. That day she also met the late Joe Thompson, one of the last remaining Black string band originators. Thompson would become the band's mentor, teaching them how to play Black old-time music.[62] As Giddens writes in her liner notes for "Track 1—'Lights in the Valley' (Live) by Joe & Odell Thompson" for the *Oxford American* in 2018:

> Joe would take out his fiddle, strike the strings with his left hand to make sure it was in tune, and he would say, "Boys, what we gonna start with tonight? Let's play 'John Henry.'" The question was always asked and answered in the same sentence, and we were always "boys," myself included. We played the same tunes over and over, and Joe never instructed in so many words. If we were getting it right, he kept playing. If we weren't, he'd stop and say, "You know, I believe we're going a little fast" or "a little slow," and we knew to pay closer attention.[63]

That these three young artists would find each other at a Black string music festival is not as unexpected as it may seem. As Robinson recounts, "There were maybe 200 or 300 mostly white people there, so it wasn't like we were, um, unapparent to each other."[64] Despite the fact that Black Americans have historically participated in a variety of roots-based musical styles, there are few in the Americana scene. Karl Hagstrom Miller argues that toward the end of the nineteenth century, and into the first two decades of the twentieth century, Southern Blacks and whites played the same music. Any categorical distinctions that were made, that is, blues versus country, were based on race alone. According to Miller, "Southern musicians performed a staggering variety of music in the early twentieth century. Black and white artists played blues, ballads, ragtime, and string band music, as well as the plethora of styles popular throughout the nation: sentimental ballads, minstrel songs, Tin

Pan Alley tunes, and Broadway hits." Of particular note is the fact that Blacks, alongside whites, created string music that evolved into what we now call country music. As Miller states, "Both black and white artists recorded examples of the string band styles that had developed throughout the South. String bands utilizing combinations of fiddles and guitars were among the major features of old-time catalogues."[65] Even so, there are few Black musicians working in the contemporary Americana scene or Black fans attending Americana concerts. As Flemons explains, "The idea of country got left behind. If you look at black people in popular culture now, there aren't many country blacks. Black is usually a very urban thing. The idea of being black, where black people live, what they do, is all based around the urban center." He adds, "Blacks will either create something or invent something and make an American music form out of it, and when it becomes too popular, they move on and go to the next thing."[66] The lack of Black interest in earlier forms of Black American musical expression fuels Giddens's passion to both share her music with new audiences and convert nonbelievers into believers.

The Carolina Chocolate Drops' music video for the song "Country Girl" from 2012's *Leaving Eden* is a tribute to Giddens's Greensboro, North Carolina, childhood, and an aural and visual love letter to the American South. For those outside of the South, particularly the Carolinas, who see country culture, including country music, as the domain of white people, this video shows a different reality where people of all races, ages, and genders share a love of Black string music. By the time the Carolina Chocolate Drops produced their first music video, Robinson had left the band, and founding members Giddens and Flemons were joined by multi-instrumentalist Hubby Jenkins, cellist Leyla McCalla, and beatboxer Adam Matta. The video, however, focuses on Giddens, Flemons, and Jenkins, who stroll down a dark country road, instruments in hand, and into a packed summer country barn dance. When the trio arrives, the crowd lets out a roar—they will be providing the entertainment, after all—that cues the music. The exuberant hugs and smiles exchanged between young and old, Black and white, give way to shots of Giddens in pigtails, perhaps a representation of a younger version of herself. The rest of the video alternates between the barn dance and various shots that appear to represent both the adult and childhood Giddens. The video features myriad signifiers of country life: Giddens, Flemons, and Jenkins eating at a BBQ joint, piling into the back of a pickup truck, and frolicking in stacks of hay. These are juxtaposed with scenes of a smiling Giddens, singing by herself in the Carolina dusk or standing by as her mother serves a bountiful feast. The old-time costume design, particularly in the case of Flemons, who wears a pink plaid shirt with brown suspenders, trousers, bowler hat, and pipe, allows the audience to read the past in the present. Giddens uses the video to not only show that string music is Black music too but also to suggest that being a "country girl" allows for cross-racial experiences.[67] Southern musical spaces are white *and* Black, and country music continues to bring Black and white people together, as it has historically. Giddens has referred to North Carolina, as a bridge: "I think North Carolina is a bridge state. I feel like what I do as an artist is bridge things. I bridge classical and secular. I bridge Black to white."[68] This idea of the bridge suggests a slightly different approach to Lordi's ambivalence. Rather than Clark's attraction and simultaneous resistance to playing the blues, Giddens sees herself as existing in the middle between oppositional forces. She is not resisting anything. She is instead introducing seemingly incongruous ideas and sounds, and challenging the audience to come to the conclusion that no bridge is needed. Or, as Ellison stated half a century ago, "It must, however, be pointed out that due to the close links which Negro Americans have with the rest of the nation these cultural expressions are constantly influencing the larger body of American culture and are in turn influenced by them. Nor should the existence of a specifically 'Negro' idiom in any way be confused with the vague, racist terms 'white culture' or 'black culture'; rather it is a matter of diversity within unity." This classic Ellisonian idea, of Blacks and whites embracing their shared American experience, which he has referred to alternatively as "diversity within unity" and as the "complexity of American Experience," is one that is still difficult to imagine for some.[69] As Marc Conner and Lucas Morel state, "Ellison explicitly saw his mission as a writer to be to chronicle the America that could be, the America that is always promised and still unrealized."[70] With the Carolina Chocolate Drops, Giddens demonstrates Ellison's point to twenty-first-century audiences.

In 2013 Giddens participated in *Another Day, Another Time: Celebrating the Music of Inside Llewyn Davis* at Manhattan's Town Hall. She performed two stirring numbers: the traditional folk song "Waterboy" and "S'iomadh Rid" ("The Dhith Om / Ciamar a Nì Mi"), a song that falls within the realm of Scottish mouth music.[71] T Bone Burnett, the executive music producer for the Coen brothers film *Inside Llewyn Davis*, was so impressed with Giddens's performances that he offered to produce her solo album on the spot, and made good on his promise by following up on the telephone two weeks later.[72] Giddens was poised to begin production on the next Carolina Chocolate Drops record, but Burnett's offer gave her pause: "But then T Bone said to me that this is my time. Did I agree? I trusted the energy that was around me and I trusted the judgment of one of the greatest producers in the world within my genre saying, 'Let's do a record'. So I thought, who am I to say no to this opportunity? Also, I have been given a voice that I have taken care of, and so I feel there's a responsibility to that." *Tomorrow Is My Turn* (2015), a collection of covers by, or made famous by, a diverse group of women that include Dolly Parton, Nina Simone, Patsy Cline, and Sister Rosetta Tharpe, is the result of her apprenticeship with Burnett. Giddens explains, "When I got the phone call from T Bone about recording a solo album, he asked me what my dream record would be. At that time, I really hadn't been thinking about a solo album, but I did have this idea in the back of my mind about songs that didn't really fit in with Carolina Chocolate Drops—songs of, from and about women in Americana throughout the decades."[73] Burnett has since invited her to perform at "The Gospel Tradition: In Performance at the White House" in his role as executive music director, and he asked her to be one of five band leaders (the others are Elvis Costello, Marcus Mumford, Jim James, and Taylor Goldsmith) for *Lost on the River: The New Basement Tapes*, a compilation of previously unfinished and unreleased Bob Dylan songs.[74] While Giddens's apprenticeship with Burnett is not the sort where he is charged with teaching her an instrument, or how to sing, or even how to be a performer (she already had that sort of apprenticeship with Joe Thompson), he has acted as a mentor who has presented Giddens with exciting opportunities for career development that even she had not imagined. Burnett saw her talent, forged a working relationship with her, and swiftly opened doors to her solo career: "He's been my fairy godfather," she says. "We have a pretty good batting average so far. He creates a great situation for you, but you have to take it. I never knew that's what I needed."[75] Burnett's expansive approach to creative expression supports Giddens's diverse musical interests. Unlike Clark's mentors, who expected him to fulfill a specific musical role that he outgrew rather quickly, Burnett decided to work with Giddens *after* seeing her perform a song made famous by a Black American female folk singer who emerged during the civil rights movement *and* a traditional Scottish folk song in Gaelic. He then invited Giddens to work in yet another style of music—gospel—for the White House event. Notably, Giddens served with the Tennessee Arts Commission's 2019 Traditional Arts Apprenticeship Program, as a gourd banjo master with her apprentice, eleven-year-old Uma Peters.

While Burnett understands that Black artists can perform in many styles, Giddens's foray into Scottish mouth music has prompted racialized musical policing by some members of the music press. When in an interview with the *Calgary Herald* Eric Volmers asks Giddens if her interest in Scottish folk music is due to her possessing some Scottish ancestry, she responds, "This is one of the reasons I love doing mouth music because it always brings that up: 'Do you have a Scottish background?' When a white guy does blues, no one ever asks him 'Do you have African-American in your background?' He just does the blues. Why do I get asked if I have a reason to do this music? I like the music. It's a part of my culture, because it's a part of North Carolina culture. That's all the ownership I need."[76] Although Giddens has taken on the burden of educating audiences about the complicated cross-racial history of American folk music, which is, of course, reflective of the various complicated cross-racial histories of American *people,* she is understandably exasperated by the suggestion that her authenticity is in question simply because of the color of her skin: "There are so many musics that are such a mixture of different cultures and experiences, and there is so much of that in the American lexicon that I think that is definitely a part of what you would think of as the American voice. And that history is so hidden, the true strain of American voices. The idea of blacks speaking Gaelic, for example; that happened, but you would never think of that."[77] The notion that Black and white Americans have a shared history that has directly influenced the course of American culture (literature, music, food, religion, and more), and will continue to do so, is fraught for many.

Giddens's statement is reminiscent of Ellison's response to Irving Howe's 1963 article in *Dissent,* "Black Boys and Native Sons," in which he took a moment to address white people in general who wrote about Blacks in lazy and intellectually dishonest ways: "Prefabricated Negroes are sketched on sheets of paper and superimposed upon the Negro community; then when someone thrusts his head through the page and yells, 'Watch out there, Jack, there're people living under here,' they are shocked and indignant."[78] The *Calgary Herald* writer certainly expressed surprise at Giddens's reaction to his question about her ancestry. The echoes of Ellison's words can be heard in Clark's and Giddens's own words and music. Both Clark and Giddens have taken Ellisonian approaches vis-à-vis musical apprenticeship and artistic experimentation to undermining stereotypical ideas of monolithic Black artistic expression. However, they still face ongoing struggles for artistic freedom within the dominant paradigm of authentic Black cultural production. It will be their continued acts of resistance, large and small, that will aid them as they—like the blues queens, country blues performers, twentieth- and twenty-first-century musical acts such as Big Mama Thornton and Amy Winehouse, and representational blues artists in fiction such as Shug Avery and "Robert Johnson"—reclaim and assert their individual power.

Afterword

In *Fictional Blues,* I have argued for the blues as a narrative art through which its makers invent and reinvent themselves by engaging autobiographical and biographical fictions. Stories and storytelling fuel blues expression, motivating questions about why these tales (objectively "true" or not) are of enduring interest to listeners of all kinds, and how blues narratives are disseminated in words and sounds.

These questions resonate in the various folkloric tellings and retellings of the Stagolee tale, documenting the 1895 murder of Billy Lyons by Lee Shelton, through ballads, blues songs, and printed media. Here we have a story that is reasonably compelling on its face, but it is really the gaps—the details no one knows—that allow other people to contribute, making it their own. This occurred with the Stagolee narrative, as everyday people embellished the original story, adding details that sounded like they could have happened, and then passing them along for others to do the same. Soon, early twentieth-century folklorists and ethnomusicologists, such as John and Alan Lomax, documented these narratives, keeping track of subsequent versions. Eventually, scholars from the late twentieth and early twenty-first century such as John Russell David, whose 1976 "Tragedy in Ragtime: Black Folktales from St. Louis" was the first scholarly work to identify Lee Shelton as the basis for the Stagolee folk tale, worked to gather more information about the real events. In *Stagolee Shot Billy*, published in 2003, Cecil Brown explores the tale's impact on African American culture, and American culture more generally.

Stories inspired by Stagolee sometimes feature a bad man or woman like Mamie Smith's narrator in her song "Crazy Blues" who threatens to "shoot . . . a cop";[1] the unnamed cheating girlfriend in Texas bluesman Mance Lipscomb's song "Freddie"; Luzana Cholly from *Train Whistle Guitar* by Albert Murray; and Shug Avery and Squeak from *The Color Purple* by Alice Walker. At other times, stories about important blues figures resemble the Stagolee tale due to the lack of available information about the subjects, and efforts by outsiders to fill in the gaps. This happened with Robert Johnson and other early twentieth-century bluesmen and women, as 1960s-era blues revival critics and scholars attempted to learn more about the foundational blues players. As these researchers pieced together the backstories, they added new and exciting but sometimes apocryphal elements. For example, the notion that Robert Johnson might have actually sold his soul to the devil was based on a suspect interview with Son House in 1966. The specter of tall-tale telling also occurred in the aftermath of Big Mama Thornton's silences in the face of Robert Neff's and Anthony Connor's prying questions about her experiences with the white music industry figures who exploited her, leaving Esther Phillips to tell Thornton's story for her.

The fictional and real-life bluesmen and women in *Fictional Blues* sometimes use autobiographical fictions and constructed personas to participate in their own mythmaking—Mamie Smith, Bessie Smith, Ma Rainey, Peetie Wheatstraw, and Jack White are a few examples—while others invent and reinvent themselves using autobiographical fictions to correct the record. These subjects resist the myths that are placed on them by others. Robert Johnson does this as a character in *Reservation Blues*. All of the women in chapter 2—Shug and Squeak in *The Color Purple*, Big Mama Thornton when she reclaims her power by taking credit for her role as the songwriter for "Ball and Chain," and Amy Winehouse through her song lyrics—use autobiographical narrative to tell their own stories. In his as-told-to book *I Say Me for a Parable: The Oral Autobiography of Mance Lipscomb Texas Bluesman*, Mance Lipscomb resists his chronicler's colonizing agenda, and Gary Clark Jr. and Rhiannon Giddens fight for their creative freedoms through their corrective autobiographical narratives.

While *Fictional Blues* is focused on the blues—a historically rich site for colorful narratives told by, and about, fictional and real-life blues makers alike—the ideas embedded in my theorizing of fictionalized autobiographical blues self-invention are portable. That is, questions about how musical artists reconfigure how they exist in the world—how they act, how they are seen—through the autobiographical and biographical fictions they tell, can be examined in varied musical genres including hip-hop, country, pop, and rock. And through these artists' self-inventive acts, where they craft new versions of themselves for public consumption, they are seen and received in fresh, new ways.

In 2019's *Serving the Servant: Remembering Kurt Cobain*, released three days before the twenty-fifth anniversary of grunge rock legend Kurt Cobain's 1994 suicide, Nirvana's former manager Danny Goldberg reveals a version of Cobain unfamiliar to most. Fitting effortlessly into Allan Moore's theory of "authenticity of expression," in which he "convey[ed] the impression that his/her utterance is one of integrity," during the first few years of the 1990s, Cobain was viewed by fans and critics alike as an exemplar of punk rock authenticity: honest, self-deprecating, and appropriately skeptical about his own fame and about celebrity in general.[2] But what perhaps cemented his legend more than anything else—besides the nature of his early death—was Cobain's persona as an extremely talented artist who quite accidentally stumbled into international fame and considerable critical and financial success. It is this version of Cobain—the sensitive young man who is self-medicating, in part, due to his overwhelming fame decidedly *not* of his own making—that supports the notion that his suicide was an inevitable by-product of toxic celebrity culture. Goldberg tells a different story: Cobain was much more calculating about the band's success than his fans or the rock press understood. In fact, according to Goldberg, in his first meeting with the band in 1990, after asking if they wanted to continue releasing music through Sub Pop—a well-regarded, Seattle-based indie record label with punk rock credibility but minimal resources to groom a band for mainstream success—Cobain articulated a resounding "Absolutely not."[3] Yet it is the fictional autobiography—the one in which Cobain is an unwitting victim of fate—that, paradoxically, helped his celebrity grow. The more he appeared to be a reluctant star, the more young people gravitated toward him, fueling his ever-increasing popularity. This is not to suggest that Cobain secretly loved fame, but it does demonstrate that he wished for his band to connect with a large audience. As Goldberg says in an NPR interview, "Reflecting on Kurt Cobain's 'Crystalline Understanding' 25 Years Later," "He had an exquisite sense of balance of how to stand for something without being boring, how to be entertaining without being shallow. He was almost kind of 24/7 reinventing this Kurt Cobain persona."[4] It was that persona that helped to create his legend, showing how the crafting of a fictional autobiographical narrative really does effectively invent a self. For Nirvana fans, and a significant portion of the 1990s rock press, Cobain was indeed a victim of the fame and fortune he never wanted—true or not.

In 2019 Gary Clark Jr. also reinvented himself through carefully constructed autobiographical narratives about his life as a Black man in the United States. At the beginning of Gary Clark Jr.'s video for his song "This Land" from his 2019 release *This Land,* we see flashes of a rural Texas town through the eyes of a young Black boy. Over the acoustic strains of a different song, "The Governor," the camera cuts between the boy and shots of an American flag and a Lone Star flag hanging side by side, rows of worn clapboard houses, an Elgin Seventh-day Adventist Church billboard instructing people to "Exercise Daily. Run from Satan. Walk w/th God," and a cluster of small Confederate flags attached to two rusted metal mailboxes. As the images shift, we see imperceptible changes in the boy's expression—moving from neutral to concerned. The music ends, and there is a long shot of a bonfire, viewed from a considerable distance, perhaps by the same boy, or a collective of young Black boys and girls. The flames rise, the boy wades into the deep, swampy waters, and we hear Clark's guitar.[5] Thus begins Clark's startlingly bold video for his unapologetic, and uncharacteristically incendiary, song about America's racist past and present: "This Land."

This song and video are Clark's latest salvos in his war on his image as the future of twenty-first-century American blues music. As we saw earlier in *Fictional Blues,* Clark has talked openly about his frustrations with the expectations of blues fans and critics who want him to fit within the narrow bounds of authentic blues expression. His acts of autobiographical self-fashioning, and his corrections to his biographical record—namely his contention that given his middle-class background and his emergence as an artist at the beginning of the twenty-first century, it would be decidedly inauthentic for him to lay claim to the Delta blues—have mainly been focused on finding ways to assert his artistic freedom. Clark has told stories about himself to carve out a space for his experimentation with varied musical genres. Not content to be a blues savior, he pushed the narrative of a socioeconomic childhood experience out of step with the blues, and he forged unexpected collaborations with hip-hop and pop artists, embracing a more polished persona as a genre-crossing singer-songwriter and guitarist. But his storytelling has moved into a new direction: in "This Land," his autobiographical renderings now reside at the intersection of the personal and the political.[6]

As Clark states in an interview with *Rolling Stone,* he wrote "This Land" in reaction to an encounter with his racist neighbor who wondered aloud if Clark was really the owner of his fifty-acre ranch: "He was very disrespectful to me in front of my kids. And I don't play with that shit. He started saying, 'You don't live here. There's no way you could live here. Who really owns this place?'" While in previous interviews Clark has mentioned that he grew up in a middle-class neighborhood in Austin, Texas, and was offered a full scholarship to attend the University of Texas at Austin, he had not previously discussed his many experiences with racism while growing up. As he tells *Rolling Stone,* he remembers "being called nigger every day, people wanting to touch my hair, throwing shit in my mailbox, rolling up to my house with Confederate flags, saying, 'Nigger, go back to Africa,' writing 'nigger' on my fence." "This Land" creates a space for Clark to revise his autobiographical narrative, exposing his political side. Before this moment in his career, it appeared that, at least publicly, Clark embraced his uncomplicated narrative as a young, laid-back Black guitar hero who grew up in socioeconomic privilege, had white musical mentors, and presumably had relatively few overt experiences with racism. "This Land" undermines that storyline, allowing his fans and the music press to see that despite Clark's celebrity and wealth he is like any other Black person in America: "It pissed me off. I got a good chunk of property. I worked my ass off to be able to buy a place that my people can enjoy and run around—and to have this guy question me?"[7]

In response to his neighbor's racist aggression, Clark wrote a song in which he is able to have the last word. His autobiographical expression expands as he tells new stories about himself in his *Rolling Stone* interview, and in lyrics such as:

I told you, "There goes the neighborhood"
Now Mister Williams ain't so funny
I see you looking out your window
Can't wait to call the police on me.[8]

By including shots in the video for "This Land" of young Black boys and girls intercut with jarring images of Confederate flags, nooses, shackles, cotton, fire, and snakes, Clark includes himself in communities of Black people who encounter racism regardless of their class positions or how comfortable they are in white spaces. Clark's narrative is not based entirely on new events, however. The racism he has faced is longstanding and extensive. And like other successful Black people, he finds that his money, a white spouse, and his biracial children cannot shield him.

Clark's solution, of sorts, at the end of the video is worth noting. After a long and blistering guitar solo against the backdrop of a glowing bonfire in the darkness, as the children watch as the Confederate flags, shackles, and nooses burn, the music abruptly stops and the camera focuses on a dead snake and a charred Confederate flag.[9] There is daylight now, and the camera lands on an end table with a gun sitting on top of its case. The young boy goes outside of his house to find Clark sitting on the porch playing his acoustic guitar. The boy sits down in front of him. The boy and Clark are both more relaxed, even at times betraying faint smiles. Clark sings the beginning of his song "The Governor":

Well, you can meet my friend the governor
He the one that makes the law
If you meet him face to face
You gon' be the one at fault.[10]

The governor appears to be a name for Clark's gun. While Childish Gambino's video for "This Is America" uses images of gun violence to critique America's violent gun culture, Clark's video suggests an embrace of the use of a firearm as a response to the threat of racial violence toward Black bodies.[11] The small smile that Clark shares with the young boy reminds the audience of the shy but affable young blues-rock guitarist who burst onto the blues scene almost a decade ago. That version of himself is still in there, but this reinvented self is what is foregrounded in this song and video.

Fictional Blues engages the invented and reinvented selves of fictional and real-life bluesmen and women. These blues makers have important stories to tell—tales that demonstrate who they are to their readers, listeners, and viewers, as well as to themselves. The autobiographical and biographical fictions also allow their identities to shift, as they confront the hostile forces that attempt to undermine, limit, or prevent their artistic or personal expression from fully flowering. The blues tradition is truly a narrative one, and it is through storytelling that bluesmen and women are able to find artistic and personal success.

Notes

INTRODUCTION

1. Alan Light, "True to the Red, White and Black," *New York Times*, June 10, 2007, https://www.nytimes.com/2007/06/10/arts/music/10light.html.

2. Mieke Bal, *Narratology: Introduction to the Theory of Narrative* (Toronto: University of Toronto Press, 1997), 5.

3. Gérard Genette, *Narrative Discourse: An Essay in Method*, trans. Jane E. Lewin (Ithaca, NY: Cornell University Press, 1980); Bal, *Narratology;* William Nelles, *Frameworks: Narrative Levels and Embedded Narrative* (New York: Peter Lang Publishing, 1997); John Barth, *The Friday Book: Essays and Other Nonfiction* (Baltimore, MD: The Johns Hopkins University Press, 1984).

4. Barth, *Friday Book*, 224, 221.

5. Barth, *Friday Book*, 226–27.

6. Barth, *Friday Book*, 221.

7. Bal, *Narratology*, 55.

8. Barth, *Friday Book*, 221.

9. For additional study about the classic blues and blueswomen, see Daphne Duval Harrison, *Black Pearls: Blues Queens of the 1920s* (New Brunswick, NJ: Rutgers University Press, 1993); and Angela Davis, *Blues Legacies and Black Feminism* (New York: Pantheon Books, 1998).

10. Elijah Wald, *The Blues: A Very Short Introduction* (Oxford: Oxford University Press, 2010), 1–2.

11. Wald, *Blues*, 4–5, 4.

12. Wald, *Blues*, 6.

13. See Leroi Jones, *Blues People: Negro Music in White America and the Music That Developed from It* (New York: William Morrow, 1963); Samuel A. Floyd Jr., *The Power of Black Music: Interpreting Its History from Africa to the United States* (New York: Oxford University Press, 1995); and Eileen Southern, *The Music of Black Americans: A History* (New York: W. W. Norton, 1997).

14. See Elijah Wald, *Escaping the Delta: Robert Johnson and the Invention of the Blues* (New York: HarperCollins, 2004); Albert Murray, *The Hero and the Blues* (Columbia: University of Missouri Press, 1973); and Ralph Ellison, *Shadow and Act* (New York: Vintage Books, 1964).

15. Wald, *Blues*, 5–6, 6.

16. For some examples of blues as dance music, see Albert Murray, *Stomping the Blues* (Cambridge, MA: Da Capo Press, 2000); and David Wondrich, *Stomp and Swerve: American Music Gets Hot, 1843–1924* (Chicago: A Cappella Books, 2003).

17. For further conversation about the "cult of authenticity," see Benjamin Filene, *Romancing the Folk: Public Memory and American Roots Music* (Chapel Hill: University of North Carolina Press, 2000), 49. Important books focused on the country/rural blues include William Barlow, *Looking Up at Down: The Emergence of Blues Culture* (Philadelphia, PA: Temple University Press, 1989); Francis Davis, *The History of the Blues: The Roots, the Music, the People* (Cambridge, MA: Da Capo Press, 1995); and Jeff Todd Titon, *Early Downhome Blues: A Musical and Cultural Analysis* (Chapel Hill: University of North Carolina Press, 1994).

18. Wald, *Escaping the Delta*, 72.

19. Barlow, *Looking Up at Down*; Wald, *Blues*, 63; For an important discussion about blues music and the African American Great Migration, see Farah Jasmine Griffin, *"Who Set You Flowin'?": The African-American Migration Narrative* (New York: Oxford University Press, 1995), 52–64.

20. Jones, *Blues People*, 17.

21. Houston A. Baker Jr., *Blues, Ideology, and Afro-American Literature: A Vernacular Theory* (Chicago: University of Chicago Press, 1984), 197.

22. Robert Palmer, *Deep Blues* (New York: Viking Press, 1981), 18.

23. "Living Blues Magazine," Center for the Study of Southern Culture, southernstudies.olemiss.edu/publications/living-blues/.

24. For further discussion about romance in the blues, see Wald, *Escaping the Delta;* Patricia Schroeder, *Robert Johnson, Mythmaking, and Contemporary American Culture* (Urbana: University of Illinois Press, 2004); Paige A. McGinley, *Staging the Blues: From Tent Shows to Tourism* (Durham, NC: Duke University Press, 2014); and Marybeth Hamilton, *In Search of the Blues: Black Voices, White Visions* (London: Jonathan Cape, 2007).

25. Allan Moore, "Authenticity as Authentication," *Popular Music* 21, no. 2 (2002): 211–20, 214, 214, JSTOR.

26. Roger Davis Gatchet, "'I've Got Some Antique in Me': The Discourse of Authenticity and Identity in the African American Blues Community in Austin, Texas," *Oral History Review* 39, no. 2 (2012): 214–15, 216–17.

27. Jennifer Lynn Stoever, *The Sonic Color Line: Race and the Cultural Politics of Listening* (New York: New York University Press, 2016), 11.

28. E. Patrick Johnson, *Appropriating Blackness: Performance and the Politics of Authenticity* (Durham, NC: Duke University Press, 2003), 163.

29. Corey Harris, "Can White People Play the Blues?" *Blues Is Black Music!*, May 10, 2015, bluesisblackmusic.blogspot.com/2015/05/can-white-people-play-blues.html.

30. Moore, "Authenticity," 218, 214–18, 211–18.

31. Sidonie Smith and Julia Watson have noted in their opening chapter in *Reading Autobiography: A Guide for Interpreting Life Narratives* (Minneapolis: University of Minnesota Press, 2010), 2, that the term "autobiography" "describes writing being produced at a particular historical juncture, the period prior to the Enlightenment in the West." In a twentieth-century context, and beyond, it makes better sense to use the term "autobiographical narrative" or "life writing." However, sometimes I use the term "autobiography" to discuss a non-book-based form of autobiographical expression. In those cases, I leave the word intact. See Paul John Eakin, *Fictions in Autobiography: Studies in the Art of Self-Invention* (Princeton, NJ: Princeton University Press, 1988), 3; Timothy Dow Adams, *Telling Lies in Modern American Autobiography* (Chapel Hill: The University of North Carolina Press, 1990); Herbert Leibowitz, *Fabricating Lives: Explorations in American Autobiography* (New York: Alfred A. Knopf, 1989); and Sidonie Smith and Julia Watson, *Getting a Life: Everyday Uses of Autobiography* (Minneapolis: University of Minnesota Press, 1996).

32. In African American folklore, the rabbit's foot is considered to be a good luck charm.

33. Philip Auslander, "Musical Personae," *TDR: The Drama Review* 50, no. 1 (T 189) (Spring 2006): 102.

34. In addition to Auslander's and McGinley's work, also see Titon, *Early Downhome Blues*; and Dennis Jarrett, "The Singer and the Bluesman: Formulations of Personality in the Lyrics of the Blues," in *Write Me a Few of Your Lines: A Blues Reader*, ed. Steven C. Tracy (Amherst: University of Massachusetts Press, 1999), 195–200.

35. Smith and Watson, *Reading Autobiography*, 72–73.

36. See Daphne A. Brooks, *Bodies in Dissent: Spectacular Performances of Race and Freedom, 1850–1910* (Durham, NC: Duke University Press, 2006); Stephanie Leigh Batiste, *Darkening Mirrors: Imperial Representation in Depression-Era African American Performance* (Durham, NC: Duke University Press, 2011); Uri McMillan, *Embodied Avatars: Genealogies of Black Feminist Art and Performance* (New York: New York University Press, 2015).

37. W. C. Handy, *Father of the Blues: An Autobiography* (New York: Macmillan, 1941), 78.

38. Barbara Welter, "The Cult of True Womanhood: 1820–1860," *American Quarterly* 18, no. 2, part 1 (1966): 152, JSTOR.

39. Angela Y. Davis, *Blues Legacies and Black Feminism: Gertrude "Ma" Rainey, Bessie Smith, and Billie Holiday* (New York: Pantheon Books, 1998), 39.

40. Toni Cade Bambara, *Gorilla, My Love* (New York: Random House, 1972). Some sources state that "Mississippi Ham Rider" was originally published in the *Massachusetts Review* in 1960, and others say 1964. It appears that the 1960 date is an error, however, as a search of the archived *Massachusetts Review* on JSTOR finds that "Mississippi Ham Rider" was indeed published in 1964.

41. F. Davis, *History*, 108.

42. Bambara, *Gorilla, My Love*, 51, 48, 47, 48.

43. Bambara, *Gorilla, My Love*, 50, 51.

44. Bambara, *Gorilla, My Love*, 52, 55, 56.

45. Bambara, *Gorilla, My Love*, 55–56, 56, 56.

CHAPTER 1: THE NARRATIVE BLUES TRADITION

1. According to Cecil Brown, he found the 1903 version of the Stagolee myth in the files of W. K. Wilgus in Los Angeles in 1995. It was sent by the folklorist G. Legman to someone with the initials D. R. W. in 1955. So even though this might be the earliest iteration of the Stagolee ballad, it does not appear to have been collected until decades after Ella Scott Fisher's version.

2. John A. Lomax and Alan Lomax, *American Ballads and Folk Songs* (New York: Dover Publications, 1994), 93–94, 94–95.

3. "Shot in Curtis' Place," *St. Louis (MI) Globe-Democrat*, December 26, 1895, Newspapers.com.

4. Given the similarities between the two forms, throughout this chapter, I sometimes use the terms "ballad" and "song" interchangeably.

5. Cecil Brown, *Stagolee Shot Billy* (Cambridge, MA: Harvard University Press, 2003), 1, 221.

6. Brown, *Stagolee;* D. Quentin Miller, "Playing a Mean Guitar: The Legacy of Staggerlee in Baldwin and Morrison," in *James Baldwin and Toni Morrison: Comparative Critical and Theoretical Essays*, ed. Lovalerie King and Lynn Orilla Scott (New York: Palgrave Macmillan, 2006).

7. Miller, "Playing," 123.

8. "Ma" Rainey with Her Georgia Band, "Stack O' Lee Blues / Yonder Comes the Blues," Paramount, 1926; "Amy Winehouse—'Stagger Lee' (cover) HD @ Arena Anhembi, São Paulo, Brazil," YouTube, uploaded by livyak, January 16, 2011, https://www.youtube.com/watch?time_continue=3&v=1yGe4rCmIo&feature=emb_logo.

9. "Stack Lee's Trial," *St. Louis (MI) Globe-Democrat*, July 14, 1896, Newspapers.com.

10. Here and elsewhere, I am indebted to the research contained in two key texts for my discussion about Stagolee: Cecil Brown's *Stagolee Shot Billy*, and John Russell David, "Tragedy in Ragtime: Black Folktales from St. Louis" (PhD diss., Saint Louis University, 1976), which was the first scholarly work to identify Lee Shelton as the basis for the Stagolee folk tale; Derek McCulloch and Shepherd Hendrix, *Stagger Lee* (Portland, OR: Image Comics, 2006) 225; Brown, *Stagolee*, 4.

11. Greil Marcus, *Mystery Train: Images of America in Rock 'n' Roll Music* (New York: Plume, 1997).

12. Brown, *Stagolee*, 7; Richard Bauman, *Story, Performance, and Event: Contextual Studies of Oral Narrative* (Cambridge: Cambridge University Press, 1986), 2.

13. David C. Rubin, *Memory In Oral Traditions: The Cognitive Psychology of Epic, Ballads, and Counting-Out Rhymes* (New York: Oxford University Press, 1995), 9.

14. Lomax and Lomax, *American Ballads*, 94.

15. Rubin, *Memory*, 6, 7.

16. Lomax and Lomax, *American Ballads*, 96.

17. David, "Tragedy in Ragtime," 160, 177, 178.

18. David, "Tragedy in Ragtime," 196, 198; Brown, *Stagolee*, 35.

19. David, "Tragedy in Ragtime," 175.

20. David, "Tragedy in Ragtime," 283; Lomax and Lomax, *American Ballads*, 93, 99.

21. David, "Tragedy in Ragtime," 170; Lomax and Lomax, *American Ballads*, 97.

22. Lomax and Lomax, *American Ballads*, 98, 97, 94–95, 98, 99, 99, 96.

23. Lomax and Lomax, *American Ballads*, 99.

24. "Smith, Mamie," in *Harlem Renaissance Lives: From the African American National Biography*, ed. Henry Louis Gates Jr. and Evelyn Brooks Higginbotham (New York: Oxford University Press, 2009), 458–59.

25. Albert Murray, *Train Whistle Guitar* (New York: Vintage Books, 1999), 11, 13, 13, 12, 13.

26. Murray, *Train Whistle Guitar*, 99, 99, 99.

27. Ethel Waters and Charles Samuels, *His Eye Is on the Sparrow* (New York: Doubleday, 1951), 160, 161.

28. In chapter 4, "From John Anthony Gillis to Jack White: A Study in Blues Self-Invention," I have a longer conversation about White's voicing of the bad man in his White Stripes song "Ball and Biscuit." White Stripes, "Ball and Biscuit," *Elephant*, V2/Third Man Records, 2003.

29. In African American folklore, the seventh son of a seventh son is blessed with the gift of clairvoyance. See W. E. B. Du Bois, *The Souls of Black Folk*, ed. Henry Louis Gates Jr. and Terri Hume Oliver (New York: W. W. Norton, 1999).

30. Lomax and Lomax, *American Ballads*, 99.

31. John W. Roberts, *From Trickster to Badman: The Black Folk Hero in Slavery and Freedom* (Philadelphia: University of Pennsylvania Press, 1989), 200.

32. David, "Tragedy in Ragtime," 291, 291.

33. Paul Garon, *The Devil's Son-in-Law: The Story of Peetie Wheatstraw and His Songs* (Chicago: Charles H. Kerr Publishing, 2003), 32.

34. David Honeyboy Edwards et al., *The World Don't Owe Me Nothing: The Life and Times of Bluesman Honeyboy Edwards* (Chicago: Chicago Review Press, 2000), 104–5, 105.

35. Robert Palmer, *Deep Blues* (New York: Viking Press, 1981), 58–59.

36. David Evans, *Tommy Johnson* (London: Studio Vista, 1971), 22–23.

37. Palmer, *Deep Blues*, 59; Henry Louis Gates Jr., *The Signifying Monkey: A Theory of African American Literary Criticism* (Oxford: Oxford University Press, 1989), 6, 22.

38. Elijah Wald, *Escaping the Delta: Robert Johnson and the Invention of the Blues* (New York: HarperCollins Publishers, 2004), 3.

39. Wald, *Escaping the Delta*, 3.

40. Mance Lipscomb and Glen Alyn, *I Say Me for a Parable: The Oral Autobiography of Mance Lipscomb, Texas Bluesman* (New York: W. W. Norton, 1993), 267, 271.

41. Albert Murray, "Jazz Lips: on Louis Armstrong," *New Republic*, November 22, 1999, https://newrepublic.com/article/114391/albert-murray-reviews-louis-armstrong-his-own-words.

42. G. Thomas Couser, *Vulnerable Subjects: Ethics and Life Writing* (Ithaca, NY: Cornell University Press, 2004); Carole Boyce Davies, "Collaboration and the Ordering Imperative in Life Story Production," in *De/Colonizing the Subject*, ed. Sidonie Smith and Julia Watson (Minneapolis: University of Minnesota Press, 1992), 3–19; Sidonie Smith and Julia Watson, eds., *De/Colonizing the Subject* (Minneapolis: University of Minnesota Press, 1992); Alison Ravenscroft, "Recasting Indigenous Lives along the Lines of Western Desire: Editing, Autobiography, and the Colonizing Project," in *The Routledge Auto/Biography Studies Reader*, ed. Ricia Anne Chansky and Emily Hipchen (London: Routledge, 2016), 168–74.

43. Couser, *Vulnerable Subjects*, 37, 36.

44. Sidonie Smith and Julia Watson, *Reading Autobiography: A Guide for Interpreting Life Narratives* (Minneapolis: University of Minnesota Press 2010), 67.

45. Ravenscroft, *Recasting*, 173, 173.

46. Smith and Watson, *Reading*, 67.

47. Lipscomb and Alyn, *I Say*, 31–32.

48. Bauman, *Story*, 2.

49. Lipscomb and Alyn, *I Say*, 25.

50. Lipscomb and Alyn, *I Say*, 25.

51. Lipscomb and Alyn, *I Say*, 51, 51.

52. Murray, *Train Whistle Guitar*, 100.

53. Lipscomb and Alyn, *I Say*, 52.

54. Lipscomb and Alyn, *I Say*, 25–26, 52, 26, 26, 400–401.

55. Lipscomb and Alyn, *I Say*, 26.

56. Lipscomb and Alyn, *I Say*, 26.

57. Lipscomb and Alyn, *I Say*, 267.

58. For further conversation about the Lomaxes' intentional marketing of Lead Belly as an exemplar of rural folk authenticity, see Benjamin Filene, *Romancing the Folk: Public Memory and American Roots Music* (Chapel Hill: University of North Carolina Press, 2000), 58–74.

59. Lipscomb and Alyn, *I Say*, 267, 267–68, 268, 268, 269.

60. Lipscomb and Alyn, *I Say*, 268.

61. David, "Tragedy in Ragtime," 195.

62. Brown, *Stagolee*, 67.

63. Lipscomb and Alyn, *I Say*, 268.

64. Lipscomb and Alyn, *I Say*, 269, 269.

65. Bauman, *Story*, 21.

66. Edwards et al., *World Don't Owe Me Nothing*, 105.

67. Lipscomb and Alyn, *I Say*, 271, 271.

68. Lipscomb and Alyn, *I Say*, 29–30, 35.

69. Allan Moore, "Authenticity as Authentication," *Popular Music* 21, no. 2 (2002): 211–20, JSTOR.

70. Lipscomb and Alyn, *I Say*, 35, 271.

71. Lipscomb and Alyn, *I Say*, 271.

72. Lipscomb and Alyn, *I Say*, 270.

73. Lipscomb and Alyn, *I Say*, 270.

74. Lipscomb and Alyn, *I Say*, 270.

75. Lipscomb and Alyn, *I Say*, 268, 270, 268, 270, 268, 270.

76. Lipscomb and Alyn, *I Say*, 191–92, 192, 192, 194–95, 195, 270, 209, 137.

77. See John W. Blassingame, *The Slave Community: Plantation Life in the Antebellum South* (New York: Oxford University Press, 1979); Gilbert Osofsky, ed., *Puttin' On Ole Massa: The Slave Narratives of Henry Bibb, William Wells Brown, and Solomon Northup* (New York: Harper Torchbooks, 1969); and Langston Hughes and Arna Bontemps, eds., *The Book of Negro Folklore* (New York: Dodd, Mead, 1958).

78. David, "Tragedy in Ragtime," 12.

79. Lipscomb and Alyn, *I Say*, 137.

80. David, "Tragedy in Ragtime," 12–13, 15.

81. Murray, *Train Whistle Guitar*, 12.

82. "Lyrics for Stack O' Lee Blues by Ma Rainey," Musixmatch, last modified May 6, 2019, https://www.musixmatch.com/lyrics/Ma-Rainey/Stack-O-Lee-Blues.

83. According to John Russell David, "Tragedy in Ragtime;" Brown, *Stagolee;* and Stacy I. Morgan, *Frankie and Johnny: Race, Gender, and the Work of African American Folklore in 1930s America* (Austin: University of Texas Press, 2017), 24–26, the ballad "Frankie and Johnny" likely originated from real-life African American prostitute Frankie Baker's 1899 murder of her pimp (and lover) Allen Britt in St. Louis, Missouri, after discovering his affair with Alice Pryor.

84. Brown, *Stagolee*, 145, 11, 23, 51, 145; "Lyrics for Stack O' Lee Blues by Ma Rainey."

85. Most sources, including the seminal work Sandra R. Lieb, *Mother of the Blues: A Study of Ma Rainey* (Amherst: University of Massachusetts Press, 1981), have suggested that Rainey was born on April 26, 1886, in Columbus, Georgia. However, through Columbus, Georgia, June 1900 census records, Dutch scholar Karl Gert zur Heide has found that she was actually born four years earlier in Alabama. Karl Gert zur Heide, "Ma Rainey—Part 1," *Doctor Jazz Magazine*, no. 208, March 2010, 9.

86. Daphne Duval Harrison, *Black Pearls: Blues Queens of the 1920s* (New Brunswick, NJ: Rutgers University Press, 1993), 34.

87. Harrison, *Black Pearls*, 34, 35.

88. Harrison, *Black Pearls*, 17, 35.

89. Lieb, *Mother of the Blues*, 18; Derrick Stewart-Baxter, *Ma Rainey and the Classic Blues Singers* (New York: Stein and Day, 1970), 42.

90. Chris Albertson, *Bessie* (New Haven: Yale University Press, 2003), 7.

91. William Barlow, *Looking Up at Down: The Emergence of Blues Culture* (Philadelphia: Temple University Press, 1989), 165; Albertson, *Bessie*, 11–12.

92. Barlow, *Looking Up*, 166; Albertson, *Bessie*, 14–16, 19.

93. Albertson, *Bessie*, 25, 27, 38.

94. Barlow, *Looking Up*, 167; Angela Davis, *Blues Legacies and Black Feminism* (New York: Pantheon Books, 1998), 319.

95. Bessie Smith and Her Blue Boys, "Send Me to the 'Lectric Chair," Columbia Records, 1927; Bessie Smith, "Hateful Blues," Columbia Records, 1924. In an e-mail conversation with Elijah Wald on 3/9/20, he confirmed that the line is "Gonna take my Wade & Butcher, gonna cut him through and through," not "Gonna take my weddin' butcher, gonna cut him through and through," as Wade & Butcher was a popular brand of razors at the time. Also, while Perry Bradford is credited as the composer of "Hateful Blues" on the label of the original seventy-eight, according to Wald (and the Library of Congress), Ely or Eli Johnson likely wrote it, and Bradford registered it in the name of Ethel Bradford, Library of Congress, *Catalog of Copyright Entries*, part 3, issues 5–6 (Washington, D.C.: Copyright Office), 435.

96. Albertson, *Bessie*, 43–44.

97. Paul Oliver, *Bessie Smith* (New York: A. S. Barnes, 1971), 24, 41–42; Harrison, *Black Pearls*, 52.

98. John W. Work, *American Negro Songs* (New York: Bonanza Books, 1940), 32.

99. Lieb, *Mother of the Blues*, 3.

100. Harrison, *Black Pearls*, 35; Albertson, *Bessie*, 12; Lieb, *Mother of the Blues*, 10, 23.

101. "Discovered at Last—'Ma' Rainey Mother of the Blues!" *Chicago Defender*, February 2, 1924, A10, ProQuest.

102. Albertson, *Bessie*, 14, 14.

103. Stewart-Baxter, *Ma* Rainey.

104. Albertson, *Bessie*, 44; Lieb, *Mother of the Blues*, 17.

105. See Marybeth Hamilton, *In Search of the Blues: Black Voices, White Visions* (London: Jonathan Cape, 2007); Ted Gioia, *Delta Blues: The Life and Times of the Mississippi Masters Who Revolutionized American Music* (New York: W. W. Norton, 2008).

106. Lynn Abbott and Doug Seroff, *The Original Blues: The Emergence of the Blues in African American Vaudeville* (Jackson: University Press of Mississippi, 2017), 264.

107. Elijah Wald, *The Blues: A Very Short Introduction* (Oxford: Oxford University Press, 2010), 22.

108. "Smith, Mamie," in *Harlem Renaissance Lives*, 458–59.

109. "Mamie Smith to Appear Wednesday at Municipal Auditorium with Her Famous Jazz Hounds," *Savannah Tribune*, February 5, 1921, Readex, America's Historical Newspapers.

110. Wm. E. Ready, "From $20.00 per Week to $1,000 Ptr [*sic*] Night: This Is What Happened to Mamie Smith in the Short Space of Three Years," *Topeka (KS) Plain Dealer*, October 14, 1921, Readex, America's Historical Newspapers.

111. Teresa DiTirro, "Researchers Confirm Blues Legend Mamie Smith Was Born in Cincinnati," *Local 12 News*, November 15, 2018, https://local12.com/news/local/researchers-confirm-blues-legend-mamie-smith-was-born-in-cincinnati.

112. Ready, "From $20.00 Per Week."

CHAPTER 2: SHUG, BIG MAMA, AND AMY

1. *Afterword* Michael Spörke, *Big Mama Thornton: The Life and Music* (Jefferson, NC: McFarland Publishers, 2014), 105–6; "Gunsmoke Blues—Muddy Waters, Big Mama Thornton, Big Joe Turner, George 'Harmonica' Smith," uploaded by musadiggari, YouTube, March 30, 2015, https://www.youtube.com/watch?v=_ATwmyuhmeY.

2. Big Mama Thornton, "Ball and Chain," *Ball and Chain: Big Mama Thornton, Lightning Hopkins, Larry Williams*, Arhoolie Records, 1968.

3. Big Brother and the Holding Company, "Ball and Chain," *Cheap Thrills*, Columbia Records, 1968.

4. "Gunsmoke Blues."

5. Elijah Wald, *The Blues: A Very Short Introduction* (Oxford: Oxford University Press, 2010), 25–26.

6. Daphne Duval Harrison, *Black Pearls: Blues Queens of the 1920s* (New Brunswick: Rutgers University Press, 2000), 6.

7. For a further discussion about the vaudeville/classic blues, see Harrison, *Black Pearls*; and Lynn Abbott and Doug Seroff, *The Original Blues: The Emergence of the Blues in African American Vaudeville* (Jackson: Jackson University Press of Mississippi, 2017).

8. Karen Brodkin, *How Jews Became White Folks and What That Says about Race in America* (New Brunswick, NJ: Rutgers University Press, 2010).

9. LeRoi Jones, *Blues People: Negro Music in White America and the Music That Developed from It* (New York: William Morrow, 1963), 87, 87; emphasis in source.

10. Stephen Calt and Gayle Wardlow, *King of the Delta Blues: The Life and Music of Charlie Patton* (Newton, NJ: Rock Chapel Press, 1988), 215–21.

11. Elijah Wald, *Escaping the Delta: Robert Johnson and the Invention of the Blues* (New York: HarperCollins Publishers, 2004), 232; Hazel Carby, "Policing the Black Woman's Body in an Urban Context," special "Identities" issue, *Critical Inquiry* 18, no. 4 (1992): 755, https://www.law.columbia.edu/sites/default/files/microsites/gender-sexuality/Gender_Justice_Fall_2018/carby_policing_the_black_womans_body.pdf.

12. Harrison, *Black Pearls*, 64, 22, 22.

13. "Mothers Taking Innocent Daughters to Houses of Ill Fame: To Play Piano Still Our Christians' Cry of White Slave Is Heard in the Community—What about the Black Ones?," *Chicago Defender*, March 26, 1910, 1, ProQuest.

14. Carby, "Policing the Black Woman's Body," 739, 741.

15. Angela Davis, *Blues Legacies and Black Feminism* (New York: Pantheon Books, 1998), 13.

16. Carby, "Policing the Black Woman's Body," 754–55.

17. Leigh Gilmore, *Autobiographics: A Feminist Theory of Women's Self-Representation* (Ithaca, NY: Cornell University Press, 1994), 42, 41–42, 42, 42.

18. "Esther Phillips," Yale University Oral History of American Music, November 13, 2014; "Big Mama Thornton," Yale University Oral History of American Music, November 13, 2014.

19. Alice Walker, *The Color Purple* (New York: Harcourt, 2003), 45, 45–46, 49.

20. Walker, *Color Purple*, 80, 81, 81.

21. Hazel V. Carby, "It Jus Be's Dat Way Sometime: The Sexual Politics of Women's Blues," in *The Jazz Cadence of American Culture*, ed. Robert G. O'Meally (New York: Columbia University Press, 1998), 481. Originally published in *Radical America* 20, no. 4 (1986): 9–24.

22. Walker, *Color Purple*, 49.

23. Walker, *Color Purple*, 43–44, 55, 54.

24. Judith Butler, *Gender Trouble: Feminism and the Subversion of Identity* (New York: Routledge, 2006), 194–95.

25. Walker, *Color Purple*, 72.

26. Walker, *Color Purple*, 53.

27. Walker, *Color Purple*, 53, 53.

28. Walker, *Color Purple*, 120–21, 121.

29. Walker, *Color Purple*, 121, 121–22, 122.

30. Walker, *Color Purple*, 49.

31. Definition of "womanist": "(1) Responsible. In charge. *Serious.* (2) A woman who loves other women, sexually and/or nonsexually. . . . Sometimes loves individual men, sexually and/or nonsexually" (xi). For a full definition of "womanist," see Alice Walker, *In Search of Our Mothers' Gardens: Womanist Prose* (New York: Harcourt, 1983).

32. Walker, *Color Purple*, 82, 82, 39, 81.

33. Walker, *Color Purple*, 83.

34. Walker, *Color Purple*, 83.

35. Walker, *Color Purple*, 83.

36. Walker, *Color Purple*, 82.

37. Walker, *Color Purple*, 95, 95.

38. Walker, *Color Purple*, 95, 96, 96.

39. Walker, *Color Purple*, 96, 96.

40. Walker, *Color Purple*, 97, 93, 93, 97.

41. Walker, *Color Purple*, 96, 98.

42. Frederick Douglass and Harriet Jacobs, *Narrative of the Life of Frederick Douglass, an American Slave and Incidents in the Life of a Slave Girl* (New York: Modern Library, 2004), 108.

43. Walker, *Color Purple*, 93.

44. Walker, *Color Purple*, 99, 30, 30, 82–83, 98.

45. Davis, *Blues Legacies*, 53.

46. Davis, *Blues Legacies*, 45–46.

47. Davis, *Blues Legacies*, 239, 239, 47.

48. Jim Windolf, "Stand by Them," *New York Times*, June 12, 2009, https://www.nytimes.com/2009/06/14/books/review/Windolf-t.html.

49. Davis, *Blues* Legacies; Harrison, *Black Pearls;* Sandra R. Lieb, *Mother of the Blues: A Study of Ma Rainey* (Amherst: University of Massachusetts Press, 1981).

50. "Gunsmoke Blues."

51. Robert Neff and Anthony Connor, *The Blues: In Images and Interviews* (New York: Cooper Square Press, 1999), 50.

52. Spörke, *Big Mama*, 5, 7, 10, 151, 152, 24–25; "Big Mama Thornton," 5.

53. Jerry Leiber and Mike Stoller with David Ritz, *Hound Dog: The Leiber and Stoller Autobiography* (New York: Simon & Schuster, 2009), 67.

54. Leiber, Stoller, and Ritz, *Hound Dog*, 94; Don Robey of Peacock Records estimated that "Hound Dog" sold between 500,000 and 750,000 copies. Sporke, *Big Mama*, 26. Later Johnny Otis suggested that he was the producer, and he was supposed to receive one-third of the songwriting credit and half of the publishing. Lieber and Stoller admitted that they had offered Otis one-third of the mechanical rights on record sales, but after a lawsuit Otis was unable to receive a publishing or songwriting credit, barring him from making a substantial sum from the remake; Sporke, *Big Mama*, 35.

55. Maureen Mahon, "Listening for Willie Mae 'Big Mama' Thornton's Voice: The Sound of Race and Gender Transgressions in Rock and Roll," *Women and Music: A Journal of Gender and Culture* 15 (2011): 4, 5, Project MUSE.

56. "Big Mama Thornton 1970," uploaded by WGBH Stock Sales, YouTube, November 11, 2009, https://www.youtube.com/watch?v=IJlBo5KJ3b4.

57. Daphne A. Brooks, *Bodies in Dissent: Spectacular Performances of Race and Freedom, 1850–1910* (Durham, NC: Duke University Press, 2006), 4.

58. Stephanie Leigh Batiste, *Darkening Mirrors: Imperial Representation in Depression-Era African American Performance* (Durham, NC: Duke University Press, 2011), 6–7.

59. Neff and Connor, *Blues*, "Introduction."

60. The transcript of the interview with Big Mama Thornton and the digitized interview with Esther Phillips are the result of archival research I conducted at the Yale University Oral History of American Music archive in the fall of 2014.

61. Linda Shopes, "Making Sense of Oral History," *Oral History in the Digital Age*, April 8, 2015, http://ohda.matrix.msu.edu/2012/08/making-sense-of-oral-history/.

62. Mahon, "Listening," 6.

63. Linda Shopes, "'Insights and Oversights': Reflections on the Documentary Tradition and the Theoretical Turn in Oral History," *Oral History Review* 41, no. 2 (2014): 261, OhioLINK.

64. Brooks, *Bodies in Dissent*, 4.

65. Sharon O'Brien, "A Short Reflection on Teaching Memoir and Oral History," *Oral History Review* 25, no. 1–2 (Summer/Fall 1998): 113, JSTOR.

66. "Big Mama Thornton," 7, 15, 15.

67. Steve Huey, "Esther Phillips," n.d., https://www.allmusic.com/artist/esther-phillips-mn0000271029/biography; Spörke, *Big Mama*, 19–20.

68. "Esther Phillips," Yale.

69. "Esther Phillips," Yale.

70. "Esther Phillips," Yale.

71. Cyril Cordor, "Amy Winehouse," n.d., https://www.allmusic.com/artist/amy-winehouse-mn0000627026/biography; Alex Ritman, "Amy Winehouse Doc Pushes Late Singer Back into U.K. Album Charts," July 9, 2015, https://www.hollywoodreporter.com/news/amy-winehouse-uk-charts-doc-807521.

72. Steve Kandell, "Amy Winehouse: Rock Myth, Hard Reality," *Spin*, July 25, 2011, https://www.spin.com/2011/07/amy-winehouse-rock-myth-hard-reality/.

73. John Aizlewood, "Amy's on Her Best Behaviour . . . But It's Not Quite Rehab, No, No, No," *Evening Standard*, February 20, 2007, 3, LexisNexis Academic, https://www.lexisnexis.com/hottopics/lnacademic/?.

74. Judy Jarvis, "Amy Winehouse's Pain Is Listener's Gain," *Lancaster New Era*, April 19, 2007, 3, LexisNexis Academic.

75. Jon Pareles, "Critic's Choice: New CDs," *New York Times*, March 12, 2007, late ed., 4, LexisNexis Academic.

76. Baz Dreisinger, *Near Black: White-to-Black Passing in American Culture* (Amherst: University of Massachusetts Press, 2008), 3.

77. Gayle Wald, *Crossing the Line: Racial Passing in Twentieth-Century U.S. Literature and Culture* (Durham, NC: Duke University Press, 2000), 16.

78. Dreisinger, *Near Black*, 7.

79. Dreisinger, *Near Black*, 7, 16.

80. Amy Winehouse, "Some Unholy War," *Back to Black*, Island Records, 2006.

81. Amy Winehouse, "Me & Mr Jones," *Back to Black*, Island Records, 2006; Billy Paul, "Me and Mrs. Jones," *360 Degrees of Billy Paul*, Philadelphia International Records, 1972.

82. Davis, *Blues Legacies*, 13.

83. A rough trajectory of Winehouse's relationship with Fielder-Civil is as follows: When they first became involved, in 2005 he had a girlfriend. After a few months, he returned to his girlfriend. Winehouse fell into a depression, and wrote *Back to Black* almost entirely about Fielder-Civil. They eventually reunited, and were married in May 2007. Mitch Winehouse, *Amy: My Daughter* (New York: itbooks, 2012).

84. "Wino Arrested; Pop Hates on Doherty," *St. Petersburg (FL) Times*, December 19, 2007, 2B, LexisNexis Academic.

85. Daphne A. Brooks, "'This Voice Which Is Not One': Amy Winehouse Sings the Ballad of Sonic Blue(s)face Culture," *Women & Performance: A Journal of Feminist Theory* 20, no. 1 (2010): 37, 49, 54, 54, 54, https://www.tandfonline.com/doi/full/10.1080/07407701003589337.

86. Robert Palmer, *Deep Blues* (New York: Viking Press, 1981), 60.

87. Ted Gioia, *Delta Blues: The Life and Times of the Mississippi Masters Who Revolutionized American Music* (New York: W. W. Norton, 2008), 299; Davis, *Blues Legacies*, 38.

88. Amy Winehouse, "You Know I'm No Good," *Back to Black*, Island Records, 2006.

89. Sidonie Smith and Julia Watson, *Reading Autobiography: A Guide for Interpreting Life Narratives* (Minneapolis: University of Minnesota Press, 2010), 72–73.

90. Amy Winehouse, "Wake Up Alone," *Back to Black*, Island Records, 2006.

91. Amy Winehouse, "Rehab," *Back to Black*, Island Records, 2006.

92. Amy Winehouse, "Tears Dry on Their Own," *Back to Black*, Island Records, 2006.

CHAPTER 3: "I WAS ASTOUNDED AT WHAT I HEARD"

1. *The Search for Robert Johnson*, directed by Chris Hunt (New York: Columbia Music Video, 1992), DVD.

2. Barry Lee Pearson and Bill McCulloch, *Robert Johnson: Lost and Found* (Urbana, IL: University of Illinois Press, 2003), 6.

3. Rick Bragg, "Court Rules Father of the Blues Has a Son," *New York Times*, June 17, 2000, https://www.nytimes.com/2000/06/17/us/court-rules-father-of-the-blues-has-a-son.html.

4. Mack McCormick began researching Robert Johnson in 1972 for a book titled Biography of a Phantom, which he never completed. Also see Gayle Dean Wardlow, *Chasin' That Devil's Music, Searching for the Blues* (Milwaukee: Backbeat Books, 1998), in which Wardlow tells the story of how he found Johnson's birth certificate during the late 1960s.

5. Elijah Wald, *Escaping the Delta: Robert Johnson and the Invention of the Blues* (New York: HarperCollins Publishers, 2004), 111–14.

6. Francis Davis, *The History of the Blues: The Roots, the Music, the People* (Cambridge, MA: Da Capo Press, 2003), 126; Patricia R. Schroeder, *Robert Johnson, Mythmaking, and Contemporary American Culture* (Urbana: University of Illinois Press, 2004), 19; Pearson and McCulloch, *Robert Johnson*, 6.

7. Ted Gioia, *Delta Blues: The Life and Times of the Mississippi Masters Who Revolutionized American Music* (New York: W. W. Norton, 2008), 51.

8. See John Fahey, *Charley Patton* (London: Studio Vista, 1970); Wald, *Escaping the Delta*. Davis, *History*.

9. Davis, *History*, 99.

10. *Fresh Cream* (1966) by Eric Clapton's band Cream, Led Zeppelin's 1969 BBC session cover of the Robert Johnson tune "Travelling Riverside Blues," and *Let It Bleed* (1969) by the Rolling Stones all demonstrate the afterlives of Johnson's *King of the Delta Blues Singers* (1961).

11. Pearson and McCulloch, *Robert Johnson*, 3.

12. See Stephen Calt and Gayle Dean Wardlow, "Robert Johnson," 78 *Quarterly* 1, no. 4, (1989): 40–50, https://archive.org/details/78QuarterlyNo4/mode/2up; Peter Guralnick, *Searching for Robert Johnson: The Life and Legend of the "King of the Delta Blues Singers"* (New York: Dutton, 1989); Samuel Charters, *Robert Johnson* (New York: Oak, 1973); and Paul Oliver, *Blues Fell This Morning: The Meaning of the Blues* (New York: Horizon, 1960).

13. Pete Welding, "Hell Hound on His Trail," *Down Beat Music '66* (1966): 76, BGSU Music Library and Bill Schurk Sound Archives.

14. Pearson and McCulloch, *Robert Johnson*, 88.

15. Sherman Alexie, *Reservation Blues* (New York: The Atlantic Monthly Press, 1995); Walter Mosley, *RL's Dream* (New York: W. W. Norton, 1995); Geoffrey Becker, "Black Elvis," in *The Best American Short Stories*, ed. E. L. Doctorow (New York: Houghton Mifflin, 2000); T. Coraghessan Boyle, *Greasy Lake and Other Stories* (New York: Viking Penguin, 1985).

16. Bob Dylan, *Chronicles: Volume One* (New York: Simon & Schuster, 2004), 282.

17. Eric Clapton, *Clapton: The Autobiography* (New York: Broadway Books, 2007), 40.

18. Keith Richards and James Fox, *Life* (New York: Little, Brown and Company, 2010), 94.

19. Clapton, *Clapton*, 40.

20. Dylan, *Chronicles*, 283.

21. Marybeth Hamilton, *In Search of the Blues: Black Voices, White Visions* (London: Jonathan Cape, 2007), 18, 9.

22. Samuel Charters, *The Country Blues* (New York: Rinehart & Company, 1959); Hamilton, *In Search*, 181–82.

23. Hamilton, *In Search*, 182–83.

24. Hamilton, *In Search*, 185, 185–187.

25. Hamilton, *In Search*, 8, 182, 189.

26. Richards and Fox, *Life*, 82–83.

27. Hamilton, *In Search*, 189.

28. Richards and Fox, *Life*, 94.

29. Dylan, *Chronicles*, 282–83.

30. Dylan, *Chronicles*, 286.

31. Sandra R. Lieb, *Mother of the Blues: A Study of Ma Rainey* (Amherst: University of Massachusetts Press, 1981); Chris Albertson, *Bessie* (New Haven, CT: Yale University Press, 2003); and Derrick Stewart-Baxter, *Ma Rainey and the Classic Blues Singers* (New York: Stein and Day, 1970).

32. Richards and Fox, *Life*, 84–85, 110.

33. Schroeder, *Robert Johnson*, 69.

34. Schroeder, *Robert Johnson*, 69.

35. Boyle, *Greasy Lake*, 147, 147.

36. Schroeder, *Robert Johnson*, 71.

37. Schroeder, *Robert Johnson*, 70; Boyle, 150–51.

38. Boyle, *Greasy Lake*, 151.

39. Schroeder, *Robert Johnson*, 48.

40. Boyle, *Greasy Lake*, 152.

41. Mosley, *RL's Dream*, 100.

42. Mosley, *RL's Dream*, 9, 44.

43. Mosley, *RL's Dream*, 130, 176, 132–33, 133.

44. Mosley, *RL's Dream*, 135, 135.

45. Alexie, *Reservation Blues*, 6.

46. Mosley, *RL's Dream*, 136, 138, 138.

47. Mosley, *RL's Dream*, 141–42, 143.

48. Mosley, *RL's Dream*, 192–95, 195.

49. Pearson and McCulloch, *Robert Johnson*, 6–7; Wald, *Escaping the Delta*, 108.

50. Mosley, *RL's Dream*, 193, 266.

51. Alexie, *Reservation Blues*, 3, 3.

52. Schroeder, *Robert Johnson*, 125.

53. Alexie, *Reservation Blues*, 15.

54. Alexie, *Reservation Blues*, 4–5, 6, 264, 10, 199, 6, 6, 8–9.

55. Alexie, *Reservation Blues*, 11, 21–24.
56. Alexie, *Reservation Blues*, 33, 49.
57. Alexie, *Reservation Blues*, 173, 174.
58. Alexie, *Reservation Blues*, 174, 174, 174–175.
59. Alexie, *Reservation Blues*, 200–201.
60. Alexie, *Reservation Blues*, 211, 211, 216.
61. Alexie, *Reservation Blues*, 225, 269.
62. Alexie, *Reservation Blues*, 303, 304.
63. Becker, "Black Elvis," 1.
64. Stanley Booth, "A Hound Dog, to the Manor Born," *Esquire Classic*, February 1, 1968, https://classic.esquire.com/article/1968/2/1/a-hound-dog-to-the-manor-born.
65. Becker, "Black Elvis," 4, 5, 5, 5, 5; emphasis in source.
66. Becker, "Black Elvis," 6, 1.
67. Becker, "Black Elvis," 6.
68. Schroeder, *Robert Johnson*, 2.
69. Becker, "Black Elvis," 8, 8, 9, 9, 9, 4.
70. Becker, "Black Elvis," 9.
71. Becker, "Black Elvis," 9.

CHAPTER 4: FROM JOHN ANTHONY GILLIS TO JACK WHITE

1. Ben Blackwell, "How Jack, Jack, Brendan and Patrick Became the Raconteurs," Tremble Under Boom Lights, June 29, 2012, https://trembleunderboomlights.blogspot.com/2012/06/how-jack-jack-brendan-and-patrick.html.
2. *It Might Get Loud*, directed by Davis Guggenheim (New York: Sony Pictures Classic, 2009), DVD.
3. Sarfraz Manzoor, "The New Review Q&A: Jack White," *Guardian*, March 13, 2010, https://www.theguardian.com/music/2010/mar/14/jack-white-stripes-interview-northern-lights.
4. In the late 1950s and into the mid-1960s, blues music was not popular with mainstream, white audiences. Rather, its popularity rested mainly among white American folk revivalists who focused on acoustic country blues to the exclusion of amplified urban blues. Urban Black audiences were interested in urban blues, and two books that also demonstrated early 1960s interest in blues music were LeRoi Jones, *Blues People: Negro Music in White America and the Music That Developed from It* (New York: William Morrow, 1963); and Ralph Ellison, *Shadow and Act* (New York: Vintage Books, 1964).
5. William Bowers, "The White Stripes/De Stijl Album Review," Pitchfork.com, June 17, 2002, pitchfork.com/reviews/albums/8650-the-white-stripesde-stijl/.
6. There were white U.S. blues-rock musicians, and integrated U.S. blues-rock bands, that also participated in 1960s–70s blues revivalism in ways that mirrored the white British rockers. Significant U.S. white blues rock musicians include Canned Heat; ZZ Top; the Electric Flag, featuring Buddy Miles, a Black drummer, and Mike

Bloomfield, a white guitar player; Johnny Winter; the Doors; the Paul Butterfield Blues Band; Ry Cooder; Janis Joplin and Big Brother and the Holding Company; and the Grateful Dead. Captain Beefheart was another young white blues rocker who, like White, approached the blues in an unconventional way. White is also a fan of his work. Born Don Van Vliet, he birthed the Beefheart persona and created myths about himself that rivaled the early twentieth-century blues legends; Dave Sanjek, "Life in the Fast and Bulbous Lane: Captain Beefheart (1941–2010)," *Popular Music and Society* 35, no. 2 (2012): 301–13, Academic Search Complete..

7. Steve Jelbert, "The Stars, the Stripes; Detroit's The White Stripes are Setting the Tone for the Next Wave of British Pop," *Evening Standard*, April 11, 2003, Lexis-Nexis Academic.

8. Jim Abbott, "Foundation Gives Blues Pioneers a Helping Hand." *Chicagotribune.com*, Tribune Newspapers: Orlando Sentinel, February 24, 2006, articles.chicagotribune.com/2006-02-24/features/0602240300_1_traditional-blues-practitioners-music-maker-relief-foundation-white-stripes.

9. Alan Light, "Still True to the Red, White and Black," *New York Times*, June 10, 2007, https://www.nytimes.com/2007/06/10/arts/music/10light.html.

10. Jim DeRogatis, "White Riot," *Guitar World*, July 2002, http://www.jimdero.com/News2002/GWWhiteStripes.htm.

11. Henry Louis Gates Jr., *The Signifying Monkey: A Theory of African-American Literary Criticism* (New York: Oxford University Press, 1989), 6, 22.

12. John Mulvey, "The Same Boy You've Always Known: A Jack White Interview," *Uncut*, June 19, 2012, https://www.uncut.co.uk/blog/wild-mercury-sound/the-same-boy-youve-always-known-a-jack-white-interview.

13. See Benjamin Filene, *Romancing the Folk: Public Memory & American Roots Music* (Chapel Hill, NC: University of North Carolina Press, 2000), 58–74; Keith Richards and James Fox, *Life* (New York: Little, Brown and Company, 2010), 82–83; and Marybeth Hamilton, *In Search of the Blues: Black Voices, White Visions* (London: Jonathan Cape, 2007), 189.

14. White masks himself out of Blackness as opposed to the literal and figurative blacking up discussed, for example, in Eric Lott, *Love and Theft: Blackface Minstrelsy and the American Working Class* (New York: Oxford University Press, 1995); and W. T. Lhamon Jr., *Raising Cain: Blackface Performance from Jim Crow to Hip Hop* (Cambridge, MA: Harvard University Press, 2000).

15. Ted Gioia, *Delta Blues: The Life and Times of the Mississippi Masters Who Revolutionized American Music* (New York: W. W. Norton, 2008), 49.

16. Gioia, *Delta Blues*, 51.

17. Gioia, *Delta Blues*, 49.

18. Francis Davis, *The History of the Blues: The Roots, The Music, The People* (Cambridge, MA: Da Capo Press, 1995) 102.

19. David Evans, *Tommy Johnson* (London: Studio Vista, 1971), 22–23.

20. Robert Palmer, *Deep Blues* (New York: The Viking Press, 1981), 60.

21. W. C. Handy, *Father of the Blues: An Autobiography* (New York: Macmillan, 1941), 78.

22. Davis, *History of the Blues*, 26.

23. Handy, *Father of the Blues*, 123, 126.

24. Robert C. Ruark, "Legend Takes Beating on Conditions under Which Handy Wrote His Blues," *Scripps-Howard*, March 31, 1947, The Blues Archive, Special Collections, University of Mississippi Libraries.

25. Ruark, "Legend."

26. There is a body of autobiographical literature by Black American blues musicians, including W. C. Handy, *Father of the Blues: An Autobiography* (New York: Macmillan, 1941); B. B. King with David Ritz, *Blues All around Me: The Autobiography of B. B. King* (New York: HarperCollins, 1996); and Ethel Waters and Charles Samuels, *His Eye Is on the Sparrow* (New York: Doubleday, 1951). An earlier generation of white musicians has also engaged the blues in their autobiographies, such as Mezz Mezzrow; see Mezz Mezzrow and Bernard Wolfe, *Really the Blues* (New York: New York Review Books Classics, 1946).

27. Bob Dylan, *Chronicles: Volume One* (New York: Simon & Schuster, 2004), 282–83.

28. Eric Clapton, *Clapton: The Autobiography* (New York: Broadway Books, 2007), 40.

29. Richards and Fox, *Life*, 94.

30. Clapton, *Clapton*, 40; Dylan, *Chronicles*, 282–83; Richards and Fox, *Life*, 94; Kurt Loder, "The White Stripes at the Zoo with Kurt Loder," MTV.com, n.d, https://www.mtv.com/bands/w/white_stripes/news_feature_060603/.

31. Baz Dreisinger, *Near Black: White-to-Black Passing in American Culture* (Amherst: University of Massachusetts Press, 2008), 3, 94.

32. Clapton, *Clapton*, 40; Dylan, *Chronicles*, 282–83.

33. Richards and Fox, *Life*, 103–4, 104.

34. Clapton, *Clapton*, 64, 80.

35. In 1957 Norman Mailer wrote a controversial essay for *Dissent* called "The White Negro." Norman Mailer, "The White Negro: Superficial Reflections on the Hipster," *Dissent* (1957), 279, https://www.dissentmagazine.org/wp-content/files_mf/1353950503Mailer_WhiteNegro.pdf. He defines a white hipster persona whose interest and participation in Black American music is a way of solving his existential crisis: life versus death, rebellion versus conformity. Mailer claims, "So there was a new breed of adventurers, urban adventurers who drifted out at night looking for action with a black man's code to fit their facts. The hipster had absorbed the existentialist synapses of the Negro, and for practical purposes could be considered a white Negro." Mailer further suggests that whites are attracted to Black cultural expression and Black style out of the recognition that Black people are somehow more alive and, therefore, have better access to their emotions. It follows that this Black core, uncontaminated by modernity, makes for a less inhibited artistic expression. The idea that, due to their collective experience with racial, socioeconomic, and political oppression, Black Americans can teach white people how to live authentically, to stand apart rather than succumbing to conformity, still undergirds white reception of Black artistic production. Proximity to Black bodies is an important part of the equation. In the hipster model, it is not enough to enjoy jazz or blues music; hipsters also desire a unique physical proximity to Blacks, leading to a closer imitation of their cultural style.

36. Ulrich Adelt, *Blues Music in the Sixties: A Story in Black and White* (New Brunswick, NJ: Rutgers University Press, 2010), 68.

37. Andrew Perry, "Double Fantasy," originally published in *Mojo*, February 2002, https://www.whitestripes.net/articles-show.php?id=09; David Fricke, "The Mysterious Case of the White Stripes: Jack White Comes Clean," *Rolling Stone*, September 8, 2005, https://www.rollingstone.com/music/news/white-on-white-2005 0908; Austin Scaggs, "Jack White, Rock Innocent: Rolling Stone's 2003 Interview," *Rolling Stone*, February 2, 2011, https://www.rollingstone.com/music/news/jack-white-rock-innocent-rolling-stones-2003-interview-20110202; Alexis Petridis, "Jack White: 'I Don't Like to Take the Easy Way Out, on Anything I Do.'" *Guardian*, April 13, 2012, https://www.theguardian.com/music/2012/apr/13/jack-white-solo-project-blunderbuss.

38. See also Perry, "Double Fantasy"; Loder, "White Stripes"; Scaggs, "Jack White," Tobias de la Manzana, "An Interview with Jack White [Musician] 'Your Furniture's Not Dead,'" *Believer*, May 2003, https://believermag.com/an-interview-with-jack-white/; Davis, *History of the Blues*; Palmer, *Deep Blues*; Albert Murray, *Stomping the Blues* (New York: Da Capo Press, 2000).

39. Perry, "Double Fantasy."

40. Keith Phipps, "The White Stripes," *A.V. Club*, April 9, 2003, https://bwww.avclub.com/article/the-white-stripes-13805.

41. Ivan Chopik, "Joe Bonamassa Interview," *Guitar Messenger*, November 10, 2007, https://www.guitarmessenger.com/interviews/joe-bonamassa-interview/; Molly Lambert, "Grading the Charts: The Top 10 Songs in . . . THE BLUES," January 8, 2013, https://grantland.com/hollywood-prospectus/the-top-10- songs-in-the-blues/.

42. Loder, "White Stripes."

43. After their marriage ceremony in 1996, Jack White took Meg's racially inflected last name as his own.

44. Phipps, "White Stripes."

45. Handy, *Father of the Blues*, 78.

46. Palmer, *Deep Blues*, 18–19; Davis, *History of the Blues*, 3–5.

47. Isabel Wilkerson, *The Warmth of Other Suns: The Epic Story of America's Great Migration* (New York: Vintage Books, 2010), 10.

48. Vron Ware and Les Back, *Out of Whiteness: Color, Politics, and Culture* (Chicago: University of Chicago Press, 2002), 255, 255, 257.

49. Pop art is now viewed as one "large, Western movement in the arts," according to David McCarthy, *Pop Art* (Cambridge: Cambridge University Press, 2000), 8–14. So when I discuss the movement, I talk about it as one Western movement rather than differentiating between the British and American versions.

50. Fricke, "Mysterious Case."

51. Simon Frith and Howard Horne, *Art into Pop* (London: Methuen, 1987), 104.

52. Frith and Horne, *Art into Pop*, 18.

53. Dick Hebdige, *Subculture: The Meaning of Style* (London: Methuen, 1979), 52.

54. Frith and Horne, *Art into Pop*, 101, 101.

55. Richard Harrington, "The White Stripes, Plain and Simple," *Washington Post*, March 29, 2002, final ed., T13+, LexisNexis Academic.

56. "The White Stripes—Seven Nation Army + The Dead Letter (Live)," YouTube, uploaded by MiMundoROCKIN, December 30, 2010, https://www.youtube.com/watch?v=Qdqah7AMyS8.

57. H Bar C is a ranchwear company that began in 1897. H Bar C clothed numerous performers in Hollywood westerns, including Roy Rogers, Gene Autry, John Wayne, Elvis Presley, and John Travolta.

58. Frith and Horne, *Art into Pop*, 18.

59. "White Stripes—Seven Nation Army."

60. Son House's 1965 recording of "Death Letter Blues" was a reworked version of his 1930 Paramount Records tune "My Black Mama—Part II."

61. Phipps, "White Stripes."

62. "White Stripes—Seven Nation Army."

63. McCarthy, *Pop Art*, 18.

64. McCarthy, *Pop Art*, 19; "The White Stripes—Seven Nation Army."

65. Mulvey, "Same Boy."

66. Gil Kaufman, "Lens Recap: White Stripes' 'Button,'" *MTV*, October 13, 2003, https://www.mtv.com/news/articles/1479718/lens-recap-white-stripes-button.jhtml 21.

67. "The White Stripes—Hardest Button to Button," uploaded by White Stripes, YouTube, May 26, 2009, https://www.youtube.com/watch?v=K4dx42YzQCE.

68. "White Stripes—The Hardest Button to Button (The Simpsons Version)," uploaded by Peka 1337, YouTube, May 11, 2015, https://www.youtube.com/watch?v=dUx3kDnT-p8.

69. Fricke, "Mysterious Case."

70. Susan Sontag, "Fascinating Fascism," *New York Review of Books*, February 6, 1975, https://www.nybooks.com/articles/archives/1975/feb/06/fascinating-fascism/?pagination=false&printpage=true.

71. Mulvey, "Same Boy."

72. Mulvey, "Same Boy."

73. White Stripes, "Ball and Biscuit," *Elephant*, V2/Third Man Records, 2003.

74. Jack White, "Founding Father: Charley Patton," *Observer*, March 21, 2010, 25, LexisNexis Academic.

75. Brian Hiatt, "The Decade's Dirty Bluesman: Jack White on the Stripes' Rise, the Industry's Fall and His Next Move," *Rolling Stone*, January 6, 2010, https://www.rollingstone.com/music/news/the-decades-dirty-bluesman-jack-white-on-the-stripes-rise-the-industrys-fall-and-his-next-move-20100106, par. 11.

76. *The White Stripes: Under Great White Northern Lights*, directed by Emmett Malloy (Nashville, TN: Third Man Films, 2009), DVD.

77. Elijah Wald, *Escaping the Delta: Robert Johnson and the Invention of the Blues* (New York: HarperCollins Publishers, 2004), 221, 221; White, "Founding Father," 25.

78. Grace Elizabeth Hale, "Hear Me Talking to You: The Blues and the Romance of Rebellion," *Beyond Blackface: African Americans and the Creation of American Popular Culture, 1890–1930*, ed. W. Fitzhugh Brundage (Chapel Hill: University of North Carolina Press, 2011), 239–40.

79. White, "Founding Father," 25.

80. Palmer, *Deep Blues*, 44.

81. Wald, *Escaping the Delta*, 71.

82. Andrew Legg, "A Taxonomy of Musical Gesture in African American Gospel Music," *Popular Music* 29, no. 1 (2010): 103, JSTOR.

83. Legg, *Taxonomy*, 108.

84. Legg, *Taxonomy*, 118.

85. Palmer, *Deep Blues*, 44.

86. White Stripes, "Ball and Biscuit."

87. Legg, *Taxonomy*, 110, 110.

88. White Stripes, "Ball and Biscuit."

89. Legg, *Taxonomy*, 112.

90. Hale, "Hear Me Talking," 239–40.

91. White Stripes, "Ball and Biscuit."

92. Rebecca Leung, "Choosing Music over Religion: Watch the Episode," *CBS News*, February 8, 2005, https://www.cbsnews.com/news/choosing-music-over-religion/.

93. John Harris, "Rocker Man," *Observer*, January 18, 2004, https://www.theguardian.com/music/2004/jan/18/popandrock.shopping.

94. Muddy Waters, "I'm Your Hoochie Coochie Man," Chess Records, 1954.

95. Josh Eells, "Jack Outside the Box: Jack White Is the Coolest, Weirdest, Savviest Rock Star of Our Time," *New York Times Magazine*, April 5, 2012, https://www.nytimes.com/2012/04/08/magazine/jack-white-is-the-savviest-rock-star-of-our-time.html.

96. Mulvey, "Same Boy."

97. Scott Lapatine, "Jack White Does Have a Sense of Humor," *Stereogum*, September 7, 2006, https://www.stereogum.com/3316/jack_white_does_have_a_sense_of_humor/news/.

98. Jay Barmann, "Twitter, Instagram Severely Frowned Upon While Jack White Is On Stage at Outside Lands," August 7, 2012, https://sfist.com/2012/08/07/twitter-instagram-severely-frowned.php; Matthew Perpetua, "Jack White Totally Pisses Off New York Crowd," BuzzFeed, September 29, 2012, https://www.buzzfeed.com/perpetua/jack-white-totally-pisses-off-new-york-crowd?utm_term=.hvz3RlK90#.io4lY6Q1W.

99. Paul Jay, "Posing: Autobiography and the Subject of Photography," in *Autobiography and Postmodernism*, ed. Kathleen Ashley et al. (Amherst: University of Massachusetts Press, 1994), 195, 196, 196.

100. Jay, "Posing," 199, 196–197.

101. Jay, "Posing," 191.

102. Given the mythology around Mozart's early death at thirty-five, and his fondness for scatological humor, he is an inspired choice for a collaboration between Jack White and Insane Clown Posse.

103. Eells, "Jack Outside the Box."

104. John Aizlewood et al., "The 50 Worst Artists in Music History," *Blender*, April 26, 2007, https://kittyradio.com/community/threads/the-50-worst-artists-in-music-history-blender.26713/.

105. "Lech Mich Im Arsch," uploaded by OfficialTMR, YouTube, August 30, 2011, https://www.youtube.com/watch?v=OyzjVL5tFno.

106. Paul John Eakin, *Fictions in Autobiography: Studies in the Art of Self-Invention* (Princeton, NJ: Princeton University Press, 1988), 3.

107. "Lech Mich Im Arsch."

108. Camille Dodero, "Sound of the City: Q&A Violent J," *Village Voice*, September 1, 2011, https://www.villagevoice.com/2011/09/01/qa-violent-j-talks-jack-white-lick-me-in-the-arse-and-why-doesnt-think-insane-clown-posse-is-really-getting-a-better-public-reception-these-days/; "Lech Mich Im Arsch."

109. "Jack White—Freedom at 21," uploaded by JackWhiteVEVO, YouTube, July 16, 2012, https://www.youtube.com/watch?v=s92smjLq_38&feature=player_embedded.

110. "Jack White–Freedom at 21."

111. Jay, "Posing," 197, 199.

CHAPTER 5: THE BLUES APPRENTICESHIP

1. Patrick Doyle, "Gary Clark Jr.: The Chosen One," *Rolling Stone*, December 24, 2013, https://www.rollingstone.com/music/music-news/gary-clark-jr-the-chosen-one-193001/.

2. "Traditional Arts Apprenticeship Program," Tennessee Arts Commission—Folklife, https://tnfolklife.org/traditional-arts-apprenticeship-program/; "Artist Development Grants," South Carolina Arts Commission, https://www.southcarolinaarts.com/artist-development/grants/.

3. "West Virginia Folklife Apprenticeship Program," West Virginia Humanities Council, http://wvhumanities.org/folklifeapprenticeships/.

4. "Folk Arts Apprenticeship," Mississippi Arts Commission, https://arts.ms.gov/grants/grants-for-individuals/folk-arts-apprenticeship/; "Apprenticeship Program," Virginia Folklife Program, https://www.virginiafolklife.org/apprenticeship-program/; Maida Owens, introduction to "Keeping It Alive: Cultural Conservation through Apprenticeship," Louisiana Folklife Program, https://www.louisianafolklife.org/LT/Virtual_Books/Keeping_It/creole_book_keep_intro.html.

5. "Apprenticeship in the Folk & Traditional Arts Program," Texas Folklife, https://www.texasfolklife.org/apprenticeships.

6. "John Cephas and Marc Pessar," Virginia Folklife Program, https://www.virginiafolklife.org/apprenticeship_team/john-cephas-and-marc-pessar/.

7. "West Virginia Folklife Apprenticeship Program."

8. Jennifer Gardner, "Apprenticeship Shines Light on History of Blues and Black Gospel," *Charleston Gazette-Mail*, July 29, 2018, https://www.wvgazettemail.com/life/apprenticeship-shines-light-on-history-of-blues-and-black-gospel/article_0fdf1b1d-4434-5a13-aa8e-19d1f9f681a5.html.

9. Tony Russell, "Eddie Kirkland Obituary," *Guardian*, April 21, 2011, https://www.theguardian.com/music/2011/apr/21/eddie-kirkland-obituary.

10. Bond interview.

11. Bond interview.

12. Bond interview.

13. Bond interview.

14. Bond interview.

15. Bond interview.

16. Robert G. O'Meally, *The Craft of Ralph Ellison* (Cambridge, MA: Harvard University Press, 1980), 78.

17. According to Mark Anthony Neal, *Soul Babies: Black Popular Culture and the Post-Soul Aesthetic* (New York: Routledge, 2002), 103, the postsoul ethos posits that "the generations(s) of black youth born after the early successes of the traditional civil rights movement are in fact divorced from the nostalgia associated with those successes and thus positioned to critically engage the movement's legacy from a state of objectivity that the traditional civil rights leadership is both unwilling and incapable of doing." For further discussion, please see Greg Tate, *Flyboy in the Buttermilk: Essays on Contemporary America* (New York: Simon and Schuster, 1992); Nelson George, *Buppies, B-boys, Baps, and Bohos: Notes on Post-soul Black Culture* (Cambridge, MA: Da Capo Press, 2001); and Trey Ellis, "The New Black Aesthetic," *Callalloo* 38 (Winter 1989): 234, JSTOR.

18. Ralph Ellison, *The Collected Essays of Ralph Ellison* (New York: Modern Library, 1995), 497.

19. David Grazian, *Blue Chicago: The Search for Authenticity in Urban Blues Clubs* (Chicago: University of Chicago Press, 2003); Adam Gussow, *Journeyman's Road: Modern Blues Lives from Faulkner's Mississippi to Post-9/11 New York* (Knoxville: University of Tennessee Press, 2007); Roger Davis Gatchet, "'I've Got Some Antique in Me': The Discourse of Authenticity and Identity in the African American Blues Community in Austin, Texas," *Oral History Review* 39, no. 2 (2012): 207–29, JSTOR.

20. Jennifer Lynn Stoever, *The Sonic Color Line: Race and the Cultural Politics of Listening* (New York: New York University Press, 2016).

21. According to Arnold Rampersad, *Ralph Ellison: A Biography* (New York: Vintage Books, 2008), with the exception of a small number of young Black fiction writers, such as James Alan McPherson and Ernest Gaines, or critics such as Robert Stepto and John Wright, Ellison did not champion young Black writers in the press or recommend them for fellowships and grants. However, Rampersad writes, "in the late 1980s and early 1990s, Ralph could argue that many, if not most, of the best younger writers were in a sense his artistic progeny" (548). In *Heroism and the Black Intellectual: Ralph Ellison, Politics, and Afro-American Intellectual Life* (Chapel Hill, NC: The University of North Carolina Press, 1994), Jerry Gafio Watts similarly argues that "the works of Robert Stepto, Ishmael Reed, Robert O'Meally, Lawrence Levine, Melvin Dixon, John Callahan, Kimberly Benston, Mae Henderson, Houston Baker, Stanley Crouch, Henry L. Gates, Gerald Early, Michael Harper, Darryl Dance, Horace Porter, Alan Ballard, Leon Forrest, Gary Giddens, and James Alan McPherson, among others, testify to the resurgence of an Ellisonian cultural outlook since the middle 1970s" (63).

22. Allan Moore, "Authenticity as Authentication," *Popular Music* 21, no. 2 (2002): 211–20, JSTOR.

23. Moore, "Authenticity," 218.

24. Moore, "Authenticity," 214; emphasis in source.

25. Leroi Jones, *Blues People: Negro Music in White America and the Music That Developed from It* (New York: William Morrow, 1963), 130, 214, 87.

26. Ralph Ellison, *Shadow and Act* (New York: Vintage Books, 1964), 251.

27. Ellison, *Shadow*, 255, 58.

28. For a discussion about Ellison's various personal, artistic, and intellectual apprenticeships, see O'Meally, *Craft;* Watts, *Heroism;* and Timothy Parrish, *Ralph Ellison and the Genius of America* (Amherst: University of Massachusetts Press, 2012).

29. Ellison, *Collected Essays*, 682–83.

30. "The Moynihan Report (1965)," n.d., Blackpast, https://www.blackpast.org/african-american-history/moynihan-report-1965/.

31. Ellison, *Collected Essays*, 683.

32. Ellison, *Shadow*, 218.

33. Emily J. Lordi, *Black Resonance: Iconic Women Singers and African American Literature* (New Brunswick, NJ: Rutgers University Press, 2013), 68; Ellison, *Shadow*, 216–18, Lordi, *Black*, 68.

34. Lordi, *Black*, 68.

35. Peter Mongillo, "Gary Clark Jr.'s Electric Style," *Austin American-Statesman*, October 28, 2012, first ed., D01, LexisNexis Academic; Doyle, "Gary Clark Jr."

36. Neil McCormick, " I'm Just Playing Nasty, Wailing Lead," *Daily Telegraph*, July 12, 2012, 1st ed., national ed., 22, LexisNexis Academic.

37. Josep Pedro, "An Intercultural History of Blues in Austin, Texas: From the Negro District to the Global Rock Circuit," *Atlantic Studies* 14, no. 1 (2017): 74, 74–75, MLA International Bibliography.

38. Doyle, "Gary Clark Jr."

39. David Smyth, "I Got the 21st Century Blues," *Evening Standard*, March 1, 2013, 1st ed., national ed., 42, 43, LexisNexis Academic.

40. Nate Chinen, "Guitarist Takes a Victory Lap," *International Herald Tribune*, final ed., 13, October 25, 2012, LexisNexis Academic.

41. "Gary Clark Jr.—Bright Lights," uploaded by CrossroadsGuitar, YouTube, January 28, 2011, https://www.youtube.com/watch?v=x_ZeDn-hHGE.

42. Grazian, *Blue Chicago*, 36; Moore, "Authenticity," 218.

43. Gussow, *Journeyman's Road*, 111, 111.

44. E. Patrick Johnson, *Appropriating Blackness: Performance and the Politics of Authenticity* (Durham, NC: Duke University Press, 2003), 4.

45. Gussow, *Journeyman's Road*, 111; Johnson, *Appropriating Blackness*, 4; Grazian, *Blue Chicago*, 36.

46. Jon Pareles, "Blak and Blu," Rolling Stone, October 23, 2012, https://www.rollingstone.com/music/music-album-reviews/blak-and-blu-244909/.

47. Smyth, "I Got the 21st Century Blues."

48. Doyle, "Gary Clark Jr."

49. Ellison, *Shadow*, 252.

50. Nate Chinen, "Always at Home, Wherever He Plays," *New York Times*, October 22, 2012, https://www.nytimes.com/2012/10/23/arts/music/gary-clark-jr-releases-blak-and-blu-an-eclectic-album.html.

51. Chinen, "Always at Home."

52. Jonathan Landrum Jr., "Gary Clark Jr. Talks Evolving beyond Blues, Show Anxiousness," *AP*, October 21, 2015, https://apnews.com/c7f3a04240f24a2893ad-f2a4ed889033.

53. Jewly Hight, "Review: Gary Clark Jr., 'The Story of Sonny Boy Slim,'" NPR, September 2, 2015, https://www.npr.org/2015/09/02/436304859/first-listen-gary-clark-jr-the-story-of-sonny-boy-slim.

54. Corbin Reiff, "Gary Clark Jr. Gets in Touch with His Soulful Side on The Story of Sonny Boy Slim," A.V. Club, September 11, 2015, https://music.avclub.com/gary-clark-jr-gets-in-touch-with-his-soulful-side-on-t-1798184844.

55. "Foo Fighters—Making of What Did I Do, God as My Witness," uploaded by Miguel Costa, YouTube, April 12, 2015, https://www.youtube.com/watch?v=Jz_CVNaWKBk.

56. Tom Mann, "Gary Clark Jr on His New Album, Meg Mac, and Working with Foo Fighters, Beyonce and the Rolling Stones," *Faster Louder*, September 11, 2015.

57. Jonah Bayer, "15 Iconic SG Players," *Gibson*, March 4, 2009, https://www.gibson.com/News-Lifestyle/Features/en-us/15-iconic-sg-players-304.aspx.

58. Lordi, *Black Resonance*, 69, 69.

59. Rampersad, *Ralph Ellison*, 27–28.

60. Clive Davis, "New Face of Old Timey," *Sunday Times*, 1st ed., national ed., 25, January 24, 2010, LexisNexis Academic.

61. Tommy Tomlinson, "Rhiannon Giddens & The Making of NC's Most Beautiful Voice," Our State, n.d., https://www.ourstate.com/rhiannon-giddens/; Eric Volmers, "Rhiannon Honours Great Ladies of Song," *Calgary Herald*, July 22, 2015, C1, LexisNexis Academic.

62. Dan Craft, "Good to the Last Drop: The Carolina Chocolate Drops Celebrate a Forgotten American String Band Tradition," *Pantagraph*, March 19, 2009, D1, LexisNexis Academic.

63. Rhiannon Giddens, "Track 1—'Lights in the Valley' (Live) by Joe & Odell Thompson," *Oxford American* 103 (2018), https://www.oxfordamerican.org/magazine/item/1637-lights-in-the-valley.

64. Craft, "Good to the Last Drop."

65. Karl Hagstrom Miller, *Segregating Sound: Inventing Folk and Pop Music in the Age of Jim Crow* (Durham, NC: Duke University Press, 2010), 1, 218.

66. Doug Pullen, "Carolina Chocolate Drops," *El Paso Times*, February 22, 2009, LexisNexis Academic.

67. "Carolina Chocolate Drops—Country Girl [Official Video]," uploaded by ccdrops, YouTube, May 9, 2012, https://www.youtube.com/watch?v=FVIaiADsyYo.

68. Tomlinson, "Rhiannon Giddens."

69. Ellison, *Shadow*, 263; Ellison, *Collected Essays*, 464.

70. Marc C. Conner and Lucas E. Morel, eds., *The New Territory: Ralph Ellison and the Twenty-First Century* (Jackson: University Press of Mississippi, 2016), 5.

71. Tony Clayton-Lea, "Rhiannon Giddens's Female History of Americana," *Irish Times*, February 5, 2015, 13, LexisNexis Academic; "Rhiannon Giddens—S'iomadh Rid (The Dhith Om / Ciamar A Ni Mi)—HD (1080p)," uploaded by AllMusicWorld, YouTube, September 22, 2014, https://www.youtube.com/watch?v=8RtToobOS8o.

72. Volmers, "Rhiannon"; Dave Gil de Rubio, "Like a Rolling Stone: Rhiannon Giddens Talks about New Projects," *Leo Weekly*, September 9, 2015, https://www.leoweekly.com/2015/09/like-a-rolling-stone-%e2%80%a8rhiannon-giddens-talks-about-new-projects/.

73. Clayton-Lea, "Rhiannon."

74. Jon Bream, "Rhiannon on a Roll," *Star Tribune Minneapolis*, May 2, 2015, LexisNexis Academic; de Rubio, "Like a Rolling Stone."

75. Bream, "Rhiannon on a Roll."

76. Volmers, "Rhiannon."

77. Bernard Zuel, "An Authentic Voice," *Sydney Morning Herald*, February 12, 2016, 1st ed., 9, LexisNexis Academic.

78. Ellison, *Shadow*, 123.

AFTERWORD

1. "Mamie Smith—Crazy Blues (1920)," uploaded by TheLandOfMarcos, YouTube, August 13, 2009, https://www.youtube.com/watch?v=qaz4Ziw_CfQ.

2. Allan Moore, "Authenticity as Authentication," *Popular Music* 21, no. 2 (2002): 214, JSTOR.

3. Daniel Goldberg, *Serving the Servant: Remembering Kurt Cobain* (New York: Ecco, 2019), 15.

4. Rachel Martin and Vince Pearson, "Reflecting on Kurt Cobain's 'Crystalline Understanding' 25 Years Later," NPR, April 5, 2019, https://www.npr.org/2019/04/05/709603031/reflecting-on-kurt-cobains-crystalline-understanding-25-years-later.

5. "Gary Clark Jr—This Land [Official Music Video]," uploaded by garyclarkjr, YouTube, January 10, 2019, https://www.youtube.com/watch?v=9KgNaRQ_J-c.

6. Patrick Doyle, "Gary Clark Jr.: The Chosen One," *Rolling Stone*, December 24, 2013, https://www.rollingstone.com/music/music-news/gary-clark-jr-the-chosen-one-193001/.

7. Patrick Doyle, "The Anger Inside Gary Clark Jr.," *Rolling Stone*, February 7, 2019, https://www.rollingstone.com/music/music-features/gary-clark-jr-new-album-racism-donald-glover-789997/.

8. "Gary Clark Jr—This Land."

9. "Gary Clark Jr—This Land."

10. Gary Clark Jr., "The Governor," *This Land*, Warner Brothers Records, 2019.

11. "Childish Gambino—This Is America (Official Video)," uploaded by Donald Glover, YouTube, May 6, 2018, https://www.youtube.com/watch?v=VYOjWnS4cMY.

Index

Page numbers in *italics* refer to figures.

AC/DC, 205
Adams, Timothy Dow, 12, 174
Adelt, Ulrich, 153
African American folk tradition: rabbit's foot as lucky in, 13, 223n32; Robert Johnson legend and, 111–112, 131; seventh son of seventh son in, 34, 153, 170, 173–75, 225n29. *See also* oral storytelling
African American Great Migration, 156
Afro-alienation, 93–94
Aizlewood, John, 99–100
Alabama Blues Project, 187, 190, 194
Alabama/Georgia State Council on the Arts Apprenticeship, 187–88
Alabama Shakes, 184
Albertson, Chris, 58, 59, 120
Alexie, Sherman, 5, 15, 21, 113–15, 127, 130–36, 142
Alloway, Lawrence, 158
Alyn, Glyn, 37–38, 40, 45–48, 49–52
Amanfu, Ruby, 184
American Ballads and Folk Songs (Lomax & Lomax), 26
American Primitive (blues guitarist), 147
"America the Beautiful" (Charles), 205
Another Day, Another Time (2013), 209
Antibalas, 101
Antone, Clifford, 10, 200
Apollo Theater, 93
Appalachian State University, 207
apprenticeship. *See* blues apprenticeship
Armstrong, Louis, 37, 147
Arnold, Kokomo, 141
Art 1963 (art exhibition), 158
"As the Spirit Moves Mahalia" (Ellison), 199

Auerbach, Dan, 184
Auslander, Philip, 14
authenticity of blues: authenticity of execution, 196–97; authenticity of expression, 9–10, 215; authenticity paradigm and power imbalance, 201–2; "Black Elvis" and racialized blues authenticity, 137–42; boundaries of, 118; concept overview, 7–11; Elijah Wald on, 8, 9, 73; Jack White's alternative blues persona, 144–46, 155–58, 167–75; in master-apprentice dynamic, 185–87, 193–203, 211–12; Moore on, 9–11, 196, 201; narrative blues tradition and, 20, 30, 36, 45–46, 58–65, *61*; narrative fictionality and, 104; Winehouse and Black musical authenticity, 71–72, 100–105. *See also* autobiographical fictions; blues apprenticeship
autobiographical fictions, 67–107; autobiographics, 75–76, 86; constructed autobiography, 83–90; deliberate fabrications for, 1–2; fictionalized autobiographical and biographical storytelling, 70–75; first-person narrative example, 76–80; gender issues of female blues persona, 20, 72–75; invented personas for, 2–4, 9–14; "Mississippi Ham Rider," 16–19; music and memory, 81–83; narrated "I" and, 105–7; narrative within narrative, 110; storytelling as correcting the record, 67–70, 90–92; Winehouse's persona aligned with factual autobiography, 98–107. *See also The Color Purple*; Johnson, Robert; oral storytelling; White, Jack
autobiography/autobiographical narrative, defined, 223n31. *See also* narrative blues tradition

Bacharach, Burt, 180
Back, Les, 156
Back Road to the Blues (*RL's Dream* book within book), 124
Back to Black (Winehouse), 71, 98, 100, 101, 232n83
bad man trope: bad man archetype and, 19, 26–34, 36–37, 41–47, 52–53; bedeviled bluesman and, 19, 29–31, 34–36, 52; Jack White and "Ball and Biscuit," 167–75; Lipscomb's "Freddie" character and, 41–52, 131, 214; overview, 19–20. *See also* Stagolee legend
Baker, Frankie, 227n83
Baker, Houston, 8–9
Bal, Mieke, 3, 4
Baldwin, James, 27
"Ball and Biscuit" (White Stripes), 22, 34, 167–75
"Ball and Chain" (Thornton; Joplin), 68, 73, 91–93
Bambara, Toni Cade, 16–19
Bankston, Dick, 36
Baraka, Amiri (LeRoi Jones), 6, 8, 72, 197
Barrett, Syd, 158
Barth, John, 3
Batiste, Stephanie, 14, 93
Bauman, Richard, 28, 38, 43
Beck, Jeff, 154, 158, 162
Becker, Geoffrey, 21, 113, 115, 137–42
Beyoncé, 175, 180, 203
Biggie Smalls, 177
Big Mom (*Reservation Blues* character), 132–36
Bilal, 203
Black Banjo Gathering (Appalachian State University), 207
"Black Boys and Native Sons" (Howe), 211
"Black Elvis" (Becker), 21, 113–14
Black Keys, 184
Black Pearls (Harrison), 70
Black Sabbath, 205
Black Swan Records, 54
Blak and Blu (Clark), 202–3
Blake, Peter, 163
Bland, Bobby "Blue," 8
Blassingame, John W., 51
Blender.com: on Insane Clown Posse, 178; on Winehouse, 100
Blue Chicago (Grazian), 201
The Blues (Elijah Wald), 5–6
The Blues (Neff & Connor), 93–98
Blues, Ideology, and Afro-American Literature (Houston Baker), 8–9
blues apprenticeship, 183–212; authenticity in master-apprentice dynamic and, 185–87, 193–203, 211–12; Bond and, 187–94; Clark and, 184, 185, 195–97, 200–206,

209, 212; Ellison and, 185, 194–203, 206–12, 242n21; gender in, 188, 192–94; Giddens and, 183–85, 195–97, 206–12; interracial/cross-racial roles in and, 184–88, 195–202, 209–12; invention and reinvention, overview, 22–23, 183–84; postsoul ethos and, 195, 242n17; state arts commissions/humanities foundations, 22, 185–87, 190, 194, 211
blues as narrative art. *See* narrative blues tradition
Blues Fell this Morning (Oliver), 117
"The Blues Had a Baby and They Named It Rock and Roll" (Waters & McGhee), 140
bluesmen. *See individual names of bluesmen; individual names of male artists*
blues music: audience of, 11–13, 235n4; defining, 5–7; Discovery/Encounter/Re-assessment phases of, 116–20; Jack White and blues vocals, 167, 170–75; Mamie Smith as first Black woman blues recording artist, 60; naming of, 56–59; revivalism (1990s), 35, 39; revivalism (1960s–70s), 16, 21, 36, 59, 116–20, 235n6; sonic (blues)face culture, 103. *See also* authenticity of blues; Delta blues style; *individual blues musicians*
"Blues People" (Ellison), 197
Blues People (Jones/Baraka), 8, 72, 197
blueswomen. *See* gender and female blues persona; *individual names of blueswomen; individual names of female artists*
Blunderbuss (Jack White), 22, 143, 146, 175–76, 184, 185
BMI, 68
Boarding House Reach (Jack White), 143
Bonamassa, Joe, 154
Bond, Debbie, 22, 187–94
Bontemps, Arna, 51
Bowers, William, 144
Bowie, David, 10
Boyle, T. C., 21, 113–15, 120–24, 142
Bradford, Ethel, 228n95
Bradford, Perry, 60, 228n95
Bramhall, Doyle, II, 201
Britt, Allen, 227n83
Brooks, Daphne, 14, 93, 103–4
Brooks, George (Fletcher Henderson), 55
Broonzy, Big Bill, 40, 117
Brown, Cecil, 26–27, 28, 53, 214, 224n1, 224n10
Brown, James, 28
Brown, Sterling, 54
Brown, Willie, 36, 72
Bruce, Joseph (Violent J), 178–79
Brymn, Tim, 54
Buddy Guy Blues Band, 92
Bunch, William (Peetie Wheatstraw), 2, 34–35, 214
Bunch of Blackberries (talent show), 53
Burnett, Chester (Howlin' Wolf), 22, 72, 105, 111, 148, 154, 161, 183, 189
Burnett, T Bone, 184, 209–10
Butler, Judith, 79–80, 103

Cade, Toni (Bambara), 16–19
Calgary Herald, Giddens interview, 212
California Rhythm and Blues Caravan, 93
Calloway, Cab, 27
Calt, Stephen, 112
Can't You Hear the Wind Howl? (film), 111
Captain Beefheart, 236n6
Carby, Hazel, 8, 73, 74–75, 78
Carolina Chocolate Drops, 23, 183, 206, 208–10. *See also* Giddens, Rhiannon
Carr, Leroy, 117
Celie. *See The Color Purple*
Cephas, John, 186
"Change the Joke and Slip the Yoke" (Ellison), 198
Charles, Ray, 205
Charleston Gazette-Mail, on blues apprenticeship, 187
Charters, Samuel, 112, 117, 121
Chess Records, 93
Chicago Defender: "Mothers Taking Innocent Daughters to Houses of Ill Fame to Play Piano Still Our Christians' Cry of White Slave Is Heard in the Community," 73–74; on Rainey, 58
Childish Gambino, 218
Chronicles (Dylan), 114, 115, 151–52
Clapton, Eric: *Clapton: The Autobiography*, 114, 151–53; *Crossroads Eric Clapton Guitar Festival 2010* (DVD), 201; Jack White and, 144, 151–54, 158, 166; Robert Johnson's influence on, 21, 109–11, 113–16

Clark, Gary, Jr.: autobiographical fictions by, 3, 5; blues apprenticeship and, 22, 184, 185, 195–97, 200–206, 209, 212, 215–19
Clark, W. C., 200
Clark, Wink, 109
Cline, Patsy, 210
clothing and costuming: authenticity of blues and, 63; of Carolina Chocolate Drops, 209; gender and female blues persona, 92–94; H Bar C, 161, 239n57; of Thornton, 92, 97–98; visual aesthetics by White Stripes and, 144, 146–53, 157–66, *163*
Cobain, Kurt, 215–16
Coca-Cola can, visual aesthetic of, 157, 165–66
Collins, Albert, 200
The Color Purple (Walker): Celie's narrative as autobiographics, 75–76, 86; gender and female blues persona, overview, 20, 69–72, 214; narrative structure, overview, 3–4; Shug Avery as narrator in, 80–83; Shug Avery as transgressive figure in, 15, 31, 76–80; Squeak (Mary Agnes) and Sophia contrasted in, 83–90; Squeak (Mary Agnes) as blues singer in, 71, 83–85. *See also* gender and female blues persona
Coltrane, John, 205
Columbia Records, 55, 59, 111, 117, 228n95
Conner, Marc, 209
Connor, Anthony, 93–98, 214
Coppola, Sophia, 180
Costello, Elvis, 210
The Country Blues (Charters), 117
"Country Girl" (Giddens), 208
Couser, G. Thomas, 37
Cox, Ida, 73, 74
Coyote Springs (*Reservation Blues* fictional band), 115, 130, 133–36
"Crazy Blues" (Mamie Smith), 19–20, 31, 60, 61, 64
Cream, 111, 144, 153, 158. *See also* Clapton, Eric
Crossing the Line (Gayle Wald), 101
"Cross Road Blues" (Robert Johnson), 35
Crossroads (film), 111
Crossroads Eric Clapton Guitar Festival 2010 (DVD), 201
Crudup, Arthur "Big Boy," 141
cultural appropriation, 22, 144, 148, 155, 180, 186

Daily Mail (London), on Winehouse, 102
Daily Telegraph (London), on Clark, 200
Dap-Kings, 101
David, John Russell, 51–52, 214, 224n10, 227n83
Davies, Carole Boyce, 37
Davies, Ray, 158
Davis, Angela, 8, 74–75, 89–91, 102
Davis, Francis, 16, 111, 150
Davis, Sammy, Jr., 103–4
Dawson, James L. (Lee Shelton's/Stagolee's jailor), 42
Dead Weather, 143, 178–79
"Death Letter Blues" (House), 154, 161–64, 239n60
Deep Blues (Palmer), 9, 113, 169
Delta blues style: defined, 169; House and, 60, 72, 111, 112, 117, 147–49, 154, 170, 183; Jack White and, 21, 144, 147–49, 154, 156, 157, 161–64, 169, 170; Patton and, 22, 72; recording of, 60; Robert Johnson and, 110–11, 114, 116–17, 124, 138; of rural bluesman, 8–9; Tommy Johnson and, 35–37
De Stijl (White Stripes), 144, 157, 160–61, 184
devil, blues myth about, 19, 29–31, 34–36, 43–44, 52, 60, 63
Devil's Son-in-Law (Peetie Wheatstraw), 2
Dissent, "Black Boys and Native Sons" (Howe), 211
Dixon, Willie, 105, 154
Dodero, Camille, 179
Doherty, Pete, 102–3
Douglass, Frederick, 87
Downbeat, on Robert Johnson, 112
"Down Hearted Blues" (Bessie Smith), 54
Doyle, Patrick, 202
Dreisinger, Baz, 100–101, 152
Dryden, Nat, 28–29
Duffy, Tim, 145

Dylan, Bob: Jack White and, 151–53; *Lost on the River*, 210; narrative blues and, 28, 40; Robert Johnson's influence on, 21, 113–16, 118–20

Eakin, Paul John, 12, 174, 179
Early, William (*RL's Dream* character), 124
Edge (David Evans), 147
Edwards, David "Honeyboy," 20, 35, 39, 43–44, 60, 110
Edwards, Rachel, 194
Eells, Josh, 175, 178
81 Theater (Atlanta), 54
Elephant (White Stripes), 22, 34, 146, 167, 173
Eliot, T. S., 198
Ellington, Duke, 27, 198
Ellison, Ralph: blues apprenticeship and, 22, 194–97, 200; Clark influenced by, 185, 195; on cross-racial engagement, 6, 197–99, 202–3, 209, 211–12; Giddens influenced by, 185, 195, 206; *Invisible Man*, 51, 95, 196, 199; narrative blues and, 51; *Ralph Ellison: A Biography*, 242n21; *Shadow and Act*, 196–97
English youth subcultures (mods, teddy boys), 158–59
Escaping the Delta (Elijah Wald), 168
Esu (Yoruban trickster god), 36, 145
Etheridge, Melissa, 73
Evans, David, 13, 112, 149
Evening Standard, on White Stripes, 144

Fabulous Thunderbirds, 200
Fahey, John, 111, 117, 147
Faster Louder, Clark interview, 205
Father of the Blues (Handy), 15–16, 149–51, 168
Fielder-Civil, Blake, 70, 102, 232n83
Fields, Doris (Lady D), 187
"50 Worst Artists in Music History" (*Blender*), 178
Fisher, Ella Scott, 25, 28, 29, 224n1
Flemons, Dom, 207, 208–9
Floyd, Samuel A., Jr., 6
Foo Fighters, 204–5
Ford, Henry, 150
Four Dancing Mitchells, 62
Fox, James, 114, 151–52
"Frankie and Johnny" ballads, 53, 227n83
Franklin, Aretha, 73
"Freddie" (Lipscomb), 41–52, 131, 214
"Freedom at 21" (Jack White), 175–81
Frith, Simon, 158, 161
"From $20.00 per Week to $1,000 ptr [*sic*] Night" (*Topeka Plain Dealer*), 63–65

Gallagher, Rory, 154
Garon, Paul, 35
"Gary Clark Jr." (Doyle), 202–3
Gatchet, Roger, 10, 195
gender, in master-apprentice relationships, 188, 192–94
gender and female blues persona, 67–107; of Bessie Smith, 5, 13, 20; blueswomen as inauthentic and, 8, 72–75, 192–94; blueswomen's struggle to make voices heard, 5; in *The Color Purple*, 20, 69–71, 75–90, 214; gender performativity, 79–80, 103; overview, 20, 69–72; of Rainey, 13, 20; of Thornton, 20, 67–71, 76, 90–98, 102, 106, 107; transgressive (bad) blueswoman persona, 5, 13, 15, 19, 30–31, 42, 48, 52–59, *57*, 76–80, 97–98; of Winehouse, 20, 69–72, 98–107
Genette, Gérard, 3
Germs, 205
Gert zur Heide, Karl, 227n85
Giddens, Rhiannon, 22–23, 183–85, 195–97, 206–12, 215
Gillis, John Anthony. *See* White, Jack
Gilmore, Leigh, 75–76, 86
Gioia, Ted, 59, 148–49
Goldberg, Danny, 215–16
Goldsmith, Taylor, 210
Gondry, Michel, 164, 165
Gordy, Berry, 160
"The Gospel Tradition," 210
"The Governor" (Clark), 218
Grainger, Porter, 54
Grammy Awards (2004), 162–64, *163*
Grazian, David, 195, 201, 202
Green, Sammy, 91
"Grinder" (song), 204
"Grinnin' in Your Face" (House), 147
Grohl, Dave, 205
"Gulf Coast Blues" (Bessie Smith), 54
Gunsmoke Blues (DVD), 67

Guralnick, Peter, 112, 113, 121
Gussow, Adam, 195, 201–2
Guy, Buddy, 184

Hadley, Elder J. J. (Patton), 148
Hager, Fred, 54
Hale, Grace, 168–69, 172
Hamer, Frank, 51
Hamilton, Marybeth, 9, 59, 116–17, 118
Hamilton, Richard, 158, 165
Hammond, John H., 109
Hammond, John Paul, 109–10
Handy, W. C.: depiction of blues and, 155; *Father of the Blues*, 15–16, 149–51, 168; Jack White influenced by, 147, 174; legacy of, 56; "Legend Takes Beating on Conditions under Which Handy Wrote His Blues" on, 150–51; "Saint Louis Blues," 149, 150
"Hardest Button to Button" (White Stripes), 164–65
Harris, Corey, 10–11
Harrison, Daphne Duval, 53, 56, 58, 70, 73, 91
"Hateful Blues" (Bessie Smith), 55, 228n95
Hawkins, Roger, 156–57
Hawkins, Taylor, 204–5
H Bar C, 161, 239n57
Heat, on Winehouse, 102
Hebdige, Dick, 159
"Hellhound on My Trail" (Robert Johnson), 35, 104
Henderson, Fletcher (George Brooks), 55
Hendrix, Jimi, 132, 135, 148, 153
"Higher Ground" (Clark; Beyoncé), 203–4
Hight, Jewly, 204
"High Water Everywhere" (Patton), 156
His Eye Is on the Sparrow (Waters), 33–34
Holiday, Billie, 73
"Homage to Duke Ellington on His Birthday" (Ellison), 198
"Homeless Blues" (Bessie Smith), 156
Honeydripper (film), 204
Hooker, John Lee, 72, 93, 118
Horne, Howard, 158, 161
"Hot Harlem Revue" (traveling variety show), 91
"Hound Dog" (Thornton; Presley), 20, 67–70, 90–92, 106, 126, 141, 231n54
House, Son: as authentic, 7, 72; Jack White influenced by, 147–49, 154, 161, 162, 166, 167, 170; mentoring by, 183; "Mississippi Ham Rider," 16–19; narrative blues and, 39, 60; Robert Johnson and, 111, 112, 117, 118, 214
Houston, Bee, 67
Howard, Brittany, 184
Howe, Irving, 211
Howlin' Wolf (Chester Burnett), 22, 72, 105, 111, 148, 154, 161, 183, 189
Hubbard, Henry "Bluesboy," 10, 200
Hurt, Mississippi John, 28, 39
Hutto, J. B., 67

"I Just Don't Know What to Do with Myself" (White Stripes), 180
"I'm Your Hoochie Coochie Man" (Waters), 174–75
Independent Group, 158
"I Need a Little Sugar in My Bowl" (Bessie Smith), 54–55
Invisible Man (Ellison), 51, 95, 196, 199
Iommi, Tony, 205
I Say Me for a Parable (Lipscomb & Alyn): "Freddie" and, 41–52, 131, 214; on Hamer, 51; on Life Story Songs, 37, 41, 50; overview, 31, 37–40, 215; on True Story Songs, 37, 46–47, 49–51, 54. *See also* Lipscomb, Mance
Island/Universal Records, 98
Isley Brothers, 28
It Might Get Loud (documentary), 144, 147

"Jack Outside the Box" (Eells, *New York Times*), 175
Jackson, Mahalia, 73, 199
Jackson, Papa Charlie, 105
Jackson, Wanda, 181
"Jack White Does Have a Sense of Humor" (*Stereogum*), 176
James, Elmore, 162
James, Jim, 210
James, Skip, 39, 111, 117
Jarrett, Dennis, 14
Jarvis, Judy, 100
Jay, Paul, 176–77, 181

Jay-Z, 167, 175, 177, 180
Jefferson, Blind Lemon, 40, 147
Jelbert, Steve, 144–45
Jenkins, Hubby, 208
Johns, Jasper, 162–63
Johnson, Blind Willie, 40
Johnson, Claud, 110
Johnson, E., 55, 228n95
Johnson, E. Patrick, 10, 202
Johnson, LeDell, 13, 35, 36, 149
Johnson, Lonnie, 117
Johnson, Louise, 72
Johnson, Robert, 109–42; aliases of, 110–11, 125; biographical information and death of, 110, 111, 121, 123–24, 125, 129–30; "Black Elvis" on, 113, 115, 137–42; blues authenticity and, 104; clothing worn by, 63; crossroads myth about, 21, 111–13, 120, 126–29, 131–32, 214; Jack White influenced by, 147, 151–52, 154, 161, 167, 174; legacy of, 2, 7–8, 21, 72, 114, 115–20; literary works on, overview, 21, 113–14; in master-apprentice relationships, 183, 188; narrative blues and bedeviled bluesman myth, 35, 43–44, 60, 63; *Reservation Blues* on, 15, 113, 115, 127, 130–36, 142; *RL's Dream* on, 15, 113–15, 124–30, 142; *The Search for Robert Johnson*, 109–11; "Stones in My Passway" on, 113–15, 120–24, 142. *See also* Delta blues style
Johnson, Tommy, 13, 35–37, 104–5, 112–13, 147–49, 174
Jones, LeRoi (Amiri Baraka), 6, 8, 72, 197
Jones, Sharon, 101
Joplin, Janis, 20, 40, 68, 73, 91–93, 125, 132, 135
Journal of American Folklore, on Stagolee legend, 28–29
Journeyman's Road (Gussow), 202
Joyce, James, 198
"Jumpin' Judy" (spiritual), 171
June, Valerie, 183–84

Kandell, Steve, 98–99
Kerrville Folk Festival, 45
Keys, Alicia, 175, 180
Kiki (*RL's Dream* character), 124, 126, 130
King, B. B., 8, 200
King, Freddie, 200
King, Willie, 187, 190–94
King of the Delta Blues Singers (Robert Johnson), 111
Kirkland, Eddie, 188, 190, 191
Knight, Kathryn, 102
Kokomo Blues Band, 188
Kweli, Talib, 203

Lancaster New Era, on Winehouse, 100
Law, Don, Sr., 122
Lazaretto (Jack White), 143
Lead Belly, 41, 63, 148, 226n58
Leake, Lafayette, 93
Leaving Eden (Carolina Chocolate Drops), 208
"Leck mich im Arsch" (Jack White & Insane Clown Posse), 22, 146, 177–80
Led Zeppelin, 92, 104, 111, 144, 154, 158
Lee, Stack. *See* Stagolee legend
"Legend Takes Beating on Conditions under Which Handy Wrote His Blues" (*Scripps-Howard*), on Handy, 150–51
Legg, Andrew, 146, 169–70, 171–72
Legman, G., 224n1
Leiber, Jerry, 90, 91, 141, 231n54
Leibowitz, Herbert, 12, 174
Lennon, John, 158
Lewis, Huey, 28
The Libertines, 102
Library of Congress, 117
Lichtenstein, Roy, 158, 165
Lieb, Sandra, 58, 59, 91, 120
Life (Richards & Fox), 114, 151–52
life writing, defined, 223n31
Lipscomb, Charles, 39
Lipscomb, Mance: as authentic, 60; autobiographical fictions and, 2, 20; biographical information, 39–41; "Freddie" as bad man trope, 41–52, 131, 214; *I Say Me for a Parable*, 31, 37–40, 215; mentoring by, 183
"Listening for Willie Mae 'Big Mama' Thornton's Voice" (Mahon), 92
"The Little Man at Chehaw Station" (Ellison), 195
Living Blues (magazine), on authenticity, 9, 202
L. L. Cool J, 177

Lockwood, Robert, Jr., 110
Loder, Kurt, 152
Lomax, Alan, 26, 28, 41, 214, 226n58
Lomax, John, 25, 26, 28, 29, 41, 214, 226n58
London Evening Standard, on Winehouse, 99–100
Lordi, Emily, 199, 205, 209
Lost on the River (T Bone Burnett), 210
Louisiana Folklife Apprenticeship Program, 186
"Love in Vain" (Robert Johnson), 110
Lynn, Loretta, 179, 181
Lyons, William "Billy," 25–26, 29, 30, 34, 42, 213

Mahal, Taj, 40, 183
Mahon, Maureen, 92
Mailer, Norman, 153, 237n35
"Makers of High Grade Suites" (Upholsterers), 154
Marcus, Greil, 28, 113, 117, 121
Maree, Ben, 36
Mary Agnes. *See The Color Purple*
Masked Marvel (Patton), 148
Matta, Adam, 208
Mayall, John, 158
MC Big K.R.I.T., 203
McCain, Jerry, 192
McCalla, Leyla, 208
McCarthy, David, 162
McCormick, Mack, 40, 110, 112, 125
McCormick, Neil, 200
McCulloch, Bill, 112–13
McGhee, Brownie, 118, 140
McGinley, Paige, 9, 14
McKune, James, 117, 118
McMillan, Uri, 14
McTell, Blind Willie, 147, 162, 167
"Me & Mr. Jones" (Winehouse), 102
"Me and the Devil Blues" (Robert Johnson), 35
Memphis Minnie, 189
mentorship. *See* blues apprenticeship
Mezzrow, Mezz, 101, 103
"Milk Cow Blues" (Arnold), 141
Miller, Aleck (Sonny Boy Williamson), 147–48
Miller, D. Quentin, 27
Miller, Irvin C., 54
Miller, Karl Hagstrom, 207–8
Mississippi Arts Commission Folk Art Apprenticeship, 185–86
"Mississippi Ham Rider" (Cade/Bambara), 16–19
Mississippi Sheiks, 147
mods (English youth subculture), 158–59
Monáe, Janelle, 203
Monsees, Eve, 200
Montgomery, Little Brother, 93
"Moonshine Blues" (Rainey), 58
Moore, Allan, 9, 11, 45, 196, 197, 201, 215
Morel, Lucas, 209
Morrison, Toni, 27
Mosley, Walter, 5, 15, 21, 113–15, 124–30, 142
Moss, Kate, 180
Mother of the Blues (Lieb), 58
"Mothers Taking Innocent Daughters to Houses of Ill Fame to Play Piano Still Our Christians' Cry of White Slave Is Heard in the Community" (*Chicago Defender*), 73–74
Motown, 160
Moynihan, Daniel Patrick, 198–99
Mozart, W. A., 22, 240n102
MTV.com, 152
Muldoon, Brian, 154
Mumford, Marcus, 210
Murray, Albert, 6, 31, 32–34, 37, 40, 214
Muscle Shoals (house band), 156
musical genres: country music, 208; gospel and the White Stripes, 146, 160, 169–72; R & B, 27–28, 69, 71, 73, 160, 184, 203, 204; rock and roll, 27–28, 91–92, 137, 140–141; Scottish mouth music, 183, 197, 209, 211; "song-speech," 172. *See also* blues music; Delta blues style; *individual names of artists*
"Musical Personae" (Auslander), 14
Music Maker Relief Foundation, 145
"My Favorite Things" (Coltrane), 205
Mystery Train (Marcus), 113, 121

narrative blues tradition, 25–65; African American folk tradition and, 13, 34, 112, 131, 153, 170, 173–75, 223n32, 225n39; as-told-to autobiography (ghostwriting), 37; autobiographical and biographical

narratives moving between fact and fiction, 30; autobiographical genre of Black and white musicians, overview, 151, 237n26; autobiography/autobiographical narrative, defined, 223n31; bad man archetype and, 19, 26–34, 36–37, 41–47, 52–53; bedeviled bluesmen and, 19, 29–31, 34–36, 43–44, 52, 60, 63; blues and improvisation, 191–92; in blues apprenticeship, 189; blues authenticity and, 20, 30, 36, 45–46, 58–65, *61*; first-person narrative, defined, 30, 32; first-person narrative example, 76–80; Moore on "first/second/third person authenticity," 9–11, 196, 201; overview, 19–20; Stagolee legend origin and, 19, 25–30, 213–14, 224n1, 224n10; storytelling tradition and, 11–14; transgressive (bad) blueswoman personae and, 19, 30–31, 42, 48, 52–59, *57*; True Story Song and, 37, 41, 43, 46–47, 49–51. *See also* authenticity of blues; oral storytelling; Stagolee legend
Narrative of the Life of Frederick Douglass (Douglass), 87
Native Son (Richard Wright), 27
Nazi banner, visual aesthetic of, 157, 165–66
Neal, Mark Anthony, 242n17
Near Black (Dreisinger), 101, 152
Neff, Robert, 93–98, 214
Negro Blues and Hollers, 117
"The Negro Family" (Moynihan), 198–99
Nelles, William, 3
The New Realists (art exhibition), 158
New Republic, on Armstrong, 37
New York Times: on Clark, 203; on Jack White, 175; on White Stripes, 1, 145
"1955" (Walker), 90
Nirvana, 205, 215
NPR (National Public Radio): on Clark, 204; on Cobain, 216

O'Brien, Conan, 175
O'Brien, Sharon, 94
Observer, on Jack White, 144, 167, 173–74
Odum, Howard, 28–29, 42
Oglesby, Xavier, 187
OKeh Records, 54, 60
Oliver, Paul, 112, 117
O'Meally, Robert G., 195
oral storytelling: African American folk tradition and, 13, 34, 112, 131, 153, 170, 173–75, 223n32, 225n39; African American myths of bad man and devil, 52; audience needed for, 126; autobiographical fictions and songs as, 92–98; dialect and, 38; "hooraw," 46, 51–52; insider's narrative in, 38–39; mythmaking from, 33–35; passing down of, 44; by Patton, 149; Stagolee legend as, 28, 31
Origins Jazz Library, 117
Orlando Sentinel, on White Stripes, 145
Osofsky, Gilbert, 51
Otis, Johnny, 91, 93, 96, 97, 101, 103, 231n54
"Out an Down" (Lipscomb), 49–50
Oxford American, Giddens in, 207

Pace, Harry, 54
Pace & Handy Music Co., 151
Page, Jimmy, 147, 154, 158, 162
Palmer, Earl, 156
Palmer, Robert, 9, 36, 113, 117, 149, 169, 171
Paolozzi, Eduardo, 158
Paramount Records, 53, 58, 72, 148
Pareles, Jon, 100, 105, 202
Parton, Dolly, 210
Patton, Charley: as authentic, 7, 72; "High Water Everywhere," 156; Howlin' Wolf influenced by, 105; Jack White influenced by, 147, 148–49, 154–56, 167–69, 180; mentoring by, 22, 183; narrative blues tradition and, 36, 60; Robert Johnson and, 111, 117
Paul, Billy, 102
Peacock Records, 191
Peacocks (band), 184
Pearson, Barry Lee, 112–13
Pedro, Josep, 200
Peewee's Café (Memphis), 151, 154
Pessar, Marc, 186
Peters, Uma, 211
Phillips, Dewey, 137
Phillips, Esther, 69, 76, 93, 94–98, 214
Phillis Wheatley Club, 74
Pickett, Wilson, 28
"Pickpocket Blues" (Bessie Smith), 104

Pitchfork.com, 144
Plant, Robert, 111
Pop art, and White Stripes visual aesthetics, 146, 157–66, *163*
"Posing" (Jay), 176–77
Powell, Willie Mae, 110
Pratt, Janie, 39
"Preaching Blues (Up Jumped the Devil)" (*Reservation Blues* song), 134
Presley, Elvis: "Black Elvis" character and, 115, 137–42; clothing and costuming, 239n57; "Hound Dog," 20, 67–70, 90–92, 106, 126, 141, 231n54; *Reservation Blues* fiction about, 135
Price, Lloyd, 28
Pridgett, Gertrude. *See* Rainey, Ma
Pryor, Alice, 227n83

Rabbit Foot Minstrels, 53, 59
race and culture: African American folk tradition, 13, 34, 112, 131, 153, 170, 173–75, 223n32, 225n29; African American Great Migration, 156; Afro-alienation, 93–94; "Black Elvis" and racialized blues authenticity, 137–42; Black-to-white passing, 86–90; blues music as cross-cultural/cross-racial, 5–7; Clark on racism, 217–19; cultural appropriation, 22, 144, 148, 155, 180, 186; historical perspective of power of Black singers, 116; "Hound Dog" as cultural theft, 20, 67–70, 90–92, 106, 126, 141, 231n54; "my man" as African American working-class argot, 102; race records and Paramount Records, 53, 58, 147; "The White Negro" on, 153, 237n35; white-to-Black passing, 100–105; Winehouse and Black musical authenticity, 71–72, 100–105
Raconteurs, 143, 176, 178
Rainey, Ma: authenticity of, 8, 72–74, 197; autobiographical fictions of, 214; Bessie Smith and, 54–56, 58–60; biographical information, 53, 227n85; blues music name and, 56–59; *The Color Purple* characters and, 78, 83, 89, 90; female blues persona as gendered, 20; as Mother of the Blues, 58; overview, 31; sexual confidence of, 15–16; "Stack-o-Lee Blues," 27, 28, 52–54; as transgressive bad woman, 13. *See also* gender and female blues persona
Rainey, Will, 53
Raitt, Bonnie, 73
Ralph Ellison: A Biography (Rampersad), 242n21
Rampersad, Arnold, 242n21
Ravenscroft, Alison, 37, 38
Reading Autobiography (Smith & Watson), 223n31
Ready, Wm. E., 63–65
Really the Blues (Mezzrow), 101
Reed, Jimmy, 161
"Reflecting on Kurt Cobain's 'Crystalline Understanding' 25 Years Later" (NPR), 216
"Rehab" (Winehouse), 69, 106–7
Reiff, Corbin, 204
Reservation Blues (Alexie), 15, 21, 113–15, 127, 130–36, 142
Revenant Records, 147
Richards, Keith: Jack White and, 151–52, 154, 158; Robert Johnson's influence on, 21, 109–11, 114–16, 118–20
Richardson, Nat, 109
Riefenstahl, Leni, 166
Rietveld, Gerrit, 160, 184
The Rise and Fall of Paramount Records (Revenant Records), 147
RL's Dream (Mosley), 15, 21, 113–14
Robbins, Everett, 54
Robert Johnson (CD), 37
Robert Johnson (Charters), 121
Robert Johnson: Lost and Found (Pearson & McCulloch), 112–13
Roberts, John W., 34
Robinson, Justin, 207, 208
Rodgers, Jimmie, 40
Rolling Stone (magazine): on blues master-apprentice relationships, 183; Clark interview, 217–19; "Gary Clark Jr.," 202–3; on Jack White, 167, 181
Rolling Stones (band), 104, 111, 144, 152, 158. *See also* Richards, Keith
Ronson, Mark, 101
"Rough and Tumble Blues" (Rainey), 89–90

Ruark, Robert C., 150–51
Rubin, David C., 28

"Saint Louis Blues" (Handy), 149, 150
Savannah Tribune, on Mamie Smith, 62, 64
Schiffman, Frank, 93
Schroeder, Patricia, 9, 121–23, 131, 139
Scorsese, Martin, 193
Scripps-Howard, on Handy, 150–51
The Search for Robert Johnson (film), 109–11
Searching for Robert Johnson (Guralnick), 113
"Send Me to the 'Lectric Chair" (Bessie Smith and Her Blue Boys), 228n95
Serving the Servant (Goldberg), 215
"Seven Nation Army" (White Stripes), 160–63, 175
sexuality: Bessie Smith and, 5, 31, 78; Jack White and, 171–73; Patton and, 149; Rainey and, 15–16; Robert Johnson and, 113, 122–23; Winehouse and, 100, 102, 104, 105; womanist ideology, 83, 230n31
Shadow and Act (Ellison), 196–97
Shaggy 2 Dope (Joseph Utsler), 178
Shelton, Lee, 26, 28–29, 34, 42, 213–14, 224n1
Sherman, Cindy, 176–77, 181
Sherman Holmes Blues Apprenticeship (Virginia Foundation for the Humanities), 185
Shines, Johnny, 22, 110, 187–90
Shirley, Wayne D., 171
Shopes, Linda, 93, 94
Shug Avery. *See The Color Purple*
Simone, Nina, 210
The Simpsons (television show), 164–65
"S'iomadh Rid" (Giddens), 209
60 Minutes (television show), 173
Small, Danny C., 54
"The Smart Set," 62
Smear, Pat, 205
Smith, Bessie: authenticity of, 8, 72, 197; autobiographical fictions of, 2, 104, 214; *The Color Purple* characters and, 83; female blues persona as gendered, 20; "Homeless Blues," 156; legacy of, 73; Lipscomb influenced by, 40; overview, 31; photo, *57*; physical presence of, 78; Rainey and, 52–56, 58–60; "Send Me to the 'Lectric Chair," 228n95; Thornton and, 71; as transgressive woman, 5, 13. *See also* gender and female blues persona
Smith, Clara, 59
Smith, Clarence (Bessie Smith's brother), 54
Smith, George "Harmonica," 67
Smith, Mamie: autobiographical fictions of, 13, 214; clothing worn by, 63; "Crazy Blues," 19, 31, *61*; female blues persona as gendered, 20; as first Black woman blues recording artist, 60; "From $20.00 per Week to $1,000 ptr [*sic*] Night" (*Topeka Plain Dealer*) on, 63–65; as inauthentic, 8; legacy of, 73; off-stage persona of, 64–65; as transgressive woman, 13; Winehouse and, 103. *See also* gender and female blues persona
Smith, Maud, 59
Smith, Sidonie, 12, 14, 37, 223n31
"Some Unholy War" (Winehouse), 102
Song of Solomon (Morrison), 27
"song-speech," 172
Sonic Highways (Foo Fighters), 204–5
Sontag, Susan, 166
Sophia. *See The Color Purple*
Soul Babies (Neal), 242n17
South Carolina Arts Commission, 185
Southern, Eileen, 6
"Spanish Flang Dang" (Lipscomb), 49
Spencer, Onah L., 34
Spin, on Winehouse, 98–99
"Spoonful" (Howlin' Wolf), 105
"A Spoonful Blues" (Patton), 105
Squeak. *See The Color Purple*
St. Louis Globe-Democrat, on Shelton murder (Stagolee legend), 26, 27
St. Petersburg Times (Florida), on Winehouse, 102
"Stackalee" (Spencer), 34
"Stack-o-Lee Blues" (Rainey), 52–54
"Stagger Lee" (Winehouse), 27
Stagolee legend: bad man trope and, 19, 26–34, 36–37, 41–52; in "Ball and Biscuit," 34; Esu (Yoruban trickster god)

Stagolee legend (*continued*)
and, 36; in *His Eye Is on the Sparrow*, 33–34; interpretations across musical genres, 27–28; oral storytelling and eventual written work, 28, 31; origin of, 19, 25–30, 213–14, 224n1, 224n10; in "Stackalee," 34; in "Stack-o-Lee Blues," 52–54; in "Stagger Lee," 27; in *Train Whistle Guitar*, 32–34, 40. *See also* narrative blues tradition
Stagolee Shot Billy (Brown), 214, 224n10
Standard Telephones and Cables (microphone), 172–73
state arts commissions/humanities foundations, apprenticeship programs of, 22, 185–87, 190, 194, 211
Stereogum (blog), 176
Stewart-Baxter, Derrick, 59, 120
Stoever, Jennifer, 10, 196
Stokes, Moses, 54
Stoller, Mike, 90, 91, 141, 231n54
Stone, Sly, 28
"Stones in My Passway" (Boyle), 21, 113–14
The Story of Sonny Boy Slim (Clark), 205
Strachwitz, Chris, 40
Sub Pop, 215–16
substance abuse: by House, 118; by Thornton, 96–98; by Winehouse, 98–99, 102–3
"Sugarbabe" (Lipscomb), 49–50
Sullivan, John Jeremiah, 65
Sumlin, Hubert, 118
Sunday Star (Washington, DC), "Homage to Duke Ellington on His Birthday," 198

"Tain't Nobody's Biz-ness If I Do" (Bessie Smith), 54–55
"Take Me Back" (Lipscomb), 49–50
Target with Four Faces (Johns), 162–63
"Tears Dry on Their Own" (Winehouse), 69, 107
teddy boys (English youth subculture), 158–59
Tennessee Arts Commission, 185, 211
Terry, Sonny, 118
Texas Folklife Apprenticeship Program, 185, 186
Tharpe, Sister Rosetta, 210
"That's All Right" (Crudup), 141
Theatre Owners Booking Association (TOBA), 53–54
There's a Riot Goin' On (Stone), 28
Third Man Records, 143, 147, 174, 178, 184
Third Man Upholstery, 154, 174
"This Is America" (Childish Gambino), 218–19
"This Land" (Clark), 216–18
"This Voice Which Is Not One" (Brooks), 103
Thomas Builds-the-Fire (*Reservation Blues* character), 130–36
Thompson, Joe, 184, 207, 210
Thompson, Odell, 207
Thornton, Willie Mae "Big Mama": autobiographical storytelling by, 5, 67–71, 76, 90–98, 106, 107, 214 (*see also* gender and female blues persona); "Ball and Chain" and, 68, 91–93, 126; Bessie Smith and, 71; "Big Mama" nickname of, 93; biographical information, 70, 71, 91; camaraderie between blues artists and, 189; gender and female blues persona, overview, 20, 69–72; "Hound Dog" and, 20, 67–69, 90–92, 106, 126, 141, 231n54; legacy of, 20; Phillips and, 69, 76, 93–98; physical image of, 92–94; struggle for artistic freedom and, 212; Winehouse and, 32, 102
"Three Quid" (Jack White), 174
"The Timbre of Sincerity" (Lordi), 199
Titon, Jeff Todd, 14, 117
Tomorrow Is My Turn (Giddens), 210
Topeka Plain Dealer, "From $20.00 per Week to $1,000 ptr [*sic*] Night" (Ready), 63–65
Townsend, Henry, 110
Townshend, Pete, 158, 159, 205
"Track 1—'Lights in the Valley' (Live) by Joe & Odell Thompson" (Giddens), 207
"Tragedy in Ragtime" (David), 51, 214, 224n10, 227n83
Train Whistle Guitar (Murray), 32–34, 40, 214
Travis, Virginia, 129
Tupac, 177
Turner, Big Joe, 67, 68, 189
Turner, Ike and Tina, 28
Tutt, Homer, 62

Twain, Mark, 198
"'Twas a Christmas morning" (Fisher), 25, 224n1
Two Part Resin, 154

United States Postal Service (Robert Johnson stamp), 111
Untitled #90 (Sherman), 176
Untitled #137 (Sherman), 176–77
Untitled #167 (Sherman), 177
Upholsterers, 154
Upside Your Head (Otis), 101
"Uptown Funk" (Ronson), 101
Utsler, Joseph (Shaggy 2 Dope), 178

Van Ronk, Dave, 119
Van Vliet, Don (Captain Beefheart), 236n6
Vaughan, Jimmie, 184, 200–201
Vaughan, Sarah, 73
Vaughan, Stevie Ray, 200
Vig, Butch, 204
Village Voice, on Violent J, 179
Violent J (Joseph Bruce), 178–79
VJM Palaver (Great Britain), on country blues, 117
Volmers, Eric, 211

"Wake Up Alone" (Winehouse), 69, 106
Wald, Elijah: on authenticity of blues, 8, 9, 73; on Bessie Smith, 228n95; *The Blues*, 5–6; narrative blues and, 36, 59, 60; Patton and, 111
Wald, Gayle, 101, 103
Walker, Alice, 2, 3–4, 5, 20, 69, 70–71, 214. *See also The Color Purple*
Wallace, Mike, 173
Waller, Fats, 8
Wardlow, Gayle Dean, 110, 112, 121, 125
Warhol, Andy, 158, 160, 165
"Waterboy" (Giddens), 209
Waters, Ethel, 13, 20, 31, 33, 60, 72, 73, 83, 147
Waters, Muddy: blues authenticity and, 8; Jack White influenced by, 148, 162, 174; master-apprentice relationships and, 183, 189, 200; Robert Johnson and, 118, 119, 120, 140; Thornton and, 67–69, 72, 93, 95
Watson, Julia, 12, 14, 37, 223n31
Watts, Charlie, 158
Welding, Pete, 112
Wells, Junior, 118
West, Kanye, 177
West Virginia Humanities Council, 22, 185–87
"What Did I Do?/God as My Witness" (Clark & Foo Fighters), 204–5
Wheatstraw, Peetie (William Bunch), 2, 34–35, 214
White, Booker, 111, 124–30, 148, 167
White, Jack, 143–87; alternative blues persona of, 144–46, 155–58; autobiographical fictions of, 1–3, 15, 22, 167–75, 214; biographical information, 153–54, 156; Captain Beefheart's influence on, 236n6; costuming and visual aesthetics by, 5, 144, 146–53, 157–66, *163*, 236n14; master-apprentice relationships of, 184; music rights owned by, 178; narrative blues by, 34, 59; number three obsession of, 174; overview of work by, 21–22, 143; relationship to Meg White, 1–2, 5, 13, 59, 144, 147–48, 173, 238n43; solo career of, 175–81; voicing Stagolee and vocals of, 167, 170–75
White, Meg: relationship to Jack White, 1–2, 5, 13, 22, 59, 144, 147–48, 173, 238n43; White Stripes drumming by, 146, 155, 161–62, *163*, 164–65, 173
"The White Negro" (Mailer), 153, 237n35
White Stripes: "Ball and Biscuit," 34; relationship between Jack and Meg White and, 1–2, 5, 13, 22, 59, 144, 147–48, 173, 238n43; visual aesthetics by, 144, 146–53, 157–66, *163*. *See also* White, Jack
The White Stripes: Under Great White Northern Lights (film), 167
Whitney, Salem Tutt, 62
Whitney Museum of Art, 176–77
the Who, 157–59, 205
Williams, Clarence, 54
Williams, Ethel, 33
Williams, Hype, 177
Williamson, Sonny Boy (Aleck Miller), 147–48
Wilson, Ossey, 64

Winehouse, Amy, 98–107; autobiographical fictions of, 5, 15, 20, 99–100, 212, 214–15; biographical information, 98, 232n83; female blues persona as gendered, 69–72; gender and female blues persona, overview, 20, 69–72; narrated "I" used by, 105–7; narrative blues and, 27, 32; struggle for artistic freedom and, 212; substance abuse by, 98–99, 102–3; white-to-Black passing by and, 100–105. *See also* gender and female blues persona
Winehouse, Janis (Amy Winehouse's mother), 98
Winter, Johnny, 10
Wise, Atwater "Soupspoon" (*RL's Dream* character), 114, 115, 124–30
womanist ideology, 83, 230n31
Wood, Ron, 158
Work, John, III, 54, 56, 58
Worry No More (Clark), 201
Wrecking Crew, 156
Wright, Pearl, 33
Wright, Richard, 27
Wyler, Link, 67, 91

"You Know I'm No Good" (Winehouse), 69, 100, 105
Young, Angus, 205
Young, Nathan Ben, 52